The Growth Process in East Asian Manufacturing Industries

To Yen-Tsun and Yue-yuan

The Growth Process in East Asian Manufacturing Industries

A Re-examination

Chia-Hung Sun

Department of Economics, National Chung Cheng University, Taiwan

Edward Elgar
Cheltenham, UK • Northampton, MA, USA

Published by
Edward Elgar Publishing Limited
Glensanda House
Montpellier Parade
Cheltenham
Glos GL50 1UA
UK

Edward Elgar Publishing, Inc.
136 West Street
Suite 202
Northampton
Massachusetts 01060
USA

A catalogue record for this book
is available from the British Library

ISBN 1 84376 775 9

Printed and bound in Great Britain by MPG Books Ltd, Bodmin, Cornwall

Contents

List of figures

List of tables

Acknowledgements

This book could not have been completed without the assistance and encouragement of numerous people. Above all, I am grateful to my supervisor, Professor Warwick McKibbin and my former supervisor, Professor Kaliappa Kalirajan for their guidance and valuable comments. Their detailed corrections and comments on early drafts have been crucial to the successful completion of this book and have substantially improved its quality.

Professor McKibbin has provided me with constant support and stimulation throughout the writing of this book. I very much appreciate his taking on the responsibility of supervising my study and especially respect his willingness to listen and his seriousness in academic research.

Professor Kalirajan, who is now at the Foundation for Advanced Studies on International Development (FASID) in Tokyo, introduced me to the latest econometric modelling and the fascinating field of productivity measurement and analysis. He is a person who always has time for his students and who has generously helped me on other non-academic matters, including my visits to the University of California at Santa Cruz and FASID in Tokyo. His encouragement and support have always been there.

I would like to thank the other members of my supervisory panel for their helpful comments. Professor George Fane gave me crucial advice on the specification of the empirical model. The detailed and critical comments received from Professor Hal Hill on Chapters 5 and 6 are greatly appreciated.

The main findings of this book have been presented at the Research School of Pacific and Asian School (RSPAS) and the Asia Pacific School of Economics and Management (APSEM) PhD Seminars on many occasions and at the conference of the Australasian Meeting of the Econometric Society in Brisbane, Australia, July 2002 and the 2nd Hellenic Workshop on Efficiency and Productivity Measurement in Patras, Greece, May 2003. The encouragement and comments from academics, fellow students and conference participants are gratefully acknowledged. Special thanks go to Professors Jong-Wha Lee and Raghbendra Jha, and to Dr Ross McLeod for their valuable suggestions at the Graduate Students Workshop organised by the Economics Division, RSPAS, Australian National University (ANU) and the Korea University.

Dr Hsiao-chuan Chang, Dr Tingsong Jiang, Dr Kanhaiya Singh, Dr Vladimir Smirnov and Dr Yi-Ping Tseng provided me with their research experiences at different stages in the writing of my book. Ms Qun Shi and Mr Jeremy Nguyen always encouraged me and offered their friendship. Jeremy Nguyen especially assisted me on numerous occasions, including with English writing and computer skills.

I would like to thank Professor Nirvikar Singh, who invited me to the University of California at Santa Cruz in June 2001 and provided constructive comments on an early draft of this book. I also wish to thank FASID for sponsoring my visit to Tokyo to continue my collaboration with Professor Kaliappa Kalirajan.

I wish to thank the people at the Directorate-General of Budget, Accounting and Statistics of the Executive Yuan, Taiwan and the staff of the International Economic Data Bank at the ANU who generously provided the data for this book. My special thanks go to Ms Jing-Ru Chen and Carol Kavanagh for their excellent editorial support throughout the writing of this book.

The arrival of my daughter, Yue-yuan, on Valentine's Day in 2001 has given me lots of joy, love and fun and significantly enriched my life in Canberra. Finally, I would like to express my deepest gratitude to my parents for their consistent support.

Chiayi, Taiwan, August 2004
Chia-Hung Sun

1. Introduction

1.1 THE BACKGROUND

The fact that the East Asian newly industrialised countries (NICs) of Hong Kong, South Korea (henceforth Korea), Singapore and Taiwan have succeeded in maintaining high output growth over the past three decades has often been characterised as an economic miracle. During 1970–97, the annual growth rates of gross domestic product (GDP) for Singapore, Taiwan, Korea and Hong Kong (from 1976) were on average 8.2 per cent, 8 per cent, 7.7 per cent and 6.6 per cent respectively. In terms of manufacturing output growth, among the East Asian economies, Korea enjoyed the highest average annual output growth rate of 13 per cent, followed by Singapore with 9.8 per cent and Taiwan with 8.8 per cent.[1]

However, some recent empirical studies on total factor productivity (TFP) growth, including Kim and Lau (1994), Young (1995) and Collins and Bosworth (1996), have shown that the economic miracles of these economies can be sufficiently explained by factor accumulation, that is, labour and capital. More specifically, Kim and Lau (1994) indicated that the extraordinary economic record was mainly fuelled by rapid accumulation of labour and capital. Using growth accounting, Young (1995) also argued that the spectacular economic performance in East Asia was not as impressive as previously thought and that the economic success was nothing more than intensive factor accumulation. Krugman (1994) described the East Asian economic miracle as having been realised mainly by perspiration with little inspiration. The implication of these findings is that such a spectacular performance would soon come to an end due to little progress in TFP; namely, economic growth would not be sustainable without TFP growth (Solow, 1957; Denison, 1962; Jorgenson and Griliches, 1967).

In contrast, studies by the World Bank (1993), Sarel (1995), Thomas and Wang (1996), Klenow and Rodriguez-Clare (1997), Hsieh (1999, 2002) and others, showed that TFP growth was an important contributor to the rapid and sustained economic growth in East Asian economies.[2] This author claims that due to different data sets selected, different sample periods covered and different methodologies used, the set of TFP studies described above have produced differing analyses with respect to TFP growth in East Asian countries, suggesting that it has not yet been possible to determine its role in the East Asian economic miracle. From a policy perspective, the assessment of TFP growth is important as it serves as a guide for allocating resources and investment decision making. Another feature of the studies that have questioned the role of TFP progress in the East Asian economic miracle is that they predominantly focus on the performance of the overall economy and pay little attention to manufacturing industries. By contrast, a report by the World Bank (1993, p. 24) points out that 'export-push strategies have been by far the most successful combination of fundamentals and policy interventions and hold the most promise for other developing countries'. The use of aggregate data at the economy level ignores sectoral TFP performance and has limited the scope of the former studies; the World Bank report reinforces the significant role played by the manufacturing sector in the East Asian economic miracle.

Therefore, it can be seen that the earlier conclusions about the East Asian economic miracle deserve further investigation. To ascertain the role of TFP growth in East Asia, this study will examine disaggregated data at the 3-digit industry level and apply a uniform data set and a better methodology, to re-examine TFP growth in the manufacturing sectors of Hong Kong, Korea, Japan, Singapore and Taiwan.

1.1.1 Growth Accounting

Despite its wide popularity, growth accounting has been seriously questioned as an appropriate means of explaining the role of technological progress in the East Asian economic miracle. In contrast to Krugman's and Young's hypothesis, Chen (1997) considers the concept of TFP growth in detail and asserts that it should not be regarded as technological change because TFP growth on the basis of growth accounting is defined as disembodied, exogenous and Hicks-neutral technological change.[3] Rodrik (1998) has particular concerns about the assumption of an elasticity of substitution between labour and capital of one for East Asian economies. If the true elasticity of substitution is less than one, this implies that technical change is no longer Hicks-neutral and TFP growth is underestimated. Likewise, Felipe (1999) argues that an important part of technological progress is embodied in the factors of production, so that conventional TFP growth may not be convincing in terms of accounting for technological progress in East Asian economies and predicting their future.

Barro (1999) reaffirms that the practice of growth accounting is only useful if the underlying technological change is independent of the production function, namely disembodied or Hick-neutral technology.[4] Given the fact that the Solow residual derived from a production function is equivalent to the first order condition of income accounting identity, Felipe (2000) further suggests that TFP progress obtained from growth accounting cannot be interpreted as technological progress. Consequently, Rodrigo (2000) points out that the disembodied technology or knowledge should not be taken as technological change because many of the production techniques have been incorporated into physical devices and structures.

Additionally, the assumption of the empirical existence of perfect competition has been questioned, which implies that factor shares will be mismeasured under the assumption of constant returns to scale (see Hall, 1988; Morrison, 1990b; Young, 1995, p. 648).[5] Because monopoly profits are reflected in capital income, capital share will be overstated and, in turn, labour share will be underestimated. As a result, the conventional growth accounting approach of measuring factor shares is defective. Consequently, it is questionable whether growth accounting can be applied to account for the economic success in East Asia given the rapid transformation and utilisation of modern technology in recent decades. Due to methodological and conceptual problems, the conclusions of earlier TFP studies, such as Kim and Lau (1994), Young (1995) and Collins and Bosworth (1996), remain open to debate and require further investigation; this will be undertaken by this study.[6]

1.1.2 TFP Growth versus Technological Progress

The assumption that TFP growth was synonymous with technological progress in the earlier growth accounting based studies has led to the conclusion that the East Asian economies achieved an insufficient level of technological progress. This is misleading because TFP growth not only explicitly captures technological progress, but also reflects an improvement in the use of available resources and technology. Hence the traditional approach of treating TFP growth as technological progress misinterprets the nature of technological progress and ignores the importance of technical efficiency pertaining to a firm's ability to use available resources effectively. Additionally, the decomposition of output growth employed in growth accounting does not elucidate the real causes of growth, nor does it evaluate industrial policies and government regulations from the perspective of efficiency.

To distinguish the difference, Nishimizu and Page (1982) first incorporated the concept of technical inefficiency into the production process and decomposed TFP growth into technological progress and technical efficiency change; namely, TFP growth stems from a combination of technological progress and technical efficiency improvement. Technological progress stemming from innovation and technological diffusion is measured by a shift in the potential production frontier from one period to another. Technical efficiency change reflects the movement of a firm's actual output to maximum potential output, where the distance between actual output and potential output, or production frontier, is traditionally referred to as technical inefficiency.

1.1.3 Conventional Stochastic Frontier versus Varying Coefficients Frontier Model

In addition to growth accounting, a large number of econometric approaches in the literature have been suggested for measuring TFP growth to date. These estimations and specifications of production frontier or 'best practice' production function are well documented in several survey articles, such as Førsund *et al.* (1980), Bauer (1990), Coelli (1995), Kalirajan and Shand (1999) and Heshmati (2003).

Even though the conventional stochastic production frontier approach proposed by Aigner *et al.* (1977) and Meeusen and van den Broeck (1977) distinguishes TFP growth from technological progress, the assumption of the homogeneity of firms or industries in applying frontier production technology remains unwarranted. Therefore, this study employs the varying coefficients frontier model proposed by Swamy (1970) and Kalirajan and Obwona (1994) to estimate the potential production frontier and investigate TFP growth for the East Asian manufacturing industries.[7] The major differences between these two approaches lie in the underlying assumptions and estimations of production frontier. The strengths of the varying coefficients frontier model are outlined briefly as follows.

The estimation of conventional stochastic frontier is carried out by assuming that firms are homogeneous in terms of applying the best available technology. However, in practice, firms utilise the frontier production technology differently for a variety of reasons, even though best practice technology is available to all. With various firm-specific characteristics, Firm A may use its labour input most efficiently because of extensive experience in choosing and supervising its human resources while Firm B is not efficient in using its labour force or capital input, and Firm C may be best at utilising and managing its capital input. As a result, it is empirically observed that firms with the same level of inputs can achieve different levels of output with the same production technology.

Moreover, the conventional stochastic frontier approach captures the variations in intercept only and leaves the estimated coefficients of factor inputs constant, that is, a neutral shift of production frontier. To eliminate the above deficiencies, this study frees the conventional frontier model from the restrictive assumption that all firms homogeneously apply the frontier production technology. The application of the varying coefficients frontier approach facilitates the modelling of a non-neutral shift from the average production frontier, which explicitly captures the variations in intercept as well as the estimated coefficients of factor inputs and, hence, represents a significant methodological improvement.

1.2 OBJECTIVES OF THE BOOK

Several East Asian economies – Hong Kong, Korea, Singapore and Taiwan – have achieved an economic miracle of maintaining high economic growth for several decades prior to the Asian financial crisis. However, Kim and Lau (1994), Krugman (1994), and Young (1992, 1995) have recently cast doubt on this economic success. They claim that this economic achievement will virtually come to an end due to the lack of significant TFP growth. However, given methodological limitations and differences in underlying assumptions used by previous studies, it is difficult to accept the conclusion reached by such analyses. Hence, by using the varying coefficients frontier model and panel data from the United Nations Industrial Development Organisation (UNIDO) Industrial Statistics Database, the overall objective of this study is to re-examine the role of TFP growth and identify the sources of output growth in the context of the manufacturing industries of the five East Asian economies. Specific issues to be considered are to:

1. explain why TFP growth differs from technological progress, which implicitly rejects the use of growth accounting, while investigating the process of technological progress in East Asian manufacturing industries;
2. demonstrate why this study favours the use of the varying coefficients frontier model rather than the conventional stochastic frontier approach;
3. test statistically whether manufacturing industries in East Asia homogeneously applied the best practice production technology by means of the Breusch–Pagan Lagrange Multiplier (LM) test;
4. investigate the concern of TFP growth slowdown in East Asian manufacturing sectors;
5. link the possible relationships between technological progress (or technical efficiency change) and structural transformation;
6. compare TFP growth between high-tech and low-tech industries on the basis of two proposed hypotheses: (a) the conjecture that high-tech industries gain more TFP growth is investigated; (b) on examining the sources of TFP growth, the hypothesis that high-tech industries gain TFP growth mainly through technological progress and low-tech industries from technical efficiency improvement is explored;

7. perform a number of sensitivity tests to consolidate the findings of this study and a comparison with earlier TFP studies for each economy.

1.3   ORGANISATION OF THE BOOK

The remainder of the book is organised as follows. Chapter 2 reviews recent TFP studies of the manufacturing sectors in the five East Asian economies. The central theme of the review focuses mainly on the estimates of TFP growth rates, sample periods covered and estimation approaches used in previous studies. Due to different aggregations and sample periods, the number of manufacturing industries examined varies from study to study. A brief conclusion ends the chapter.

Chapter 3 discusses several popular methods used in measuring TFP growth, including the conventional stochastic frontier and meta-production function, and advances the need for an alternative approach. Next a recent method, the varying coefficients frontier model, is discussed. This is followed by a demonstration of decomposition analysis, in which output growth can be decomposed into input growth, technical efficiency change and technological progress. The empirical model, associated tests, data sources, constructions of variables and selection of deflators are also presented.

Chapter 4 first describes the characteristics of the five East Asian manufacturing sectors. Using the Breusch–Pagan LM test, the conventional assumption of the homogeneity of manufacturing industries is examined. In addition, it presents the estimated varying frontier coefficients, mean coefficients and the computer program used in this study. Applying the concept of technical efficiency, Chapter 4 also discusses how well the manufacturing industries in the East Asian economies utilised labour and capital inputs. The number of industries and sample periods covered in the study are examined and presented in Appendix A.3.

Chapter 5 identifies the sources of output growth and analyses the importance of TFP growth in different stages of economic growth in the East Asian manufacturing sectors. The average share of industries in the manufacturing sector is briefly discussed before presenting the decomposition results of long-term output growth. The detailed annual TFP growth estimates for individual industries are presented and the trends in annual TFP growth in the five manufacturing sectors are also discussed.

In Chapter 6, following Nishimizu and Page (1982), TFP growth in the five East Asian manufacturing industries is decomposed into the contribution attributed to technological progress and change in technical efficiency, which explicitly distinguishes TFP growth from technological progress. This is followed by an analysis of the long-term trends in technological progress and changes in technical efficiency, providing empirical evidence with regard to the structural transformation across East Asian manufacturing sectors.

Two hypotheses for high-tech and low-tech industries are examined. The first is that high-tech industries have a higher TFP growth. The second is that the sources of TFP growth for high-tech industries come largely from technological progress and for low-tech industries mainly from technical efficiency improvement. A comparison of the productivity growth in high-tech and low-tech industries is made to examine these hypotheses. A series of sensitivity tests for Singapore's manufacturing sector and comparisons with earlier TFP studies are also included to consolidate the findings of this study.

The final chapter summarises the main findings of this study, presents the limitations of this research and offers policy implications.

NOTES

1. Hong Kong's manufacturing sector was the only sector experiencing negative output growth (–0.2 per cent) due to the relocation of its manufacturing production to mainland China in the mid-1980s.
2. Recently, Hsieh (1999, 2002) proposed a dual approach to growth accounting, which produced a contrasting result to that of Young (1995) in the case of Singapore and Taiwan.
3. In addition, he provides several reasons, including capacity utilisation and price deflators, which are likely to be responsible for the low estimated TFP growth in East Asia due to over-adjustment in factor inputs (see Chen, 1997, pp. 32–3).
4. Addressing the possible problems of growth accounting in conjunction with various issues, such as spillover effects, increasing returns to scale, taxes and multiple types of factor inputs, Barro (1999) offers several theoretical solutions to these issues in his paper but the empirical evidence has not yet been seen.
5. Nelson and Pack (1999) pointed out that the estimates by those accumulationists are probably dependent on the extent of errors caused by the presence of biased technical change and an elasticity of substitution of less than one. Felipe and McCombie (2001) proposed constant-technology factor shares as weights to calculate the corrected growth of TFP, which avoids the above deficiencies. The TFP growth estimates over different elasticities of substitution (σ) are available in Felipe and McCombie (2001, Table 2, p. 555); for instance, if the elasticity of substitution (σ) is 0.2, the annual TFP growth rate for Taiwan will rise to 4.27 per cent.
6. Using a similar methodology to growth accounting, empirical results frequently differ. In terms of country-specific studies, the extent of TFP growth in Singapore appears the most controversial. According to Sarel (1995), Collins and Bosworth (1996) and Klenow and Rodriguez-Clare (1997), the results of annual TFP growth rates for Singapore were 2 per

cent (nearly), 1.5 per cent and 3.3 per cent respectively, over the 1975–90, 1960–94 and 1960–85 periods, which substantially contradicts Young (1995) that Singapore had little progress (0.2 per cent) in TFP during the period 1966–90.

7. The varying coefficients frontier model provides a convincing reason why output differs across firms not only due to their degree of inefficiency but also because of the different applications of the best practice production technology.

2. Literature review: total factor productivity studies on East Asian manufacturing industries

Before proceeding to the empirical model used by the current study, Chapter 2 briefly reviews recent TFP studies on East Asian manufacturing sectors. The main focus of the review is on the estimates of TFP growth rates, sample periods covered and estimation approaches. TFP survey papers are reviewed first, beginning with studies comparing the performance of East Asian manufacturing sectors, followed by country-specific studies of Hong Kong, Japan, Korea, Singapore and Taiwan. Due to different aggregations and sample periods, the number of manufacturing industries examined will vary from study to study. Comparisons of TFP growth estimates at the industry level will be carried out in Chapter 6. A brief conclusion on the nature of the studies reviewed will be drawn at the end of the chapter.

2.1 TFP SURVEYS

Chen (1997) discussed the popular TFP methodologies and raised concerns over possible problems in measuring capital input.[1] He argued that the assumption of disembodied technology appears to be problematic in the case of Singapore, which may have gained more from embodied technological change than disembodied technological change due to its speedily improved labour force and the adoption of modern technologies. The persuasive conclusion by Chen (1997) is that 'the significance of technological change in economic growth depends largely on how TFP is defined and how factor input data are measured'.

Extending Chen's (1997) arguments, Felipe (1999) reiterated the theoretical and empirical problems evidenced in recent TFP literature with respect to the application of aggregate production and growth accounting. Given the varied and conflicting results, Felipe urged caution in drawing any conclusions from these TFP estimates because of the problems and limitations associated with the methodology used in these studies. To avoid misuse of the notion of TFP growth, Felipe advocated the need for future research in understanding technological change as well as the interaction between human and physical capital.

Barro (1999) presented an extensive examination of growth accounting and demonstrated several possible problems for models with increasing returns and spillovers, various taxes and different types of factor inputs. Barro also showed how the growth accounting exercise could be expanded to endogenous growth theory, including product-varieties and quality-ladders models.[2] In a comprehensive study of TFP, Hulten (2000) broadly discussed methods used for calculating TFP growth and indicated possible extensions for future research in the wake of new growth theory. Despite the drawbacks of growth accounting, Hulten commended the idea of a TFP residual; this has provided a simple and internally consistent intellectual framework for organising data on economic growth, as well as the theory to guide economic measurement. Mahadevan (2003) debated the definition of TFP growth and its relation to the concepts of embodied and disembodied technical change. She then raised a number of issues regarding the use of the frontier and non-frontier approaches to measure TFP growth (see Mahadevan, 2003, p. 372, Figure 1). Other concerns relating to the notion of TFP growth implied by the production function and the accounting identity were also discussed.

2.2   REVIEW OF STUDIES OF EAST ASIAN MANUFACTURING SECTORS

Prior to reviewing country-specific TFP studies, this section discusses studies that have compared TFP performance across East Asian manufacturing sectors.[3] Using growth accounting with translog production function, Young (1995) examined TFP growth in the four East Asian Tigers (Hong Kong, Korea, Singapore and Taiwan), although the results for manufacturing sectors were available only for the last three economies. On the one hand, he found evidence that the Korean manufacturing sector gained TFP at an average annual rate of 3.0 per cent over the 1966–90 period while the average annual TFP growth rate for Taiwan's manufacturing sector was moderate at 1.7 per cent during the same period, mainly due to zero TFP progress in the 1970s. On the other hand, Singapore's manufacturing sector was reported to have had a TFP decline of 1 per cent during the period 1970–90 on an average annual basis.

In a study of manufacturing sectors in Korea, Turkey, Yugoslavia and Japan by Nishimizu and Robinson (1984), the TFP of the Korean and Japanese manufacturing sectors measured by the translog TFP index number grew by 3.71 per cent and 2.04 per cent over the periods 1960–77 and 1955–

73 respectively. TFP growth was considered to have made a 20.7 per cent and 17.6 per cent contribution to output growth respectively. As for the 16 individual industries, the electrical machinery industry achieved the highest average annual TFP growth of 7.25 per cent (Korea) and 4.42 per cent (Japan). However, outcomes varied substantially across the other 15 industries in these two economies.

Nadiri and Kim (1996) estimated TFP growth for the US, Japanese and Korean manufacturing sectors. Using the Törnqvist index with labour, capital, materials and research and development (R&D) as factor inputs, the average annual TFP growth for Korea and Japan based on total cost shares as weights was estimated at 0.69 per cent and 1.26 per cent respectively, over the 1975–90 period. Nadiri and Kim also provided another set of TFP estimates if conditions of perfect competition, constant returns to scale and instantaneous adjustment of all inputs were assumed to exist. The average annual TFP growth rates based on revenue shares as weights for the Korean and Japanese manufacturing sectors were 1.14 per cent and 3.15 per cent respectively.

Timmer and Szirmai (2000) also applied growth accounting to the four Asian manufacturing sectors of India, Indonesia, Korea and Taiwan, to estimate the aggregate and output–weighted TFP growth. The difference between the two TFP growth estimates was the result of a total reallocation effect due to the shift from less productive manufacturing industries towards more productive industries. Timmer and Szirmai's results show that the average annual TFP growth rate of the Korean manufacturing sector was 4.5 per cent over the period 1963–90 despite a negative reallocation effect. For Taiwan's manufacturing sector, it was 2.0 per cent for the 1963–93 period, which was partly attributable to the reallocation effect (0.3 per cent).

Taking the manufacturing sector of the United States as the reference country, Timmer (2002) argued that in 1997 the TFP level of Taiwanese manufacturing was 34 per cent relative to that of the United States, due to the rapid introduction of new technologies, leaving little time for efficient assimilation. That is, Taiwan gained little from technical efficiency improvement.

Han *et al.* (2002) applied the varying coefficients model to investigate TFP growth for 20 manufacturing industries in Hong Kong, Korea, Japan and Singapore. After decomposing output growth into input growth, technical efficiency and technological progress, they suggested that over the period 1987–93 factor accumulation accounted for most of the output growth in the four East Asian manufacturing sectors, whereas technological progress played a lesser role during the same period.[4] A summary of these TFP studies on East Asian manufacturing sectors is presented in Table 2.1.

Table 2.1   TFP studies comparing TFP performance across five East Asian manufacturing sectors

Authors	Country	Period	Method	TFP growth p.a. (%)
Nishimizu and Robinson (1984)	Japan Korea	1955–73 1960–77	Translog TFP index	2.04 3.71
Young (1995)	Korea Singapore Taiwan	1966–90 1970–90 1966–90	Growth accounting	3.0 −1.0 1.7
Nadiri and Kim (1996)	Japan Korea	1975–90 1975–90	Törnqvist index	1.26 0.69
Timmer and Szirmai (2000)	Korea Taiwan	1963–90 1963–93	Growth accounting	4.5 2.0

Note: Nadiri and Kim (1996) also provided another set of TFP growth estimates for Japan and Korea if the conditions of perfect competition, constant returns to scale and instantaneous adjustment of all inputs are assumed to be valid.

2.3   REVIEWS OF HONG KONG'S MANUFACTURING SECTOR

Compared with other East Asian manufacturing sectors, there have been relatively fewer TFP studies of Hong Kong's manufacturing sector because most TFP studies involving Hong Kong have concentrated on the overall economy; for instance, Dowrick and Nguyen (1989), Kim and Lau (1994), Young (1992, 1995), Sarel (1995), Drysdale and Huang (1997) and Hsieh (1999, 2002).

The study most relevant to the theme being reviewed is that by Kwong *et al.* (2000). They used growth accounting with translog gross output function to investigate the TFP growth of Hong Kong's manufacturing industries for the period 1984–93. The study revealed that although 15 out of 29 industries advanced in TFP, the overall manufacturing sector experienced a technology decline of 13.8 per cent during the decade.[5] Stated differently, Hong Kong's manufacturing sector in 1993 could only produce 87 per cent of the output in

1984 from the same amount of resources.[6] The implication of this unexpected finding had much to do with the liberalisation in China since 1978 and the style of Hong Kong's existing manufacturing sector (original equipment manufacturing). More specifically, manufacturers in Hong Kong were not willing to invest heavily in R&D to upgrade their technology while profits remained positive and low-cost resource facilities in mainland China could be easily accessed.

Tuan and Ng (1995) explored three major export-oriented industries, namely garments and wearing apparel, consumer electronics, and electronic parts and components. In applying the Cobb–Douglas production function with regression approach, the study found that there was little change in TFP level in the three industries except for garments and wearing apparel.[7]

Imai (2001) did not explicitly estimate TFP growth for Hong Kong's overall manufacturing sector. Instead, he disaggregated Hong Kong's economy into three sectors: non-tradable, tradable services and tradable goods (overwhelmingly dominated by manufacturing). Applying growth accounting, Imai suggested that the tradable goods sector (manufacturing) experienced high average annual TFP growth rates of 5.6 per cent and 6.0 per cent during 1981–90 and 1991–97 respectively.[8]

2.4 REVIEWS OF JAPAN

There are many TFP studies of Japanese manufacturing industries, which enable them to be classified into four categories. The first category concentrates on individual industries, for example the chemical or automobile industry. Using the translog (Törnqvist) index of cost efficiency growth to measure TFP growth, Fuss and Waverman (1990) investigated productivity growth in the motor vehicle industries of Canada, Japan and the US. They found that the TFP of the Japanese auto industry grew by an annual rate of 3.0 per cent, compared with an average annual TFP growth rate of 1 per cent for the US and Canada.[9] Furthermore, the study found that 80 per cent of TFP growth in the Japanese auto industry during the 1970–84 period was due to technical change and 20 per cent was attributed to scale economies.

Kumbhakar *et al.* (2000) discussed the time trend model and the variants of the general index model to accommodate technical change and technological biases in measuring TFP growth. They showed that the average annual TFP growth rates computed by three versions of the general index model appeared to be similar, ranging from 1.553 per cent to 1.716 per cent for the Japanese chemical industry during the period 1968–87.

The second category of studies focuses on either the Japanese manufacturing sector as a whole or individual manufacturing industries in

Japan. Nakajima *et al.* (1998) used an index number approach to estimate and decompose TFP growth into technical change and scale economy effects for 18 manufacturing industries over the period 1964–88. They found that more than 90 per cent of the gains in TFP were due to technical change and average annual TFP growth rates ranged from 2.167 per cent (food/kindred products industry) to 5.489 per cent (petroleum and coal products industry). Overall, the simple average of TFP growth rate for the entire manufacturing sector was found to be 3.731 per cent per annum.

A study analysing the sectoral shifts in the Japanese economy by Prasad (1997) found that the share of manufacturing output in the real economy GDP remained stable despite the declining share of the manufacturing sector in total employment. According to the OECD sectoral database, the average annual TFP growth rate of the manufacturing sector during the 1971–93 period was 2.8 per cent.

In an overall assessment of the Japanese economy, Sato (2002) regarded the contraction of manufacturing employment as being partly responsible for the stagnant economy in the 1990s. The average annual TFP growth rates for the manufacturing sector were found to be 2.5 per cent, 2.6 per cent and 2.2 per cent over the periods 1979–85, 1985–91 and 1991–97 respectively.[10] Yet the poor performance of the non-manufacturing sector was the main factor that pulled down overall productivity growth in the 1990s.

The success of Japanese industrialisation after World War II has attracted much attention and led to comparisons of the Japanese growth experience with other industrialised nations. If the US manufacturing sector is assumed to be the world leader in terms of production technology, an interesting question is to examine the extent of catching-up progress its Japanese counterpart has made over the past several decades. Hence, the third category of studies focuses on a bilateral comparison between Japanese and US manufacturing industries.

Norsworthy and Malmquist (1983) initially rejected the value added approach to measuring productivity growth in the US and Japan due to the failure of separability tests.[11] They then carry out a comparison of the estimates of multifactor productivity growth for US and Japanese manufacturing using the translog production function and gross output approach. Their findings revealed that average annual TFP growth rates for Japanese manufacturing were 0.91 per cent and 1.64 per cent during the periods 1965–73 and 1973–78 respectively.[12]

Jorgenson *et al.* (1987b) employed translog quantities indexes of the rates of technical change to compare the productivity growth of the Japanese and US manufacturing industries. Their empirical results showed that the estimated average annual TFP growth rates for 21 Japanese manufacturing industries varied widely, from –3.16 per cent in the petroleum and coal industry to 3.07 per cent in the electrical machinery industry over the period 1960–79. The modest annual TFP growth rate of 0.83 per cent for the overall manufacturing sector was due largely to the TFP slowdown after 1973.

Griliches and Mairesse (1990) used firm-level data to assess the contribution of R&D to productivity growth in the manufacturing sectors of Japan and the US. By assuming that value added and sales varied proportionally and capital input share was constant and equal to 0.25 for all firms in Japan, Griliches and Mairesse found that the electrical equipment and instruments industries experienced the highest annual TFP growth rates during the 1973–80 period, of 8.4 per cent and 8.1 per cent respectively.[13] On the other hand, they reported the lowest average annual TFP growth rate of 0.6 per cent in the chemical and rubber industry.

The final category of studies concentrates on a wider comparison of Japanese manufacturing industries with those of the US, Canada and Germany. Using the generalised Leontief cost function, Morrison (1990a) provided an alternative measure of TFP growth that allowed for scale economies, subequilibrium, costs of adjustment and markup behaviour, as opposed to the conventional TFP growth approach. He compared these two approaches using the data of the US, Japanese and Canadian manufacturing sectors and found that the average annual conventional TFP growth rate of the Japanese manufacturing sector was 1.223 per cent over the period 1960–81, whereas the modified TFP growth rate became 0.987 per cent.

Using a Törnqvist TFP index, Denny *et al.* (1992) found evidence that the slowdown of TFP growth was a widespread phenomenon across the manufacturing sectors of Canada, Japan and the US over the 1973–80 period. Their study found that the average annual TFP growth rates for Japanese manufacturing industries ranged from 0.23 per cent in the food industry to 3.28 per cent in precision instruments during the 1954–86 period. Moreover, there was no sign of any improvement in TFP growth in Japan in the 1980s.

2.5   REVIEW OF KOREA

One of the key issues in the series of TFP studies on the Korean manufacturing sector by Jene K. Kwon is the consideration of capital utilisation rate.[14] After incorporating the capital utilisation rate in the growth accounting framework, Kim and Kwon (1977) demonstrated that the contribution of TFP growth to output growth in the Korean manufacturing sector fell significantly from 36 per cent to 8 per cent during the period 1962–71. However, the detailed estimate of TFP growth was not available in their study.

Kwon (1986) decomposed TFP growth into technical change, non-constant returns to scale and change in capital utilisation by linking growth accounting to a cost function. The empirical result showed that during the 1961–80 period the TFP of the Korean manufacturing sector grew by 2.95 per cent per annum and contributed 15.16 per cent to output growth. More specifically, the shares attributed to TFP growth by technical change, non-constant returns to scale and change in capital utilisation were found to be 44.6 per cent, 38.1 per cent and 17.3 per cent respectively.

In employing growth accounting, Dollar and Sokoloff (1990) split labour productivity growth into capital deepening and advances in total factor productivity and analysed their relative contributions to labour productivity growth in 25 Korean manufacturing industries. They found evidence that capital deepening accounted for over 70 per cent of labour productivity growth in heavy industries, comprising iron and steel, industrial chemicals and others. In contrast, a rapid advance in total factor productivity in light, medium and natural resource industries on average explained about two-thirds of labour productivity growth.[15] The highest TFP growth was found in the leather (12.7 per cent) and other chemical (12.6 per cent) industries but the glass industry suffered a negative TFP growth rate of 4.1 per cent. Among TFP studies on Korean manufacturing industries, Dollar and Sokoloff (1990) reported the highest average annual TFP growth of 6.1 per cent for the entire manufacturing sector over the period 1963–79.

Kang and Kwon (1993) measured the TFP growth of 22 Korean manufacturing industries, using growth accounting associated with a translog cost function as well as taking account of the capital utilisation rate. They suggested that TFP for the entire manufacturing sector on average grew at annual rates of 3.43 per cent and 0.16 per cent for the periods 1963–73 and 1973–83 respectively. Input growth accounted for 84 per cent and 99 per cent of the output growth for the two corresponding periods, suggesting that the output growth in Korean manufacturing industries was mainly input-driven. Meanwhile, the decomposition of TFP growth into technical change, returns to scale and capital utilisation showed that returns to scale accounted for half of the TFP growth and technical change contributed 45 per cent during the 1963–83 period.

In applying a Cobb–Douglas production function and value added as a measure of output, Pilat (1995) first compared the level of TFP in the Korean manufacturing industry with that of the United States based on specific industry-of-origin purchasing power parities. He found that the Korean manufacturing sector's TFP had risen from 9 per cent of the US level in 1967 to more than 18 per cent in 1987. Using growth accounting, Pilat found that the TFP growth of the overall manufacturing sector exhibited an average annual rate of 4.3 per cent between 1967 and 1987. Among 13 Korean manufacturing industries, the highest average annual TFP growth rate of 10.4 per cent occurred in the electrical machinery and equipment industry.

Using the short-run generalised Leontief cost function, Park and Kwon (1995) investigated the TFP growth of 28 Korean manufacturing industries, grouped as heavy and light industries, together with the effects of markups (market power), scale economies and capacity utilisation. The empirical results showed that there was a considerable difference between conventional TFP growth (2.0 per cent) and generalised TFP growth (–1.6 per cent) for Korean manufacturing as a whole over the period 1967–89. This implied that due to the failure to distinguish the effects of scale economies and capacity utilisation in the measurement of TFP growth, the conventional TFP estimates were theoretically biased. Hence it was argued that the negative TFP growth derived from the generalised TFP measure reflected the true degree of technology decline in the Korean manufacturing sector.

In addition to examining the impact of government interventions (tariff, tax incentives and so on) on the TFP growth of the manufacturing sector in Korea, Lee (1996) also provided TFP growth estimates for 38 manufacturing industries over four separate periods: 1962–67, 1968–72, 1973–76 and 1979–83. As there was no aggregate TFP growth estimate for the entire manufacturing sector and no estimates for 38 industries over the entire period, the results for individual industries are not presented here but are available in Lee (1996, p. 408).

In a comparative study involving Korea and Taiwan, Okuda (1997) provided TFP growth estimates for Korean manufacturing industries using the growth accounting framework. The Korean manufacturing sector as a whole had an average annual TFP growth rate of 3.2 per cent for the period 1970–93. In terms of relative contribution to output growth, 22.7 per cent of output growth was attributed to TFP growth during the sample period. Moreover, the first and second highest annual TFP growth rates appeared in the metals (8.4 per cent) and machinery (7.6 per cent) industries; in contrast, the oil refinery industry did not record any progress in TFP.

Lee *et al.* (1998) applied the non-parametric Malmquist productivity index for 36 Korean manufacturing industries over the period 1967–93. Overall, the TFP of the entire manufacturing sector increased by an annual rate of 0.286 per cent. The decomposition of TFP growth revealed that technological progress (1.141 per cent per annum) was the major source of TFP progress. However, the moderate technological progress combined with low TFP growth implied that there was a deterioration in technical efficiency (–0.855 per cent per annum) over time, which was the case in many Korean manufacturing industries.

Hwang (1998) disagreed with the views of Young (1995) and others who argued that TFP performance in the East Asian manufacturing sectors was comparable with that of developed countries.   Applying two different approaches (the conventional growth accounting and augmented Solow models), Hwang showed that TFP for Korea's entire manufacturing sector increased by average annual rates of 2.06 per cent and 2.46 per cent between 1973 and 1993 respectively.[16]   Further applying Johansen's cointegration analysis, Hwang suggested that the Korean manufacturing sector could be characterised by an endogenous growth model due to increasing returns to scale in production technology or a learning-by-doing effect.

Following Hall (1988) and Harrison (1994), Kim (2000) distinguished between 'standard' TFP growth and 'true' TFP growth for 36 Korean manufacturing industries over the period 1966–88 due to the incidence of imperfect competition and non-constant returns to scale. Using Korea's *Input Output Tables* and adjusting the growth in labour input for changes in hours worked and education level, the result derived from traditional growth accounting showed that the unweighted average TFP growth of Korean manufacturing industries was 1.9 per cent per annum. After excluding the effects of imperfect competition and non-returns to scale, the true unweighted TFP growth estimate for the entire manufacturing sector was about 0.5 per cent per annum during the sample period, accounting for only 3 per cent of output growth in the Korean manufacturing sector. The detailed TFP growth rates for 36 manufacturing industries are available in Kim (2000, p. 77, Table 7).

Kwack (2000) measured the TFP growth of Korean manufacturing industries over the period 1971–93. Using the growth accounting approach, the results revealed annual TFP growth rates of 3 per cent, 4.5 per cent and 1.1 per cent in the total, heavy and light manufacturing industries respectively. The contribution of TFP growth to value added growth for the entire manufacturing sector was 21.6 per cent for the sample period but fell to 9.4 per cent in the more recent period 1989–93.

Yuhn and Kwon (2000) extended the work of Kwon and Yuhn (1990) and criticised the use of value added as a measure of manufacturing output in any productivity analysis due to its failure to satisfy the separability hypotheses. Then they applied the growth accounting approach to estimate the TFP growth of the Korean manufacturing sector as a whole. The result suggested that TFP grew by an average annual rate of 1.52 per cent between 1962 and 1981 and the contribution of TFP growth to output growth was 7.6 per cent.

Kim and Han (2001) examined the TFP growth of Korean manufacturing industries by using a stochastic production frontier approach. Following Kumbhakar *et al.* (2000), TFP growth was decomposed into four components: technical progress, changes in technical efficiency, changes in allocative efficiency and scale effects. Using the annual data for 508 manufacturing firms listed on the Korean Stock Exchange from 1980 to 1994, Kim and Han found that technical progress was a key contributor to TFP growth and that technical efficiency improvement also had a significant effect. The average annual TFP growth rate of the entire manufacturing sector was 7.3 per cent despite the decreasing trend. Among the individual industries, the fabrication industry (fabricated metal products, machinery and equipment) enjoyed the highest average annual TFP growth of 9.4 per cent during the same period, followed by textiles (7.7 per cent) and food (7.1 per cent).

Mahadevan and Kim (2003) recently applied the random coefficients model and firm-level data from 135 firms listed on the Korean Stock Exchange to estimate the TFP growth for four industries at the 2-digit level during 1980–94. Their study showed that output growth in the four manufacturing industries was increasingly productivity-driven from the mid-1980s. Note that because the sample size was relatively small and presumably based on large firms, their results may not be comparable with the present study and other studies discussed above.

2.6   REVIEW OF SINGAPORE

There have been many TFP studies on Singapore's manufacturing industries. A comprehensive survey by Mahadevan (1999) additionally offered comparisons of TFP performance in the service sector and the overall economy. Notably, Tsao (1985) first argued that the miraculous output growth in Singapore's manufacturing industries was not associated with high TFP growth in the 1970s. Tsao then applied growth accounting with the translog production function and four factor inputs, and discovered that 17 out of 28 of Singapore's manufacturing industries experienced negative TFP growth over the period 1970–79. On average, Singapore's manufacturing sector enhanced its TFP by only 0.08 per cent per annum, stemming from annual TFP growth rates of –1.18 per cent for the period 1970–73 and 0.71 per cent for 1973–79.

Wong and Gan (1994) applied the conventional growth accounting approach to examine TFP growth in 28 Singapore manufacturing industries at the 3-digit level. Using gross output and the factor inputs of capital, labour, material and energy, their results indicated that the overall manufacturing sector averaged an annual TFP growth rate of 1.6 per cent over the period 1981–90. Surprisingly, the high-tech industries such as electrical machinery and electronic products, and industrial machinery, experienced an annual decline in TFP of 0.54 per cent and 2.32 per cent respectively, while the tobacco industry obtained the highest average annual TFP growth rate of 11.22 per cent. Moreover, Wong (1993) investigated the sources of labour productivity growth and found that the TFP growth of Singapore's manufacturing industries accounted for 44 per cent of labour productivity growth in the 1980s.

Rao and Lee (1995) explored the sources of output growth in Singapore's manufacturing and services sectors and the overall economy over three distinct phases: 1966–73, 1976–84 and 1987–94. In employing conventional growth accounting, their findings showed that Singapore's manufacturing sector experienced an average annual TFP growth of –0.4 per cent and 3.2 per cent for the periods 1976–84 and 1987–94 respectively. The contribution of TFP growth to output growth increased from –5 per cent to 32 per cent over the two periods. In contrast to Kim and Lau (1994) and Young (1995), Rao and Lee concluded that the sustainability of Singapore's manufacturing sector looked optimistic.

Leung (1997) employed growth accounting to study 30 of Singapore's manufacturing industries for the period 1983–93. Unlike many existing TFP studies, Leung estimated a weighted average annual TFP growth of 2.8 per cent for the manufacturing sector as a whole. In addition, the average annual TFP growth rate of the aggregate (unweighted) manufacturing sector was calculated to be 2.0 per cent. Hence Leung suggested that an average annual TFP growth rate of between 2 per cent and 3 per cent was plausible for Singapore's manufacturing sector during the decade. With further analysis of the determinants of TFP growth, the learning-by-doing effect was not found to be significant. Leung's result coincides with the finding of the current study that there was no technical efficiency improvement in Singapore's manufacturing industries.

Bloch and Tang (1999) estimated cost-saving technical progress for 27 of Singapore's manufacturing industries at the 3-digit level in an attempt to distinguish TFP growth derived from conventional growth accounting. Although eight industries were excluded due to divergence, the findings on the other 19 industries indicated that 11 of them experienced technical progress represented by the elasticity of cost with respect to time, whereas the other eight industries suffered technical regression between 1975 and 1994. With regard to individual industries, the fast growing industry, electronic products and components, significantly gained technical progress of 6.5 per cent per annum. Moreover, 17 of the 19 industries exhibited increasing returns to scale. It was also suggested that although the largest and fastest growing industries such as electronic products and components were inclined to demonstrate a higher rate of technical progress, they experienced a greater degree of decreasing returns to scale. The estimates of TFP growth rates computed by growth accounting are also available in the Bloch and Tang study.

Mahadevan and Kalirajan (2000) applied the stochastic production frontier approach to examine TFP growth for 28 of Singapore's manufacturing industries over the period 1976–94. Although input growth emerged as a major factor driving output growth, their study found evidence of positive technological progress with negative technical efficiency change leading to positive but low and declining TFP growth in Singapore's manufacturing sector. The average annual TFP growth rates for the periods 1976–84 and 1987–94 were 0.92 per cent and –0.52 per cent respectively. More specifically, the –0.52 per cent TFP growth rate was attributable to –0.8 per cent technical efficiency change and 0.28 per cent technological progress.

In contrast to earlier TFP studies, Koh *et al.* (2002) provided the most optimistic TFP estimate for Singapore's manufacturing sector to date. They employed the conventional growth accounting approach in conjunction with the Singapore manufactured product price index (output–price deflator) and import price (material-price deflator) to estimate TFP growth for the manufacturing sector, comprising 18 industries at the 2-digit level over the period 1975–98. Their findings suggested that TFP growth for the overall manufacturing sector was 2.7 per cent per annum.

2.7 REVIEW OF TAIWAN

Before discussing the relationship between export performance and productivity growth, Chen and Tang (1990) applied growth accounting to estimate TFP growth for 16 Taiwan manufacturing industries at the 2-digit level over the 1968–82 period. Unlike conventional growth accounting, the TFP growth in their study was defined as 'a change in average cost not accounted for by the changes in input prices', in which the inputs included labour, capital and material. Chen and Tang found that four of the 16 industries experienced negative TFP growth and average annual TFP growth ranged from –0.76 per cent in the lumber and furniture industry to 4.13 per cent in the leather and fur industry. It should be noted that it is unclear whether quality improvement embodied in capital and labour inputs was adjusted in their study.

Okuda (1994) explored the impact of trade and foreign direct investment on productivity growth in Taiwan's manufacturing industries and, using a Törnqvist index, provided TFP growth estimates for 11 industries between 1978 and 1991.[17] The average annual TFP growth rate for the entire manufacturing sector was estimated at 2.6 per cent during the sample period. In terms of individual industries, the electronics industry outperformed other industries, with 5 per cent annual TFP growth. Note that the adjustments for quality improvement embodied in labour and capital inputs were not carried out in Okuda's study, suggesting a possible overstatement of TFP growth. Okuda (1997) extended his earlier study to compare the TFP performance of the Taiwanese and Korean manufacturing industries. However, the sample period covered for Taiwan's manufacturing industries only added one more year to his earlier study and the new TFP growth estimates in Table I of Okuda (1997, p. 365), are generally comparable to his previous results; hence this study is not described here any further.

Liang (1995) stressed the importance of disaggregating factor inputs due to possible measurement errors caused by the heterogeneous characteristics of inputs, for example skilled labour, unskilled labour and manager and so on. Using the translog index with gross output and four inputs (labour, capital, materials and energy), Liang examined 17 industries comprising the manufacturing sector and found the average annual TFP growth rates of overall manufacturing to be 0.12 per cent and 1.41 per cent during the periods 1973–82 and 1982–87 respectively.[18] Moreover, he found that ten industries suffered a decline in TFP in the former period and five experienced negative TFP growth during the latter.

Unlike most TFP studies, Chuang (1996) applied the regression approach to measure TFP growth for Taiwan's manufacturing sector and found that it increased at an average annual rate of 1.9 per cent between 1975 and 1990. Chuang further suggested that over 40 per cent of manufacturing output growth in Taiwan was attributable to a 'trade-induced learning' effect, which he treated as TFP growth. However, detailed TFP growth estimates for individual manufacturing industries were not provided in his study.

Extending Liang's (1995) study, Liang and Jorgenson (1999) compared TFP growth estimates for Taiwan's manufacturing industries on the basis of two different output measurements: gross output and value added output. The average annual TFP growth rates computed from value added output for the overall manufacturing sector were 2.33 per cent, 2.72 per cent and 2.46 per cent over the periods 1961–82, 1982–93 and 1961–93 respectively. Correspondingly, average annual TFP growth rates calculated from gross output appeared to be lower and turned out to be 0.2 per cent, 0.55 per cent and 0.32 per cent respectively. However, further examination and interpretation of these two distinctive sets of estimates are not available in the Liang and Jorgenson study.

Hu and Chan (1999) applied growth accounting in conjunction with human capital to estimate TFP progress in 15 Taiwan manufacturing industries. On average, TFP in the overall manufacturing sector grew at 3.1 per cent per annum (employees as labour input) or 3.4 per cent (hours worked as labour input) over the period 1979–96.[19] Because quality improvement embodied in capital and labour inputs was not adjusted, Hu and Chan's TFP growth estimates apparently overstated the extent of actual TFP growth. With regard to individual industries, the chemical industry, including chemical material products, rubber and plastics, enjoyed the highest average annual TFP growth rate of 7.1 per cent, while precision instruments and other industrial products industries experienced negative 1.3 per cent growth in TFP.

Using a Törnqvist TFP index, an official publication, *The Trends in Multifactor Productivity, Taiwan Area, Republic of China*, 2000, published by the Directorate-General Budget, Accounting and Statistics (DGBAS) provided annual TFP growth estimates as well as TFP levels for the aggregate manufacturing sector and 18 manufacturing industries from 1978 to 1998. Over this period, the average annual TFP growth of the aggregate manufacturing sector was reported to be 1.9 per cent. However, the DGBAS (Republic of China, 2000) did not allow for the effect of imperfect competition; so these official figures unavoidably overestimated the real TFP growth rates for Taiwan's manufacturing industries.

Aw *et al.* (2001) applied the multilateral TFP index proposed by Caves *et al.* (1982a) and Good *et al.* (1997) to three sets of Industrial and Commercial Census data in 1981, 1986 and 1991 in order to investigate the TFP differentials of Taiwanese firms.[20] By defining industry productivity as the market share of the weighted sum of the firm productivity levels, Aw *et al.* subsequently computed TFP growth for the nine manufacturing industries at the 2-digit level. With the exception of the transportation equipment industry, all other industries achieved TFP growth of between 7.8 per cent (clothing) and 36.6 per cent (chemicals) over the period 1981–91. At the manufacturing level, the weighted TFP growth was estimated to be 32.4 per cent during the decade (or 3.2 per cent per annum).

Färe *et al.* (1995) focused on four Taiwanese major industry groupings, comprising essential goods, chemicals, metal machinery and electrical precision equipment. Using the non-parametric DEA (Data Envelopment Analysis) approach, the TFP level of the overall manufacturing sector measured by the Malmquist TFP index increased by 3.59 per cent annually solely due to technological progress during the period 1978–89. Subsequently, Färe *et al.* (2001) extended their earlier study and calculated Malmquist productivity indexes for 16 of Taiwan's manufacturing industries between 1978 and 1992. They suggested that Taiwan's manufacturing sector had on average enhanced TFP by 2.89 per cent per annum, with 2.56 per cent attributed to technological progress and 0.33 per cent to technical efficiency improvement; that is, technological progress largely accounted for TFP growth.

A brief summary of the main findings of the TFP studies on the five East Asian manufacturing sectors reviewed in this chapter is presented in Table 2.2.

Table 2.2   *TFP studies on the manufacturing sector in the five East Asian economies*

Author	Period	Method	TFP growth p.a. (%)
Hong Kong			
Kwong *et al.* (2000)	1984–93	Growth accounting	−1.53
Imai (2001)	1981–90	Growth accounting	5.6
	1991–97		6.0
Japan			
Norsworthy and Malmquist	1965–73	Translog function with	0.91
(1983)	1973–78	gross output	1.64
Jorgenson *et al.* (1987b)	1960–79	Translog quantities index	0.83
Morrison (1990a)	1960–81	Generalised Leontief cost function	0.987
Prasad (1997)	1971–93	Not available	2.8
Nakajima *et al.* (1998)	1964–88	Index number approach	3.731
Sato (2002)	1979–85	Not available	2.5
	1985–91		2.6
	1991–97		2.2
Korea			
Kwon (1986)	1961–80	Growth accounting with a cost function	2.95
Dollar and Sokoloff (1990)	1963–79	Growth accounting	6.1
Kang and Kwon (1993)	1963–73	Growth accounting	3.43
	1973–83	with a cost function	0.16
Pilat (1995)	1967–87	Growth accounting	4.3
Park and Kwon (1995)	1967–89	Generalised Leontief cost function	−1.6
Okuda (1997)	1970–93	Growth accounting	3.2
Lee *et al.* (1998)	1967–93	Malmquist productivity index	0.286
Hwang (1998)	1973–93	Growth accounting	2.06
		Augmented Solow model	2.46

Table 2.2   (continued)

Author	Period	Method	TFP growth p.a. (%)
Kim (2000)	1966–88	Traditional growth accounting	1.9
		Modified growth accounting	0.5
Kwack (2000)	1971–93	Growth accounting	3.0
Yuhn and Kwon (2000)	1962–81	Growth accounting with a cost function	1.52
Kim and Han (2001)	1980–94	Stochastic frontier approach	7.3
Singapore			
Tsao (1985)	1970–79	Growth accounting	0.08
Wong and Gan (1994)	1981–90	Growth accounting	1.6
Rao and Lee (1995)	1976–84	Growth accounting	−0.4
	1987–94		3.2
Leung (1997)	1983–93	Growth accounting	2.8
Mahadevan and Kalirajan	1976–84	Stochastic frontier	0.92
(2000)	1987–94	approach	−0.52
Koh *et al.* (2002)	1975–98	Growth accounting	2.7
Taiwan			
Okuda (1994)	1978–91	Growth accounting	2.6
Liang (1995)	1973–82	Growth accounting	0.12
	1982–87		1.41
Chuang (1996)	1975–90	Regression approach	1.9
Liang and Jorgenson (1999)	1961–93	Growth accounting	2.46
Hu and Chan (1999)	1979–96	Growth accounting	3.1
Republic of China (2000)	1978–98	Törnqvist TFP index	1.9
Aw *et al.* (2001)	1981–91	Multilateral TFP index	3.24
Färe *et al.* (1995)	1978–89	Malmquist productivity index	3.59
Färe *et al.* (2001)	1978–92	Malmquist productivity index	2.89

2.8   CONCLUSION

As seen from the above TFP reviews, the empirical results of the studies differed significantly. Even for the same country, TFP growth estimates often varied extensively; for instance, the average annual TFP growth estimates for the entire Korean manufacturing sector ranged from –1.6 per cent in Park and Kwon (1995) to as high as 7.3 per cent in Kim and Han (2001). So, what has contributed to these discrepancies?

First: the use of different methodologies or specifications. Taking Taiwan as an example, it is found that the methods used varied from study to study. They included growth accounting, regression, DEA (Malmquist productivity index) and multilateral TFP index approaches. Although growth accounting has been widely applied in many TFP studies, different specifications for the production function could have led to different outcomes. For instance, Hu and Chan (1999) incorporated human capital into the growth accounting framework, whereas in a series of TFP studies on Korean manufacturing industries by Kwon (Kwon, 1986; Kang and Kwon, 1993; Park and Kwon, 1995; Yuhn and Kwon, 2000), he insisted on taking account of capital utilisation to estimate the growth of capital input.

Second: differences in sources of data sets and sample periods covered. Not surprisingly, different types and sources of data sets generated various outcomes; for example, Aw *et al.* (2001) used firm-level data and other studies used aggregate data at the industry level. Also, the sample periods varied across studies, which makes it difficult to compare outcomes.

Third: variations in industrial classifications or aggregations. Interestingly, these are not always the same even for the same country in the TFP studies reviewed. In the case of Singapore, 27 industries were investigated in Bloch and Tang (1999), 28 in the studies by Tsao (1985) and Mahadevan and Kalirajan (2000), and 30 in Leung (1997). In the case of Taiwan, the classifications or aggregations were even more diverse and the number of industries examined ranged from 11 to 17, as seen in section 2.7. Furthermore, in the Chuang (1996) study, estimation of TFP growth was carried out for the manufacturing sector as a whole rather than for individual industries.

Fourth: differences in variable constructions and adjustments. In relation to this, quality improvement embodied in labour and capital inputs has frequently been ignored and may have led to an overestimation of the extent of TFP growth, for instance Dollar and Sokoloff (1990) and Kim and Han (2001). In addition, the choice of 'hours worked' or 'number of employees' as the measure of labour input would give rise to different conclusions, such as Hu and Chan (1999). Lastly, it is observed that applying gross output as the measure of firm or industry performance rather than value added output in some studies would also produce discrepancies (Liang and Jorgenson, 1999; Yuhn and Kwon, 2000).

In order to examine TFP growth in the five East Asian manufacturing sectors, the current study applies the varying coefficients frontier model to avoid the limitations and strict assumptions imposed by the growth accounting and the conventional stochastic frontier approaches. Since growth accounting cannot distinguish the difference between TFP growth and technological progress, this study will follow the rationales introduced by Nishimizu and Page (1982) and use the decomposition approach outlined in Chapter 3 to demonstrate why growth accounting is inadequate and show how improvement in technical efficiency can play an important role in the process of enhancing TFP and output growth. The detailed specifications of the varying coefficients frontier approach and empirical model used are described in Chapter 3.

The current study uses a uniform data set from the United Nations Industrial Development Organisation (UNIDO) database, which covers manufacturing industries at the 3-digit level and has a consistent industrial classification for each country that will facilitate investigation of the sources of output growth in the East Asian manufacturing sectors. [21] More importantly, the adjustment of quality improvement embodied in labour and capital inputs and construction of variables will be undertaken consistently. Thus an accurate comparison of TFP growth for manufacturing industries in East Asia can be ascertained. Although the UNIDO database does not hold the data for manufacturing gross fixed capital formation (GFCF) for Taiwan, data sources for Taiwan are obtained from the official publications by the DGBAS, Taiwan, the Republic of China. The details of data sources are presented in Chapter 3.

NOTES

1. Reasons for the possible over-adjustment of factor inputs in East Asia include capacity utilisation, depreciation of the capital stock and the deflators of capital input. For details of other possible reasons, see Chen (1997, pp. 32–3).

2. In this case, TFP growth becomes the sum of exogenous technological change and endogenous expansion of varieties (or growth rate of overall quality) weighted by the labour share.

3. Apart from Young (1995), none of these TFP studies on East Asian manufacturing sectors has taken embodied technology into account, namely adjusting quality improvement embodied in capital and labour inputs. Thus, without carrying out the quality improvement adjustments, those TFP estimates are likely to be overstated.

4. Although this study is conducted concurrently with Han *et al.* (2002), the coverage of sample periods and manufacturing industries in this study is much longer and larger than Han *et al.* Also, this study adjusts quality improvement embodied in labour and capital inputs in conjunction with Young (1995) and uses manufacturing (value added and GFCF) deflators to obtain constant 1990 prices for all variables. An important partner of East Asia, Taiwan, is also included in this study.

5. Sample periods differed across the 29 industries, for example the petroleum and coal industry was from 1988–93 and the electronic parts and components industry from 1984–89. For more details, see Table 6.11.

6. One possible concern is that Kwong *et al.* (2000) used gross output (rather than conventional value added), with the inputs of material, labour, capital, utilities and factory space, to estimate TFP growth because they claimed that manufacturing value added was overstated as a result of the recent integration with mainland China in manufacturing production. An example is provided in Kwong *et al.* (2000, p. 173, footnote 4).

7. Strictly speaking, the study by Tuan and Ng (1995) is less relevant to the objective of this study. Moreover, it is unclear why there were several negative capital coefficients in their estimation results. This indicates that less capital would lead to more output, which basically contradicts economic theory. No explanations were given regarding the huge swing in TFP level and capital coefficients (or elasticities) on an annual basis, from 1.6977 to 2.9047 (constant term, represented by TFP) and from 0.2618 to 0.6300 (capital coefficient). Hence, their results must be read with great care.

8. Note that the qualitative improvement associated with labour and capital inputs was not eliminated in Imai's study, which may overstate the actual TFP growth rates. More importantly, the tradable sector cannot be completely viewed as the manufacturing sector; hence, his results should be interpreted with caution.

9. Because TFP growth measures the improvement in the efficiency of the use of inputs over time, Fuss and Waverman (1990) measured TFP growth by the growth in cost efficiency.

10. The estimates of TFP growth rates of Sato (2002) are from the *Annual Report of National Accounts* by the Japanese Economic Planning Agency.

11. Using the same data set of Norsworthy and Malmquist (1983) and non-parametric analysis, Chavas and Cox (1990) suggested that the findings of Norsworthy and Malmquist (1983) were sensitive to their parametric specification. In other words, Chavas and Cox (1990) found little evidence to support the necessity of using the gross output approach and the hypothesis of Hick non-neutral technical change.

12. If the value added approach were applied, the corresponding results would be 2.03% and 3.67% respectively.

13. The results of the Japanese manufacturing industries in Griliches and Mairesse (1990) were unweighted firm averages and many of the multinational firms were also included in the sample, so the TFP growth estimates are not comparable to other studies.

14. Other papers on the issue of the Korean manufacturing sector's productivity growth by Jene K. Kwon include Kwon (1986), Kang and Kwon (1993), Park and Kwon (1995) and Yuhn and Kwon (2000).

15. The classification of four major categories (light, heavy, medium and natural resources) is available in Dollar and Sokoloff (1990, p. 313).
16. Hwang (1998) used the index of manufacturing output as a measure of aggregate output and the total man hours worked in Korean manufacturing as a measure of labour input.
17. The original 18 industries were combined into 11 industries in order to be consistent with other statistics; for instance, the chemicals industry now comprises chemical materials, chemical products, petroleum and coal, and rubber products. The detailed aggregation of industries is available in Table VI of Okuda (1994, p. 433).
18. The results for the manufacturing industries are only available up to 1987 and can be found in Table 3 of Liang (1995, pp. 22–3).
19. Hu and Chan (1999) also reported that the human capital adjusted TFP growth rates of the manufacturing sector were correspondingly high at 5.5% and 6.0% during the sample period.
20. The details of the variables involved in the estimation are available in Aw *et al.* (2001, pp. 82–4).
21. There are some industrial aggregations in the cases of Hong Kong, Singapore and Taiwan due to missing data and the change of industrial classification.

3. Methodology and data sources

This chapter discusses the methodology, data sources and constructions of variables used in the current study. Section 3.1 briefly reviews some popular methods used to measure TFP growth, including the conventional stochastic frontier and the meta-production function. This review is followed by a discussion of a recent method that uses the varying coefficients frontier model. A major limitation in many of the earlier studies of TFP growth, particularly growth accounting based studies, is the use of TFP growth as synonymous with technological progress. This is problematic. The empirical literature indicates that TFP growth can be obtained not only through technological progress but also by improving the technical efficiency with which the chosen technology is applied. Hence, section 3.2 demonstrates the decomposition analysis in which output growth can be decomposed into input growth, technical efficiency change and technological progress, and shows that TFP growth combines the effects of technical efficiency and technological progress. More importantly, the decomposition of TFP growth is invaluable from the policy perspective because it provides relevant information to economic policy makers. The rest of the chapter relates to the current study. Section 3.3 describes the model employed and associated tests applied to it. Section 3.4 discusses data sources. Section 3.5 details the construction of variables as well as the selection of deflators. The UNIDO Industrial Statistics and industry coverage can be found in Appendix A.1.

3.1   THEORIES AND METHODOLOGY

Analysis of the sources of growth in East Asia has long been recognised to be an important issue. However, there is still no consensus on the role of TFP growth in the East Asian economies. Given that the results of empirical studies ultimately depend on the choice of methods used to estimate TFP growth, this section reviews some of the popular measures used in the literature. After a general discussion of these measures, the meta-production function approach proposed by Kim and Lau (1994) is reviewed in section 3.1.1. Section 3.1.2 discusses the stochastic frontier and three other deterministic approaches. Finally, a recent method using the varying coefficients frontier approach, which is employed by the current study, is discussed in section 3.1.3.

3.1.1 General Review of TFP Methods

Tinbergen (1942) and Solow (1957) initially proposed the conventional factor share growth accounting approach in the absolute form (TFP growth) using time series. Later, Jorgenson and his associates introduced the use of Divisia and translog indices in growth accounting, reflecting the necessity of dividing factor inputs into a number of categories. The other category of time-series approach in its relative form (TFP levels) was initiated by Jorgenson and Nishimizu (1978) and applied to international comparisons of TFP. For other applications of this approach, see Christensen *et al.* (1980, 1981), Caves *et al.* (1982a), Wolff (1991) and Dollar and Wolff (1994). Also, Nadiri and Prucha (1999) demonstrated a comparison between a dynamic factor demand model and a conventional Divisia TFP index.[1]

Although conventional factor share growth accounting has thus far received more attention in the literature, criticisms against it have been well documented in Chen (1997), Felipe (1999) and Nelson and Pack (1999), to mention a few.[2] The growth accounting approach with a detailed breakdown of the factor inputs suggested by Jorgenson *et al.* (1987a) is described briefly in Appendix A.2. The second approach to growth accounting involves estimating the factor shares through the production function using ordinary least squares (OLS) procedures. Recent examples of this research can be seen in Hall and Jones (1996) and Islam (1995). The detailed specifications, advantages and weaknesses regarding this approach are available in Islam (1999).

Kim and Lau (1994) employed the meta-production function approach to measure productivity growth in four East Asian economies in comparison to five developed OECD countries, specifying that all countries have the same meta-production function.[3] It is assumed that the efficiency-equivalent quantities of output and inputs, Y_{it}^* and X_{ijt}^*, are associated with time-varying, country- and commodity-specific augmentation factors $A_{ij}(t)$'s, $i = 1,...,n$, $j = 0,...,m$; this the production function can be expressed as

$$Y_{it} = A_{i0}(t)^{-1} F(X_{i1t}^*,...,X_{imt}^*), \quad i = 1,...,n, \tag{3.1}$$

where $F(\cdot)$ is a translog production function and $Y_{it}^* = A_{i0}(t)Y_{it}$, $X_{ijt}^* = A_{ij}(t)X_{ijt}$, $j = 1,...,m$. A further assumption is that the commodity-augmentation factors are assumed to have constant geometric form with respect to time, $Y_{it}^* = A_{i0}(1+c_{i0})^t Y_{it}$, and $X_{ijt}^* = A_{ij}(1+c_{ij})^t X_{ijt}$, where augmentation level parameters (A_{i0}'s and A_{ij}'s) and augmentation rate parameters (c_{i0}'s and c_{ij}'s) are constants and subject to a normalisation. They also add up to another equation that consisers the payment of labour input to total output. A detailed discussion of the estimation process can be found in Kim and Lau (1994, p. 244).

The comments by Rao and Lee (1995, p. 85) on the results produced by the meta-production function approach suggest that there is a difficulty in interpreting the augmentation in output and inputs in real life. It is also unclear whether Kim and Lau's results remain robust if the frontier technology of the numeraire country is changed. Further, although the hypothesis of the existence of a unique meta-production cannot be rejected for the sample of four NICs and the combined sample of NICs and G-5, an increase in the number of sample countries will eventually alter the estimated values of the relevant coefficients. Finally, the estimation method using instrumental variables has certain limitations.

Another major approach to TFP growth is the 'production frontier approach', which can be subdivided into two categories. The first category is the non-parametric approach – the Malmquist productivity index, which is widely used in empirical studies. Under this framework, TFP growth can be decomposed into several components, such as technical progress, technical efficiency change and scale efficiency change. For instance, Caves *et al.* (1982b) applied the Malmquist productivity index to compare relative productivity among countries.[4] Nevertheless, one of the major drawbacks of this approach is that empirical results are rather sensitive to outliers, which may subsequently lead to biased outcomes. For a general overview of the Malmquist productivity index, see Färe *et al.* (1994a). The second category is a parametric frontier approach. Though a number of econometric approaches have been suggested in the literature to estimate the production frontier, which shows the maximum possible output, the stochastic frontier approach popularised by Aigner *et al.* (1977) and Meeusen and van den Broeck (1977) has attracted more attention than others.

3.1.2 Stochastic Frontier Approach

Several survey articles, such as those by Førsund *et al.* (1980), Bauer (1990), Coelli (1995) and Kalirajan and Shand (1999), have provided indispensable reviews on the stochastic production frontier. The detailed specifications and estimations are described in those surveys, so only some of the key aspects will be mentioned here.

One of the features explaining the popularity of the stochastic frontier is that it allows for the possibility of a firm's performance being affected by some uncontrollable factors such as bad weather as well as controllable factors such as inefficiency. More explicitly, the symmetric component specified in the stochastic frontier approach allows for variation of the frontier across firms and captures measurement error, statistical noise and varying shocks outside the firms' control. In addition, the one-sided component captures the effects of inefficiency relative to the stochastic frontier (Aigner *et al.*, 1977). Therefore, the stochastic frontier function is specified as

$$y = f(x)\exp(v-u), \tag{3.2}$$

where the stochastic production frontier is $y = f(x)\exp(v)$ and v is assumed to be symmetric to capture the varying effects of measurement error and exogenous shocks which cause the placement of the deterministic kernel $f(x)$ to vary across firms. Technical inefficiency is captured by the one-sided error component $\exp(-u)$, $u \geq 0$. For other details of estimation, see Aigner *et al.* (1977) and Meeusen and van den Broeck (1977).

Bauer (1990) argued that there had been substantial progress towards more flexible functional forms and more varieties of systems of equations, such as cost, profit and distance functions. Even firm-specific estimates of inefficiency cound be obtained after imposing specific distributional assumptions. Coelli (1995) concluded that the proper selection of methods, using either the stochastic frontier or DEA approach, largely depended on the application being considered. In the case of agricultural studies, the stochastic frontier approach is generally preferred.

Nevertheless, the scenario of the stochastic frontier approach remains far from realistic because various constraints may affect the performance of firms, including style of management, experience of firms and scale or size of firms. For instance, a firm situated in a convenient location with good management and more experience in production will always outperform those with poor management and little experience. Put differently, firms or industries may not fully apply the best practice production technology for various reasons, including the firms' experience and ability of employees. Moreover, the ability to coordinate labour and capital is likely to differ across firms. All these factors will generate an impact on the coefficients of factor inputs (capital and labour); that is, there will be a significant variation in the estimated coefficients of capital and labour inputs, implying a non-neutral shift in the production frontier.

Kim and Han (2001) found empirical evidence of non-neutral technological progress, indicating varying coefficients of capital and labour for the manufacturing firms listed on the Korean Stock Exchange, over the period 1980–94. As opposed to the constant marginal rates of technical substitution (MRTS) of the conventional stochastic frontier, Huang and Liu (1994) argued that the MRTS at any input combination would not be constant because firms may have greater knowledge and experience with respect to the productivity of one input over another.[5] Hence, they proposed the non-neutral stochastic frontier model in which the production frontier is a non-neutral shift from the average production function. Therefore, to overcome the drawbacks of the conventional stochastic frontier, the current study applies the varying coefficients frontier model to capture differing applications of best practice technology by firms. Kalirajan and Shand (1999) detailed the strengths and weaknesses of four approaches to measuring productivity, namely DEA, stochastic frontier, stochastic varying coefficients frontier and Bayesian. The stochastic varying coefficients frontier approach stands out as being superior to others because it has the advantage of using both the DEA and stochastic frontier approaches, and can thus be viewed as a stochastic counterpart of DEA. The details of the modelling of the varying coefficients frontier will be illustrated next, and the empirical model presented in section 3.2.

Recently, Kumbhakar *et al.* (1999) have empirically compared various approaches to measuring TFP growth. They employed six variants of the time trend and general index models to derive the TFP growth for the Swedish cement industry. The three extensions of the time trend model include the standard translog model, the firm-specific technical change translog model of Cornwell *et al.* (1990), and the generalised translog model of Stevenson (1980). The other three generalised index models comprise the Baltagi–Griffin (1988) and Lee–Schmidt (1993) models. Despite some consensus among the six models on the degree of TFP growth, the model suggested by Stevenson (1980) is preferred on the basis of statistical tests and empirical results. Nevertheless, Kumbhakar *et al.* concluded that more examinations and simulations on various models were required to gain a better understanding of TFP measures.

3.1.3   Varying Coefficients Frontier Model

In contrast to the stochastic frontier approach, the varying coefficients frontier model avoids the hypothesis that firms apply inputs in a uniform manner. In practice, actual output across firms may differ due to management styles, organisational or institutional factors, and quality of labour. Empirically, given the same levels of inputs, data often show that different levels of actual output are obtained because firms have various methods of utilising the best available production technology. In order to account for such differences, it is vital to take account of the heterogeneity of firms and estimate variations in both intercepts and slope coefficients across firms and over time for the same firm. For a recent application of the varying coefficients frontier model to measuring TFP growth, see Kalirajan *et al.*

(1996), in which they have examined the impact of Chinese agricultural reforms on TFP growth.

Following Kalirajan and Obwona (1994), it is assumed that the production technology of the East Asian manufacturing industries can be represented by the Cobb–Douglas production function,

$$\ln Y_i = \beta_{0i} + \sum_{m=1}^{M} \beta_{mi} \ln X_{mi}, \quad i = 1,\ldots,N, \tag{3.3}$$

where Y_i is the output level of the ith firm, X_{mi} is the level of the mth input used by the ith firm, β_{0i} is the varying intercept term, and β_{mi} is the varying response coefficients of application of the mth input by the ith firm. Equation (3.3) indicates that the estimated response coefficients are unique to each individual firm. Put differently, the response production coefficients vary from firm to firm according to firm-specific characteristics.

Nevertheless, the estimation of equation (3.3) cannot be carried out without further assumptions imposed on the varying coefficients, because the number of intercepts and coefficients ($MN+N$) to be estimated exceeds the number of observations (N). To resolve the difficulty, the individual varying coefficients are assumed to vary from the mean coefficients; that is,

$$\beta_{mi} = \overline{\beta}_m + u_{mi}, \quad m = 1,\ldots,M \tag{3.4}$$

where $E(\beta_{mi}) = \overline{\beta}_m$, $E(u_{mi}) = 0$ and $E(u_{mi}) = \sigma_{umm}$ for $i = m$ and 0 otherwise; the varying intercept terms refer to $\beta_{0i} = \overline{\beta}_0 + u_{0i}$. With these additional assumptions, equations (3.3) and (3.4) can be rewritten as

$$\ln Y_i = \overline{\beta}_0 + \sum_{m=1}^{M} \overline{\beta}_m \ln X_{mi} + v_i, \tag{3.5}$$

where $v_i = u_{0i} + \sum_{m=1}^{M} u_{mi} \ln X_{mi}$, $E(v_i) = 0$ for all i, $Cov(v_i,v_j) = 0$ for $i \neq j$ and $Var(v_i) = \sigma_{u00} + \sum_{m=1}^{M} \sigma_{umm} \ln(X_{mi})^2$, $m = 1,\ldots,M$. In fact, this model is a special case of Swamy (1970) and identical to Hildreth and Houck's model (1968). For a general specification of the varying coefficients frontier model in terms of panel data, Swamy (1970), Hsiao (1975) and Kalirajan and Shand (1999, pp. 164–66) provide more details on this debate.

To find the estimates of $\overline{\beta}$, OLS procedure gives an unbiased but inefficient estimator. If $Var(v_i)$ is known, the best linear unbiased estimator

(BLUE) can be derived by generalised least squares (GLS). Following Hildreth and Houck's (1968) procedure, the mean response coefficients $\bar{\beta}$ can be estimated under certain assumptions of $Var(v_i)$. As for the individual response coefficients β_{mi}, Griffiths (1972) presented the actual firm-specific and input-specific response coefficient estimator for the ith observation. Drawing heavily on Kalirajan and Obwona (1994), the implications of equation (3.5) are twofold.

First, technical efficiency is achieved by adopting the best available techniques, which involve the efficient use of inputs. Therefore, the sources of technical efficiency stem from the efficient use of each input which contributes individually to technical efficiency, and any other firm-specific intrinsic characteristics which are not explicitly included may produce a combined contribution over and above the individual contributions. The former can be measured by the magnitudes of varying slope coefficients β_{mi} and the latter can be obtained by the varying intercept term.

Second, the highest magnitude of each response coefficient and the intercept constitute the production coefficients of the potential production function. These production frontier coefficients, β^*, are chosen in such a way as to reflect the production responses following the adoption of best practice techniques. Assume β_m^* is the highest response coefficient of the mth input for all firms, that is, $\beta_m^* = \max_i \{\beta_{mi}\}$, $m = 0,...,M$ and $i = 1,...,N$. Then, the potential frontier output for each firm can be expressed by

$$\ln Y_i^* = \beta_0^* + \sum_{m=1}^{M} \beta_m^* \ln X_{mi}, \quad i = 1,...,N. \tag{3.6}$$

Moreover, the characteristics of the frontier coefficients deserve further explanation. First, it is reasonable to assume that firms will not utilise all of the inputs efficiently. Despite best practice technology being available to all firms, not all will apply the same method to produce their output due to firm-specific characteristics. Consequently, technical efficiency will vary from firm to firm and the frontier coefficients (maximum coefficients of each input) may emanate from any single firm; that is to say, the frontier coefficients $\beta_1^*, \beta_2^*,...\beta_M^*$ may issue from different firms. For example, β_1^* is from the 3rd firm and β_2^* the 10th firm and so on, which implies that the 3rd firm applies its first input (say, labour) most efficiently and the 10th firm uses its second input (say, capital) more efficiently than any of the other firms. Second, the possibility that all frontier coefficients may be selected from a single firm cannot be completely ruled out. It is often observed that a firm that uses some inputs efficiently is likely to use all inputs efficiently.

According to the definition of technical efficiency by Farell (1957), the *i*th firm's technical efficiency TE_i can be estimated by the ratio of the actual output to the potential output, namely,

$$TE_i = \frac{Y_i}{\exp(\ln Y_i^*)} \qquad (3.7)$$

where the numerator Y_i denotes the actual output of the *i*th firm under the best available technology and a given set of inputs, and the denominator $\exp(\ln Y_i^*)$ refers to the estimated potential output of the *i*th firm, which is the maximum potential output calculated from equation (3.6) if the technology can always be applied efficiently by the firm. Several applications of the varying coefficients frontier model can be found in the literature, such as an examination of the demand for liquid assets in the US by Feige and Swamy (1974), technical efficiency by Kalirajan and Obwona (1994) and production capacity realisation by Kalirajan and Salim (1997). A survey article by Swamy and Tavlas (1995) developed the varying coefficients frontier model with respect to empirical applications and theoretical background.

3.2   A DECOMPOSITION ANALYSIS

Discussion of the sources of output growth has been central in the literature since Abramovitz (1956), Swan (1956), Solow (1957) and Denison (1962). The objective of the debate is to identify the relative contributions of factor inputs and technological progress towards output growth. However, the conventional growth accounting assumption that firms are operating efficiently on the production frontier contradicts what is generally observed in practice, namely firms operating below the production frontier. Firms do not always operate on the production frontier because actual output is often subject to a number of unexpected constraints, including both uncontrollable and controllable factors. The former comprise bad weather, input supply breakdowns, sudden blackouts or natural disasters and so on and the latter include poor management or inefficiency (Aigner *et al.*; 1977, Meeusen and van den Broeck, 1977). The difference between actual output and frontier output is defined as technical inefficiency (Farell, 1957).

As technical efficiency plays a role central to a firm's actual output, Nishimizu and Page (1982) first incorporated the concept of technical efficiency into the TFP growth framework. They followed the non-parametric approach proposed by Aigner and Chu (1968) and decomposed output growth into input growth, technological progress and technical efficiency change. As a consequence, TFP growth should be construed as the combination of technical efficiency change and technological progress, as demonstrated in Mahadevan and Kalirajan (1999), who also emphasised the importance of the decomposition of TFP growth, because TFP growth derived from growth accounting cannot be used synonymously with technological progress.

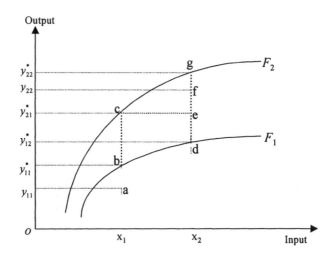

Figure 3.1   The decomposition of output growth with technical inefficiency

Once the decomposition is made, we can further examine which factor has contributed more to TFP growth in East Asian manufacturing industries. In other words, a large technical efficiency improvement stemming from a learning-by-doing effect can increase TFP growth substantially even without much technological progress. Without identifying the real factors behind TFP growth, economic policy will not effectively enhance it in the region.

In Figure 3.1, F_1 and F_2 refer to the potential production frontiers at periods T_1 and T_2, that is, the efficient production technologies from which maximum potential output is estimated from equation (3.5). The points x_1 and x_2 (in logarithms) are the levels of inputs and y_{ij} (in logarithms) is the output level, where i denotes technology (or production frontier) and j represents the level of inputs. Finally, the asterisk (*) denotes levels of output achieved when firms operate efficiently on the production frontier. For example, y_{11}^*, which is technically efficient, represents a firm achieving the frontier output by using the technology F_1 with the level of input x_1. If there is an innovation in production technology as a result of R&D or technology diffusion, technological progress occurs. Then the potential production frontier shifts from F_1 to F_2 demonstrated by $(y_{21}^* - y_{11}^*)$, which means the additional output $(y_{21}^* - y_{11}^*)$ is achieved by employing the advanced production technology (F_2) without raising input. In the context of this study, the distance between the two production frontiers $(y_{21}^* - y_{11}^*)$ measures technological progress evaluated at x_1.

In practice, a firm's output usually appears below production frontiers, as shown in Figure 3.1 – at y_{11} and y_{22} – so that the gap between y_{11} and y_{11}^* reveals the extent of technical inefficiency as described in Farell (1957). According to Figure 3.1, the decomposition of output growth $(y_{22} - y_{11})$ into input growth, a movement towards the production frontier and a shift in the production frontier can be described as follows:

$$\text{Output growth} = y_{22} - y_{11} = \overline{ab} + \overline{bc} + \overline{ef} = \overline{ab} + \overline{bc} + (\overline{eg} - \overline{fg})$$

$$= (\overline{ab} - \overline{fg}) + \overline{bc} + \overline{eg}$$

$$= [(y_{11}^* - y_{11}) - (y_{22}^* - y_{22})] + (y_{21}^* - y_{11}^*) + (y_{22}^* - y_{21}^*)$$

$$= (TE_2 - TE_1) + (\Delta TP) + (\Delta Y_x)$$

$$= \textbf{(change in technical efficiency)} + \textbf{(technological progress at } x_1) + \textbf{(input growth from } x_1 \text{ to } x_2 \text{ with production technology } F_2),$$

where the distance between frontier output y_{11}^* and actual output y_{11} indicates that firms do not operate efficiently on the production frontier and the loss in output is due to technical inefficiency measured as 'a movement towards or away from the production frontier' (Aigner *et al.*, 1977; Meeusen and van den Broeck, 1977). The gap $(y_{21}^* - y_{11}^*)$ implies that using the same amount of input x_1 but different technologies (F_1 and F_2), the increase in output is attributed to the technological progress measured as 'a shift in production frontier', that is, a vertical upward shift. The gap between y_{22}^* and y_{21}^* results from using the same technology (F_2) but with different levels of inputs, x_1 and x_2, and represents output growth due to the increase in inputs. The decomposition framework has revealed the important role played by technical efficiency in determining TFP growth.

According to the above illustration, TFP growth (TFPG) is defined as output growth not explained by input growth; that is, it comprises two components: change in technical efficiency and technological progress, $TFPG = (TE_2 - TE_1) + \Delta TP$. It is worth stressing that the decomposition of TFP growth enables an understanding of the status of production technology applied by industries (or firms). In other words, the decomposition analysis facilitates examining whether technological progress is stagnant over time and whether the given production technology has been utilised in an efficient way to realise wholly its potential. More importantly, from the policy perspective, these two components are analytically distinct and may have quite different policy implications (Nishimizu and Page, 1982). On the one hand, high rates of technological progress can coexist with deteriorating technical efficiency. On the other hand, low rates of technological progress can also coexist with high improvements in technical efficiency. If the technology has not been used to its full potential, introducing new technologies or upgrading the existing technology is wasteful (Kalirajan *et al.*, 1996).

3.3   EMPIRICAL MODEL

The current study uses the varying coefficients frontier model specified in section 3.1.3 and is based on the underlying assumption that all industries have the same opportunity to access the best available technology. A Cobb–Douglas production technology is assumed for 3-digit manufacturing industries in each East Asian economy,

$$\ln Y_i = \beta_{0i} + \beta_{1i} \ln L_i + \beta_{2i} \ln K_i, \quad i = 1,\dots,N, \tag{3.8}$$

where Y_i denotes the output level of the ith industry measured by value added, L is the labour input measured by the number of employees adjusted for quality improvement, and K_i is capital input measured by the level of capital stock adjusted for quality improvement. The varying intercept is β_{0i}, and β_{1i} and β_{2i} are the response coefficients of labour and capital inputs respectively. All variables are further discussed in section 3.5. Meanwhile, it is assumed that all the varying response coefficients are distributed with a mean and a variance, which facilitates obtaining the estimates of the coefficients, $\beta_{0i} = \overline{\beta}_0 + u_{0i}$ and $\beta_{mi} = \overline{\beta}_m + u_{mi}$, $m = 1,2$, without much difficulty, since the number of observations is usually larger than the number of estimates. Then, equation (3.8) can be rewritten as

$$\ln Y_i = \overline{\beta}_0 + \overline{\beta}_1 \ln L_i + \overline{\beta}_2 \ln K_i + v_i, \tag{3.9}$$

where $v_i = u_{0i} + u_{1i} \ln L_i + u_{2i} \ln K_i$, $E(v_i) = 0$ for all i, $Cov(v_i, v_j) = 0$ for $i \neq j$ and $Var(v_i) = \sigma_{u00} + \sigma_{u11}(\ln L_i)^2 + \sigma_{u22}(\ln K_i)^2$. The estimation procedure has been described in section 3.1.3. The empirical estimation is carried out using the computer program TERAN and the results are presented in Chapter 4.

3.3.1   Testing for Heterogeneity of Industries

One of the advantages of the varying coefficients frontier model is that industry-specific characteristics can be taken into account to obtain production frontier coefficients despite the heterogeneity of industries. Whether the given data set is sufficient to reflect such heterogeneity for the application of the varying coefficients frontier model can be tested by employing the Breusch–Pagan test. The idea of this for heteroskedasticity is that if there are some variables $z_1, z_2, ..., z_m$ that influence the error variance $Var(\varepsilon_i) = \sigma_i^2$ and if $\sigma_i^2 = f(\alpha_0 + \alpha_1 z_{1t} + \alpha_2 z_{2t} + \cdots + \alpha_m z_{mt})$, then the Breusch–Pagan test is an assessment of the hypothesis:

$$H_0 : \quad \alpha_1 = \alpha_2 = \cdots = \alpha_m = 0. \qquad (3.10)$$

Additionally, the Breusch–Pagan test does not depend on the functional form. The function $f(\cdot)$ can be any function, such as x^2 or e^x. Assume $\hat{\sigma}^2 = \sum \hat{\varepsilon}^2/n$ and S = regression sum of squares from a regression of $\hat{u}_t^2$ on $z_1, z_2, ..., z_m$. Then, $\lambda = S/2\hat{\sigma}^4$ has a χ^2 distribution with degrees of freedom m.[6] The results of the Breusch–Pagan test for the five East Asian manufacturing sectors are presented in Chapter 4.

3.4 DATA SOURCES

The data for the manufacturing sectors of Hong Kong, Japan, Korea and Singapore are obtained from the *UNIDO Industrial Statistics Yearbook* compiled by the International Economic Data Bank at the Australian National University. It contains the data on manufacturing industries at the 3-digit level on value added, number of employees and GFCF.

However, the UNIDO database does not hold the data for manufacturing GFCF for Taiwan, so the unpublished real and nominal GFCF data are obtained from the DGBAS of Taiwan.[7] Because the industrial classification of the UNIDO database differs from that of Taiwan, the UNIDO data on manufacturing value added and number of employees for Taiwan cannot be used together with the manufacturing GFCF data from the DGBAS.[8] Hence all the data on manufacturing industries for Taiwan are from the DGBAS. The value added data are from *National Income in Taiwan Area of the Republic of China* published by DGBAS, the Republic of China. The *Monthly Bulletin of Manpower Statistics* contains the number of employees for 22 Taiwanese manufacturing industries since 1979.

The construction of GDP and GFCF deflators can be derived using the nominal and real data for GDP and GFCF, which are available from the publications of national accounts in each country. Alternatively, the deflators of GFCF, GDP and manufacturing value added for the five East Asian manufacturing sectors can be obtained from *dX* for Windows 3.0, EconData.

3.5   DATA CONSTRUCTION AND ADJUSTMENT

The variables used in this study comprise manufacturing value added, number of employees and GFCF. Since manufacturing value added and GFCF are measured at current prices in the UNIDO database, it is necessary to deflate all variables into constant prices. Additionally, measuring the manufacturing value added and GFCF in local currencies precludes the adverse influences of exchange rate fluctuations, which may distort the results of output growth decomposition. More details on these variables are discussed next.

3.5.1   Output

Value added is a measure of net output, that is, gross output less the purchased (or intermediate) inputs of goods and services, which have been embodied in the value of the products. Value added avoids double counting since products purchased from other establishments are deducted as input costs. However, the survey data cannot gather all the components necessary to calculate 'pure value added'. The value added figure produced is called 'census value added' due to the missing components, namely purchased services.   Census value added is calculated by subtracting the cost of materials, supplies, purchased fuel and electricity used from the value of the gross output of manufacturing activity. Hence the actual output of each manufacturing industry in the current study is measured in census value added.

3.5.2   Labour

Theoretically, 'hours worked' is best used as a measure of labour input.[9] However, such data are unavailable from the UNIDO database. Instead, the use of wages and salaries paid to employees (employment) may be a suitable alternative measure for 'hours worked'.[10] Despite the advantages of using wages and salaries expenditure as the measure of labour input, the current study has explicitly chosen the number of employees as the labour input in this study. The major concern is whether the marginal product of labour has been enhanced as much as the growth of the real wage in the East Asian manufacturing industries. If the answer is negative, then the use of wages and salaries expenditure as the labour input apparently overstates its contribution to output growth. Consider total wages and salaries expenditure in real terms as $W = w \cdot L$, where the number of employees and real wage per worker are denoted as L and w respectively.   After logarithmically differentiating total wages and salaries expenditure with respect to time, this can be rewritten as $\dot{W}/W = \dot{L}/L + \dot{w}/w$, indicating that the growth rate of total wages and salaries expenditure equals the growth rate of number of employees plus the growth rate of real wage per worker.

In the case of the Singaporean manufacturing industries, the real growth rate of wages and salaries expenditure during the period 1970–97 was 237 per cent and the growth rate of manufacturing employees was 108 per cent; hence, the growth rate of real wage per worker turned out to be 129 per cent. If the marginal product of labour did not increase as much as the real wage per worker, the contribution of wages and salaries expenditure as the measure of the labour input to output growth would be overvalued, which accordingly implies that TFP growth would be understated.

Why has the growth of real wage per worker in the East Asian manufacturing sectors not reflected the actual growth of the marginal product of labour? First, one of the comparative advantages in the East Asian manufacturing sectors during the 1960s and 1970s was cheap labour, which attracted massive foreign direct investment to boost these economies. As Huff (1999, p. 36) described, 'Control of the labour market enabled the Singaporean government to secure international manufacturing competitiveness through limiting wage rises'. Hence, it is understood that in the 1960s and 1970s manufacturing workers were generally underpaid. Second, the rapid advance of the East Asian manufacturing sectors that followed resulted in competition with the industrialised economies in areas such as electronic products and automobiles. This was accompanied by mounting legal protection for workers such as minimum wage legislation and the rising power of trade unions, which may have caused current workers to be overpaid. Taking these two factors into account, it is suggested that the growth of real wage per worker would be comparatively higher than that of the marginal product of labour in the East Asian manufacturing industries. Therefore, instead of using wages and salaries expenditure, the current study adopts 'number of employees' as the measure of labour input to prevent the contribution of labour input from being overstated.

3.5.3 Capital Stock

The capital stock of each industry is estimated by the conventional perpetual inventory method, $K_t = K_{t-1}(1-\delta) + I_{t-1}$, where K_t and K_{t-1} denote capital stocks at time t and $t-1$, δ is the rate of depreciation and I_{t-1} is real gross investment or, more precisely, GFCF carried out at time $t-1$.[11] If the growth rate of GFCF is assumed to be stable over time, the initial capital stock K_0 can be constructed by the initial GFCF ($GFCF_0$) divided by the sum of the depreciation rate and the average real growth rate of GFCF (g) at the manufacturing level in the first ten years of the sample period, that is,

$K_0 = GFCF_0 / (g + \delta)$.[12] Due to the lack of data on the detailed components of GFCF, a simple average depreciation rate (δ) of 0.0925 is employed to depreciate capital stock for the East Asian manufacturing sectors with the exception of Singapore.   According to Hulten and Wykoff (1981), the average depreciation rate of 0.0925 is computed from the four depreciation rates of capital subinputs, comprising non-residential (0.029), construction (0.021), transport (0.182) and machinery (0.138), where land is excluded from the construction of capital stock.

For Singapore's manufacturing sector, the choice of the depreciation rate is somewhat sensitive for the empirical results.   It is believed that the depreciation rate of 0.0925 may be too low for the Singaporean manufacturing industries. To adjust in favour of the outcomes for Singapore, a higher depreciation rate of 0.1768 from Jorgenson's (1990) estimates is adopted to depreciate manufacturing capital stocks. Since the GFCF data are only available at the manufacturing industry level, the simple average depreciation rate of 0.1768 is generated from the four depreciation rates of capital subinputs: non-residential building (0.0361), machinery and equipment (0.1048), transport equipment (0.2935) and office equipment (0.2729).

In addition to Singapore's manufacturing industries, the higher depreciation rate of 0.1768 is applied to the other four economies for sensitivity tests. For instance, if the higher depreciation rate is applied to Japan's manufacturing sector, TFP growth will be increased to 0.065 over the 1965–98 period, that is, 0.2 per cent per annum. For Taiwan's manufacturing sector, it will only be 0.016 during the period 1981–99, that is, 0.1 per cent per annum. Thus, it is evident that the choice of capital depreciation rate (0.0925) would not bias the outcomes of those four East Asian manufacturing sectors.

3.5.4 Quality Adjustment for Labour and Capital Inputs

In order to capture the quality improvement embodied in labour input due to an increasing number of well educated employees, the current study adopts several labour quality improvement indices from Young (1995).   He estimated the difference between raw labour and quality-adjusted labour input using the technique suggested by Bishop *et al.* (1975) and then suggested that the average annual labour quality adjustment indices for the manufacturing sectors of Hong Kong, Korea, Singapore and Taiwan were 0.6, 1.1, 1.6 and 0.4 per cent respectively.[13] The quality-adjusted labour input in the current study is calculated as number of employees multiplied by one plus the labour quality adjustment index over time. This effectively scales up the number of employees in later years when workers become better educated.

However, as far as the labour quality adjustment index is concerned, Chen (1997) argued that the quality improvement of labour input may be over-adjusted in the case of Singapore; hence the resulting estimates for Singapore's manufacturing industries will be further examined while conducting sensitivity analyses in Chapter 6. If the labour quality improvement index is considered, for instance, the growth rate of the quality-adjusted labour input for Singapore's manufacturing sector over the period 1970–97 would be 150.8 per cent rather than 108 per cent (no adjustment). Because the labour quality adjustment index for Japan is not available in Young (1995), the adjustment index is simply assumed to be 0.5 per cent.

Similarly, the adjustment of quality improvement embodied in capital input (GFCF) is implemented using the capital quality adjustment indices from Young (1995).[14] It is suggested that the average annual capital quality adjustment indices for the manufacturing sectors of Singapore and Taiwan at the manufacturing level were 0.5 and 0.2 per cent respectively; for Hong Kong and Korea, the estimated indices were 0.3 and 0.8 per cent at the economy level, and the index for Japan's manufacturing sector is assumed to be 0.4 per cent.[15] The outcome of the adjustments can be easily ascertained. The quality adjustment for capital input will raise the growth of capital input; subsequently, it reduces the degree of TFP growth slightly. The magnitude of reduction in TFP growth due to the quality adjustments for labour and capital inputs is therefore interpreted as 'embodied technological change'.

Despite carrying out the quality adjustment for capital input, the results of this study remain subject to the extent of the utilisation of capital stock. To minimise the impact, this is implicitly assumed to be constant over the entire period. As long as the capacity utilisation of capital stock is unchanged, the estimates of TFP growth will not be affected even though the capital stocks are not completely utilised. Nevertheless, if the capital stock utilisation were decreasing over time, the growth of capital input could be overestimated, leading to TFP growth being understated.

3.5.5 Construction of Deflators

Ideally, it is preferable to use the deflators of manufacturing value added and GFCF if both are available. Alternatively, the economy GDP and GFCF deflators may be applied to deflate the variables into constant prices, although this action has encountered an unexpected problem. The difference between manufacturing value added and economy GDP deflators might be expected to be small or negligible. Yet Figure 3.2 reveals there was a significant difference between those two deflators in Japan. The economy GDP deflator in 1970 was lower than the manufacturing value added deflator but became higher from 1991. If the economy GDP deflator is used to deflate the nominal manufacturing value added, it will generate a higher real manufacturing value added in 1970 but a lower value added in 1995. Subsequently, the growth rate of manufacturing value added in Japan falls from 96.6 to 49.5 per cent during the 1970–95 period and seriously distorts the true degree of TFP growth. Hence the real manufacturing value added at constant 1990 prices is derived using the manufacturing value added deflator for all manufacturing sectors except Hong Kong.[16] Since the manufacturing value added deflator in Hong Kong is not available, there is no alternative but to use the economy GDP deflator.

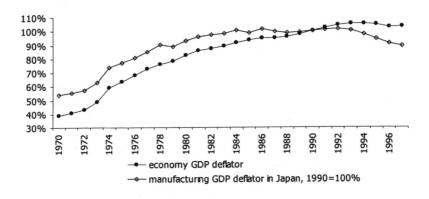

Source: Author's calculations based on dX for Windows 3.0, EconData: CEIC Database, Japan.

Figure 3.2   Economy GDP deflator versus manufacturing value added deflator at constant 1990 prices in Japan

Figure 3.3 shows the economy GFCF and manufacturing GFCF deflators at constant 1990 prices in Taiwan over the period 1970–97. Since the deflator of manufacturing GFCF is only available for Taiwan, the next step is to choose appropriate GFCF deflators for the other four economies. As with Japan, the considerable gap between economy GDP and manufacturing value added deflators exists in Taiwan but, as shown in Figure 3.3, the difference between economy GFCF and manufacturing GFCF deflators is negligible. Thus it is believed that the GFCF deflator at the economy level can be substituted as the manufacturing GFCF deflator for Hong Kong, Japan, Korea and Singapore.

The deflators of economy GDP and GFCF for Hong Kong are available from 1973 to 2000. The deflators of manufacturing value added and economy GFCF for Japan and Singapore are available from 1955 to 1999 and from 1960 to 2000 respectively. Two implicit price indices of fixed capital formation and manufacturing value added for Korea are obtainable in the national accounts from 1970 to 1997. Lastly, the manufacturing value added and GFCF deflators for Taiwan are available from 1962 to 1998 and from 1951 to 1997 respectively.

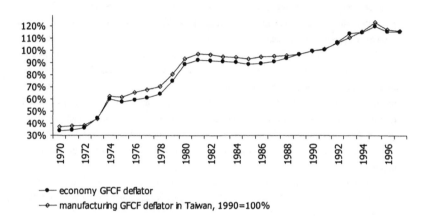

—•— economy GFCF deflator
—◇— manufacturing GFCF deflator in Taiwan, 1990=100%

Source: Author's calculations based on dX for Windows 3.0, EconData: CEIC Database, Taiwan.

Figure 3.3   *Economy GFCF deflator versus manufacturing GFCF deflator at constant 1990 prices in Taiwan*

NOTES

1. They argued that if the underlying assumptions did not hold, for example constant returns to scale, then the conventional growth accounting approach would, in general, yield biased estimates of technical change. However, the econometric approach based on general dynamic factor demand models allows for a careful testing of various features of a postulated model.
2. Moreover, Barro (1999) extended the applications of growth accounting to various scenarios, including the most recent endogenous growth model. Hulten (2000) clarified the misconception against the growth accounting approach and further explained the associated issues surrounding the approach.
3. The former consists of Hong Kong, South Korea, Singapore and Taiwan and the latter of France, West Germany, Japan, the UK and the United States.

4. They also showed that the Törnqvist and Malmquist indices yield the same result if the two underlying technologies have translog forms.

5. With the assumption that the production technology of firms can be represented by a Cobb–Douglas function, $Y = AL^{\alpha}K^{\beta}$, that is, $\ln Y = \ln A + \alpha \ln L + \beta \ln K$, the calculation of MRTS between labour and capital yields: $MRTS_{LK} = -dK/dL = -\alpha K/\beta L$. If the coefficients, α and β, are constant, then MRTS is also constant, which implies that a shift in production frontier is neutral. Graphically, it represents an upward shift in production frontier or a change in intercept term but no variations in slopes, that is, estimated response coefficients. However, if the MRTS varies due to changes in coefficients (α and β), it is referred to as a non-neutral shift in production frontier. Conventionally, the stochastic frontier approach adopts the neutral shift in production frontier, which will occur only if the MRTS between inputs remains constant. In applying the varying coefficients frontier model, the restrictive assumption of constant MRTS can be relaxed and the shift in production frontier turns out to be non-neutral. Compared with growth accounting, one of the advantages of the varying coefficients frontier approach is that it does not require strong assumptions, such as perfect competition or constant returns to scale.

6. More details on the Breusch–Pagan LM test can be found in textbooks such as Maddala, G. S. (1992) *Introduction to Econometrics*, 2nd ed. Prentice Hall, and Kennedy, P. (1998) *A Guide to Econometrics*, 4th ed. Blackwell.

7. Gratitude is extended to Mr Wu-Chi Lai of the DGBAS for providing the unpublished data for manufacturing GFCF for Taiwan. The other possible source regarding the data for GFCF is *The Trends in Multifactor Productivity, Taiwan Area, the Republic of China* published by the DGBAS of Taiwan (Republic of China, 2000) but it contains only 18 manufacturing industries due to aggregation.

8. It is found that more than half of the classifications of Taiwan's manufacturing industries are not compatible with UNIDO's International Standard Industrial Classification (ISIC).

9. For example, Jorgenson *et al.* (1987a) and Young (1992, 1995).

10. First, it can easily reflect the quality improvement in labour input over time because of a growing number of better educated employees. Second, the idea of marginal product of labour could be captured by wages and salaries expenditure if labour markets were functioning efficiently. To some extent, it might reveal the true contribution of labour input to manufacturing output. Third, because of the existence of part-time and full-time employees, the problem of counting the total number of employees or employment can be avoided.

11. Gross fixed capital formation is defined as the outlays of producers on durable real assets, such as buildings, motor vehicles, plant and machinery, roads and improvements to land. In measuring the outlays, sales of similar goods are deducted. Land is excluded from gross fixed capital formation. Included is the value of construction work done by a firm's own employees. The term 'gross' indicates that consumption of fixed capital has not been deducted from the value of the outlays.

due to the dramatic fluctuations of GFCF in several industries, which is not possible in practice. The average annual real growth rates of GFCF in the initial ten years for the manufacturing sectors of Hong Kong (1976–86), Japan (1963–73), Korea (1970–80), Singapore (1970–80) and Taiwan (1970–80) were 0.050, 0.0857, 0.2011, 0.0840 and 0.1168 respectively. Note that the average annual growth rates of GFCF are geometric *not* logarithmic.

13. The labour quality adjustment index is the difference between the average annual growth rate of raw labour and weighted labour. The index of 0.6 per cent for Hong Kong was based on the economy level and estimated for the period 1966–91. For Singapore, the estimated index was for the period 1970–90 at the manufacturing level. For Korea (1966–90) and Taiwan (1966–90), the indices were at the manufacturing level. These four indices are adopted from Young (1995, pp. 657–61, Tables V–VIII). Despite carrying out the quality adjustments, the empirical results are relatively insensitive to the choice of indices.

14. Hulten (1992), after adjusting capital input for quality improvement, found that approximately 20 per cent of the TFP growth could be attributed to embodied technological change in the US manufacturing industry over the period 1943–83.

15. See note 13.

16. In the case of Singapore, the use of the economy GDP deflator to deflate nominal manufacturing value added favours the outcome of output growth and TFP growth but this is certainly deceptive.

4. Characteristics of the five East Asian manufacturing sectors and estimates of varying coefficients

Before discussing the outcomes of the test for heteroskedasticity and estimates of varying coefficients, section 4.1 describes the characteristics of the five East Asian manufacturing sectors. The results of the Breusch–Pagan Lagrange Multiplier test are reported in section 4.2. Section 4.3 considers the estimated frontier, mean coefficients and computer program used in this study. Using the concept of technical efficiency, section 4.4 examines how well manufacturing industries in the East Asian economies utilised labour and capital inputs. The number of industries covered is discussed comprehensively in Appendix A.3. The estimated varying coefficients for selected years and the estimation result of the computer program TERAN are available in Appendix A.4.

4.1   CHARACTERISTICS OF THE FIVE EAST ASIAN MANUFACTURING SECTORS

This section presents a number of statistical indicators of individual economies to facilitate understanding of the role of the manufacturing sector in each economy. These statistics include average annual real growth rates of manufacturing value added, GFCF, capital stock, GDP and number of employees. Discussion of inflation rates (or change in GDP deflators), manufacturing share in GDP and the ratio of manufacturing GFCF to manufacturing value added is also provided.[1]

It should be noted that the value added and other variables drawn from the UNIDO database are likely to be different from those of the national accounts of individual countries.[2] According to the United Nations *International Yearbook of Industrial Statistics* (1999, pp. 7–11), the data for value added obtained from the UNIDO database are in the 'census' concept and not in the 'national accounting' concept in which manufacturing GDP and so on are measured. The 'census value added' covers only activities of an industrial nature, which is defined as the value of census output less census input. However, the national accounting value added (or, total value added) is census value added less the cost of non-industrial services plus the receipts for non-industrial services. Furthermore, the data on census value added as well as on other variables are the results of annual industrial surveys conducted by the national statistical offices in individual countries, which cover only the manufacturing establishments that were registered at those offices, so the surveys do not cover the informal sector nor very small establishments. In addition, the scope of the surveys differs from country to country. It should be noted that the calculation of growth rates in this study is done by taking a logarithmic difference in two consecutive years and all variables have been deflated at constant 1990 prices. Hence the figures reported here could be slightly different from those in the official publications.

4.1.1   Hong Kong

Figure 4.1 shows the average annual growth rates of GDP, manufacturing value added and GDP deflator in Hong Kong between 1976 and 1997. The growth rate of manufacturing value added has been negative since 1989 despite the strong and positive growth rate of the overall economy. Due to the liberalisation policy in China in 1978, there has been a rapid relocation of manufacturing production to nearby mainland China since the mid-1980s, and this has largely contributed to the negative output growth in the manufacturing sector.[3] Hong Kong's inflation rate generally fluctuated at around 8 per cent, which was higher than Japan, Singapore and Taiwan but lower than Korea.

As a result of the manufacturing relocation, the total number of employees in manufacturing industries has been shrinking since 1987, as shown in Figure 4.2. Similarly, the real growth rate of GFCF has been negative since 1989, except for 1995. At the same time, the growth rate of capital stock has been slowing down and it also became negative after 1994.

Figure 4.3 presents manufacturing share in GDP and the ratio of manufacturing GFCF to manufacturing value added in Hong Kong. It is understood that the manufacturing share in GDP has been decreasing over time since the mid-1980s. At the beginning of the 1980s, manufacturing value added still accounted for over 25 per cent of GDP but dropped to only 6.6 per cent in 1997.

The manufacturing share in GDP in the 1970s, 1980s and 1990s was on average 27.1, 20.8 and 9.8 per cent respectively. In terms of the ratio of manufacturing GFCF to manufacturing value added, the highest ratio recorded was 16.4 per cent in 1986, falling to 7.9 per cent in 1994.

Regardless of the relatively stable ratio in the past two decades, the result indicates that manufacturing GFCF was declining at a similar rate as manufacturing value added.

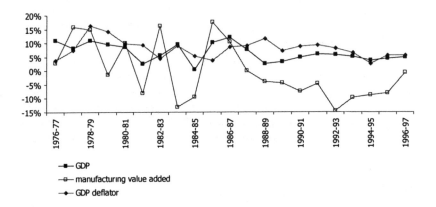

Source: Author's calculations based on dX for Windows 3.0, EconData: CEIC Database, Hong Kong and UNIDO database.

Figure 4.1   Average annual real growth rates: GDP, manufacturing value added and GDP deflator in Hong Kong, 1976–97

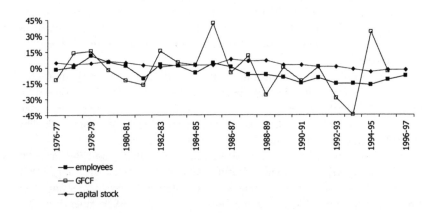

Source: Author's calculations based on dX for Windows 3.0, EconData: CEIC Database, Hong Kong and UNIDO database.

Figure 4.2   Average annual growth rates: number of employees, real GFCF and real capital stock in Hong Kong's manufacturing, 1976–97

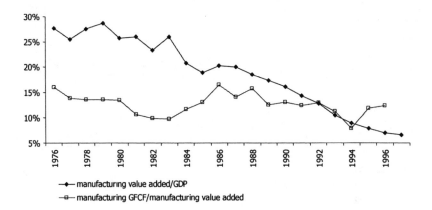

Source: Author's calculations based on dX for Windows 3.0, EconData: CEIC Database, Hong Kong and UNIDO database.

Figure 4.3   Manufacturing share in GDP and ratio of manufacturing GFCF to manufacturing value added in Hong Kong, 1976–97

4.1.2 Japan

Figure 4.4 shows the average annual real growth rates of economy GDP, manufacturing value added and GDP deflator in Japan for the 1970–97 period. The average annual growth rate of GDP was similar to that of manufacturing value added, yet the latter apparently fluctuated more than the former and even became negative in 1975, 1986, 1992–93 and 1995.   The rate of inflation was high in the early 1970s during the oil crisis but it stabilised after the late 1970s. Nevertheless, the Japanese economy has been in trouble since 1990, causing deflation over the period 1994–95.

The number of employees decreased during the periods 1974–79 and 1992–97, as seen in Figure 4.5. When fewer workers are employed, it may signal that less physical capital investment is required.   Moreover, the average annual growth rate of GFCF was negative in both the 1974–78 and 1992–94 periods, which to some degree corresponded to the fluctuation of manufacturing employment. In the end, the GFCF only grew at a rate of 0.8 per cent per annum. With regard to the growth rate of capital stock, except for 1978 and 1995 it has always been positive. However, even in these years the negative growth rates of capital stock were negligible.

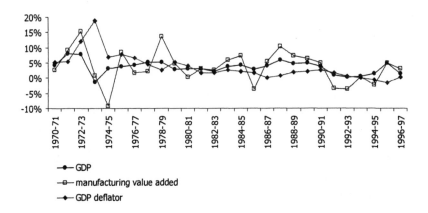

Source: Author's calculations based on dX for Windows 3.0, EconData: CEIC Database, Japan and UNIDO database.

Figure 4.4   Average annual real growth rates: GDP, manufacturing value added and GDP deflator in Japan, 1970–97

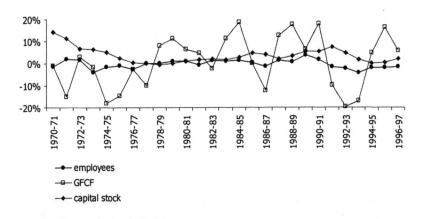

Source: Author's calculations based on dX for Windows 3.0, EconData: CEIC Database, Japan and UNIDO database.

Figure 4.5   Average annual growth rates: number of employees, real GFCF and real capital stock in Japan's manufacturing, 1970–97

Figure 4.6 presents the manufacturing share in GDP and the ratio of manufacturing GFCF to manufacturing value added during the period 1970–

97. Surprisingly, the manufacturing share in GDP ranges from 24.8 to 28.6 per cent and has been steady over the whole 27 years. To some extent, it reflects the crucial role of the manufacturing sector in Japan's economy. The ratio of manufacturing GFCF to manufacturing value added was above 20 per cent in the early 1970s but fluctuated at around 9 to 12 per cent from the late 1970s to the 1990s. The highest ratio recorded was 23.7 per cent in 1970 and the lowest ratio was 8.8 per cent in 1994. This implies that the amount of investment from Japan's manufacturers was based mostly on the actual value added produced. In other words, when the growth of valued added slowed, so did the growth of GFCF.

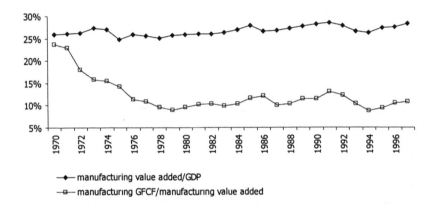

—◆— manufacturing value added/GDP
—□— manufacturing GFCF/manufacturing value added

Source: Author's calculations based on dX for Windows 3.0, EconData: CEIC Database, Japan and UNIDO database.

Figure 4.6   *Manufacturing share in GDP and ratio of manufacturing GFCF to manufacturing value added in Japan, 1970–97*

4.1.3 Korea

Apart from 1980, the Korean economy was strong over the 1971–97 period and annual growth rates of GDP even achieved double digits in a number of years, as shown in Figure 4.7. As an engine of the overall economy, the Korean manufacturing sector performed even better. The value added of the manufacturing sector on average grew by more than 20 per cent per annum during the 1971–78 period, whereas negative output growth occurred in 1979, which was a significant outlier compared with other years. Despite this outstanding economic performance, an average annual inflation rate of nearly 19 per cent prevailed throughout the 1970s. The inflation rate was under control in the 1980s and 1990s, except for 1981 and 1991. In general, it fluctuated at around 6 per cent in the 1980s, increasing to 10 per cent in 1991, but decreasing again since then. In 1997, the inflation rate fell to 2.6 per cent.

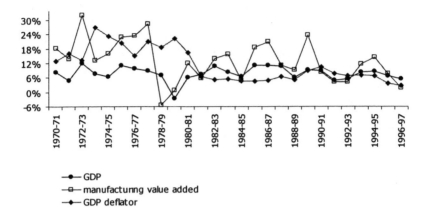

Source: Author's calculations based on dX for Windows 3.0, EconData: CEIC Database, Korea and UNIDO database.

Figure 4.7   Average annual real growth rates: GDP, manufacturing value added and GDP deflator in Korea, 1970–97

Figure 4.8 shows that except for 1971, the number of employees in the manufacturing sector grew significantly in the 1970s. The expansion of manufacturing employees slowed in the late 1970s and became negative in the early 1980s; after that, it began increasing until 1986. Numbers of employees fell during the 1989–92 period. In general, the average annual growth rate of the number of employees was negative in the 1990s. The growth rate of GFCF was 65.8 per cent in 1973 but in the subsequent year it dropped considerably, to –30.4 per cent. A similar scenario also took place in other periods, such as 1979–80; nevertheless, the trend for GFCF growth was declining, although the growth rate of capital stock remained positive during the sample period.

As shown in Figure 4.9, unlike other East Asian manufacturing sectors, the manufacturing share of GDP in Korea rose from 10.6 per cent in 1971 to 29.1 per cent in 1988. Since then, the share has been maintained at between 29 per cent and 30 per cent. The highest ratio of manufacturing GFCF to manufacturing value added occurred in 1974, and it was over 30 per cent for most of the 1970s. Apart from 1992 (36.6 per cent), the ratio ranged between 20 per cent and 30 per cent in the 1980s and 1990s.

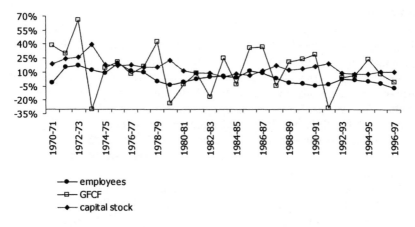

Source: Author's calculations based on dX for Windows 3.0, EconData: CEIC Database, Korea and UNIDO database.

Figure 4.8   *Average annual growth rates: number of employees, real GFCF and real capital stock in Korea's manufacturing, 1970–97*

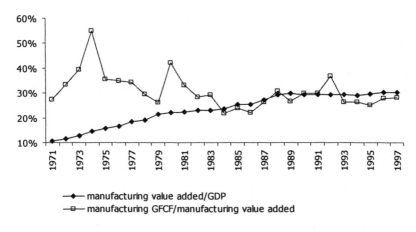

Source: Author's calculations based on dX for Windows 3.0, EconData: CEIC Database, Korea and UNIDO database.

Figure 4.9   *Manufacturing share in GDP and ratio of manufacturing GFCF to manufacturing value added in Korea, 1970–97*

4.1.4 Singapore

Figure 4.10 indicates that Singapore's economy grew spectacularly over the past three decades except for 1985, which experienced negative growth of 1.6 per cent. In terms of output growth, the manufacturing sector performed better than the overall economy in the 1970s, but the reverse occurred in the 1980s and 1990s. The manufacturing sector experienced negative output growth in 1975, 1982 and 1985. The inflation rate has been low in Singapore since the early 1980s, but deflation occurred in 1985 and 1986, due mainly to economic recession. On average, the rate of inflation was below 3 per cent during the 1980s and 1990s.

The number of employees in the manufacturing sector increased rapidly in the 1970s but experienced negative growth in the periods 1981–83 and 1985–86, as seen in Figure 4.11. In the following two years, 1987 and 1988, the number of employees grew by 11.2 and 16.2 per cent respectively. In the 1990s, there was very little growth in the number of employees. Despite sharp fluctuations in the 1970s, the average annual growth rate of GFCF was maintained at over 10 per cent in the 1970s and 1990s. After the economic recession in the period 1985–86, there was considerable growth in GFCF in 1987. The growth rate of capital stock has been positive and steady since the mid-1970s.

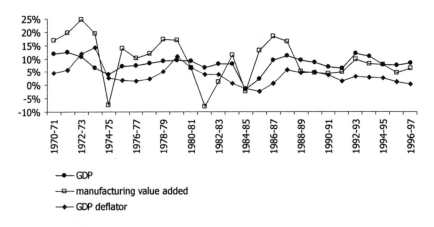

Source: Author's calculations based on dX for Windows 3.0, EconData: CEIC Database, Singapore and UNIDO database.

Figure 4.10   Average annual real growth rates: GDP, manufacturing value added and GDP deflator in Singapore, 1970–97

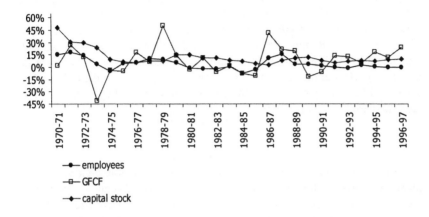

Source: Author's calculations based on dX for Windows 3.0, EconData: CEIC Database, Singapore and UNIDO database.

Figure 4.11   Average annual growth rates: number of employees, real GFCF and real capital stock in Singapore's manufacturing, 1970–97

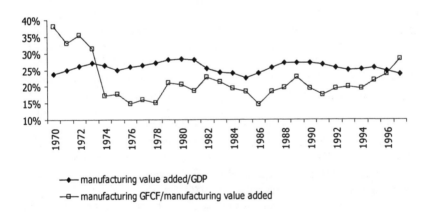

Source: Author's calculations based on dX for Windows 3.0, EconData: CEIC Database, Singapore and UNIDO database.

Figure 4.12   Manufacturing share in GDP and ratio of manufacturing GFCF to manufacturing value added in Singapore, 1970–97

According to Figure 4.12, the manufacturing share in GDP in Singapore ranged from 22.5 (1985) to 28.2 (1980) per cent during the sample period. In general, the share was above 25 per cent with the exception of the early 1970s and 1982–86 and 1996–97, when it declined slightly. The ratio of manufacturing GFCF to manufacturing value added was over 30 per cent in the early 1970s but declined to 15.1 per cent in 1978. Then, the ratio varied between 17 and 23 per cent from the 1980s until the mid-1990s. In 1997, the ratio increased to 28.3 per cent.

4.1.5 Taiwan

As with Singapore, Taiwan's economy also enjoyed double-digit growth in the early 1970s. Although the growth rates of the overall economy slowed in the 1980s and 1990s, as indicated by Figure 4.13, they have been positive over the past three decades. With respect to output growth, the manufacturing sector outperformed the entire economy in the 1970s but suffered negative growth in 1974 and 1990. Nonetheless, the economy grew more than the manufacturing sector in the 1980s and 1990s. The average annual inflation rate was about 9 per cent in the 1970s and the highest inflation rate was recorded in 1974 due to the oil crisis. The inflation rate has been approximately 3 per cent since 1982, following the second oil crisis in 1980.

Employment growth in the manufacturing sector was limited in Taiwan, as shown in Figure 4.14. Despite high employment growth in 1984, it was soon offset by negative growth in 1989 and 1990. The number of employees on average increased by 1.8 per cent per annum during the 1980s but decreased in the 1990s. Similar to other economies, the growth of GFCF in Taiwan's manufacturing industries fluctuated drastically, and even experienced negative growth in the 1976–78 and 1982–83 periods as well as in 1985. The growth rate of capital stock was roughly 15 per cent in the 1970s but it decelerated to around 8 per cent in the 1980s and 1990s.

As indicated in Figure 4.15, the share of manufacturing output was roughly 24 per cent of GDP at the outset. As an engine of Taiwan's economy, the manufacturing sector soon increased its GDP share over time. The highest share, 38.4 per cent, was recorded in 1986 and 1987 and was the highest among the five East Asian manufacturing sectors. Since then, the manufacturing share in GDP has dropped to nearly 30 per cent. The highest ratio of manufacturing GFCF to manufacturing value added occurred in 1975 and the lowest was in 1985. Average ratios were about 22, 16 and 20 per cent in the 1970s, 1980s and 1990s respectively.

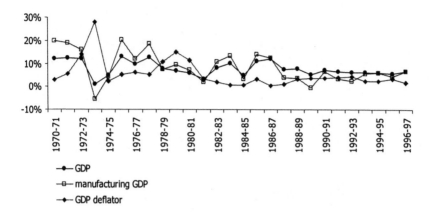

Source: Author's calculations based on dX for Windows 3.0, EconData: CEIC Database, Taiwan.

Figure 4.13 *Average annual real growth rates: GDP, manufacturing value added and GDP deflator in Taiwan, 1970–97*

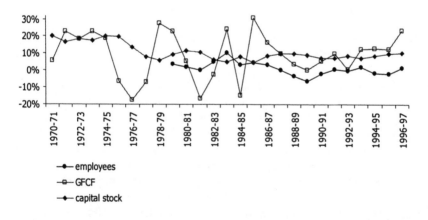

Source: Author's calculations based on dX for Windows 3.0, EconData: CEIC Database, Taiwan and the DGBAS (GFCF).

Figure 4.14 *Average annual growth rates: number of employees, real GFCF and real capital stock in Taiwan's manufacturing, 1970–97*

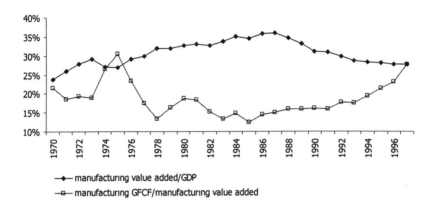

Source: Author's calculations based on dX for Windows 3.0, EconData: CEIC Database, Taiwan and the DGBAS (GFCF).

Figure 4.15 Manufacturing share in GDP and ratio of manufacturing GFCF to manufacturing value added in Taiwan, 1970–97

4.1.6 Economic Indicators in the Five East Asian Manufacturing Sectors: A Summary

Table 4.1 presents a summary of the economic indicators of the five East Asian manufacturing sectors. Among the five economies, the highest average annual growth rate of GDP over the past three decades was in Singapore with 8.0 per cent, followed by Taiwan with 7.9 per cent, Korea with 7.7 per cent, Hong Kong with 6.6 per cent and Japan with 3.6 per cent. In terms of manufacturing output growth, Korea had the highest average annual output growth rate of 13 per cent, followed by Singapore (9.4 per cent), Taiwan (8.4 per cent) and Japan (3.7 per cent). However, Hong Kong's manufacturing sector was the only one to experience –0.2 per cent output growth because of the relocation of its manufacturing production to mainland China from the mid-1980s. Correspondingly, it comes as no surprise that the growth rate of employee numbers in Hong Kong was negative (–5.1 per cent). In Japan, there was a small negative growth of –0.4 per cent in manufacturing employment. In contrast, Korea, Singapore, and Taiwan increased manufacturing employment by 4.3, 4.0 and 1.1 per cent per annum respectively. Similarly, the average annual growth rate of GFCF was negative in Hong Kong (–1.5 per cent) and relatively small in Japan (0.8 per cent), but there was substantial growth of GFCF in the other three economies, with 13 per cent in Korea, 8.3 per cent in Singapore and 8.9 per cent in Taiwan.

Table 4.1   Average annual growth rates: GDP, manufacturing value added, employees, GFCF, capital stock, average manufacturing share in GDP and GFCF share in manufacturing value added

Country	Period	GDP	Manu. value added	Employ- ees	GFCF	Capital stock	Manu. GDP/ GDP	GFCF/ value added
Hong Kong	1976–80	9.9	8.1	3.7	3.6	4.3	27.1	14.0
	1980–90	6.3	1.6	–2.9	1.4	3.5	20.8	12.7
	1990–97	5.0	–7.6	–13.2	–9.7$	–1.3	9.7	11.5$
	1976–97	6.6	–0.2	–5.1	–1.5$	2.0	18.7	12.6$
Japan	1970–80	4.3	5.0	–0.6	–4.1	4.6	25.9	14.5
	1980–90	3.9	4.5	0.9	6.3	2.8	27.0	10.8
	1990–97	2.0	0.6	–1.8	–0.2	3.0	27.6	10.8
	1970–97	3.6	3.7	–0.4	0.8	3.5	26.8	11.8
Korea	1970–80	7.3	16.3	8.9	18.3	21.5	16.2	35.7
	1980–90	8.7	13.6	3.8	12.6	10.4	25.7	27.1
	1990–97	6.9	7.5	–1.8	6.2	11.8	29.4	28.5
	1970–97	7.7	13.0	4.3	13.0	14.9	23.1	30.7
Singapore	1970–80	8.6	14.2	8.3	8.1	18.3	26.2	23.6
	1980–90	7.0	6.5	2.0	5.9	9.4	25.4	19.5
	1990–97	8.5	6.4	0.7	11.8	8.3	25.2	21.4
	1970–97	8.0	9.4	4.0	8.3	12.4	25.7	21.6
Taiwan	1970–80	9.3	12.2	NA	10.9	14.9	28.8	20.4
	1980–90	7.6	7.1	1.8	5.6	8.2	34.1	15.2
	1990–97	6.3	4.9	–0.3	10.9	8.3	28.9	20.5
	1970–97	7.9	8.4	1.1#	8.9	10.7	30.7	18.6

Notes:
1. ($) denotes the period to 1996 only and (#) the period from 1980 to 1997.
2. NA: not available and GFCF/value added is GFCF share in manufacturing value added.

Source: Author's calculations based on dX for Windows 3.0, EconData: CEIC Database, UNIDO database and the DGBAS (Taiwan's GFCF).

The growth rates of manufacturing capital stock were positive across the five manufacturing sectors; Korea recorded the highest growth rate of 14.9 per cent, followed by Singapore (12.4 per cent), Taiwan (10.7 per cent), Japan (3.5 per cent) and Hong Kong (2 per cent).   With regard to manufacturing share in GDP, on average Taiwan had the highest share at 30.7 per cent.   For Japan, Korea and Singapore, shares were somewhere between 25 and 30 per cent.   Due to the share falling below 10 per cent in the 1990s, Hong Kong's manufacturing sector on average contributed only 18.7

per cent to GDP. The average ratio of manufacturing GFCF to manufacturing value added in Korea was 30.7 per cent between 1970 and 1997; in other words, Korean manufacturing industries invested more than 30 per cent of their value added in GFCF. Both Singapore and Taiwan devoted about 20 per cent of manufacturing value added to GFCF. The investment in GFCF was lower in Hong Kong and Japan, only about 12 per cent of output. Overall, the Korean manufacturing sector had the highest average annual growth rates of manufacturing value added, GFCF and capital stock, followed by Singapore and Taiwan.

4.2   RESULTS OF THE BREUSCH–PAGAN LM TEST

In this section, the conventional assumption of homogeneously applying the best practice technology is tested by employing the Breusch–Pagan LM test outlined in section 3.3.1. Table 4.2 reports the Breusch–Pagan test statistics using the computer program SHAZAM. This test will validate statistically the use of the varying coefficients frontier model if the null hypothesis of the homogeneous application of production technology is rejected. As can be seen in Table 4.2, the hypothesis of homogeneity across industries is statistically rejected for Korean manufacturing industries apart from the period 1970–82 and the year 1997, and for Singaporean manufacturing industries except for 1974–77, 1979–80, 1983 and 1985–86. The results strongly support the specification of the varying coefficients frontier model in the cases of Korea and Singapore (Breusch and Pagan, 1979). Intuitively, the interpretation of the statistical results is that manufacturing industries in Korea and Singapore always utilised their production technology and resources in different ways despite having equal access to the frontier production technology. In other words, the actual input-specific response coefficients did vary across industries. In contrast, the conventional constant-slope frontier production function, which cannot reflect the random variation in coefficients, has been rejected through the Breusch–Pagan test.

Although Table 4.2 does not favour the manufacturing sectors of Hong Kong, Japan, and Taiwan statistically, random variation in the estimated coefficients across industries cannot be ruled out. In most cases, there are certain variations in the estimated coefficients of labour input which, despite being small, indicate that industries applied their human resources differently. Although the heterogeneity of manufacturing industries has been rejected in those three economies, modelling the variation in the labour and capital coefficients is theoretically justified.

Table 4.2   *Results of the Breusch–Pagan LM test in the five East Asian*
              manufacturing industries

Year	Hong Kong	Japan	Korea	Singapore	Taiwan
1965	—	8.797*	—	—	—
1966	—	8.196*	—	—	—
1967	—	12.105*	—	—	—
1968	—	13.627*	—	—	—
1969	—	10.327*	—	—	—
1970	—	9.752*	0.476	10.486*	—
1971	—	5.492**	0.507	12.316*	—
1972	—	3.206	0.072	16.293*	—
1973	—	1.479	1.061	9.157*	—
1974	—	4.904**	0.184	2.487	—
1975	—	3.565	0.073	4.513	—
1976	0.171	1.638	0.018	2.002	—
1977	0.344	1.587	1.983	1.304	—
1978	0.767	0.478	0.175	6.517*	—
1979	1.834	0.784	1.111	1.71	—
1980	0.482	1.346	0.164	3.726	—
1981	2.927	1.125	1.053	10.197*	1.873
1982	2.645	1.191	3.753	6.55*	0.995
1983	2.883	0.319	8.615*	1.209	1.128
1984	2.849	0.691	11.729*	9.711*	1.119
1985	1.924	0.392	10.473*	3.787	1.070
1986	13.237*	0.243	14.269*	3.915	1.155
1987	2.512	0.042	8.955*	4.93**	1.407
1988	0.505	0.534	11.750*	7.831*	1.994
1989	2.323	1.525	10.588*	8.564*	1.692
1990	0.755	4.181	10.136*	10.639*	1.613
1991	0.398	4.746**	8.378*	12.423*	1.745
1992	0.782	3.285	7.393*	11.563*	1.488
1993	0.990	0.416	5.402**	14.760*	2.502
1994	4.911**	0.791	7.444*	13.682*	3.164
1995	7.306*	0.570	12.343*	17.066*	6.322*
1996	9.738*	1.667	10.713*	15.500*	8.136*
1997	2.840	1.715	2.673	11.918*	7.228*
1998	—	2.023	—	—	5.573**
1999	—	—	—	—	1.613

Note: * and ** represent statistical significance at the 5 per cent and 10 per cent levels, where the critical values of a χ^2 distribution with 2 degrees of freedom at the 5 per cent and 10 per cent significance levels are 5.99 and 4.61 respectively.

4.3   ESTIMATES OF VARYING COEFFICIENTS

Irrespective of differences in nature across manufacturing industries at the 3-digit level, the underlying assumption of the varying coefficients frontier model is that industries have equal opportunities to access frontier technology, that is, they share the best practice production frontier. However, in practice, one observes various applications of frontier technology leading to different output outcomes. According to the specification of the varying coefficients frontier model, the frontier production function is estimated for individual economies and individual manufacturing industries by employing the computer program TERAN developed by Kalirajan and Obwona (1994) at the Australian National University. The ranges of actual response coefficients, that is, the estimated minimal and maximal (frontier) coefficients and mean coefficients of the five East Asian manufacturing sectors, are presented in Tables 4.3 to 4.7.[4] The average intercepts and labour and capital coefficients are reported at the bottom of each table. To save space, the t-ratios of the mean coefficients estimated by general least squares are not reported here; however, those t-ratios are always statistically significant at the 5 per cent or even 1 per cent level.

Table 4.3 shows the estimates of frontier and mean coefficients of production function for Hong Kong's manufacturing sector over the period 1976–97. Due to the relatively larger labour coefficients, that is, greater than 0.8 since 1992, the estimated frontier coefficients for Hong Kong were not satisfactory. The data became increasingly volatile in the 1990s, due to minute output–capital ratios in the footwear industry since 1993, negative GFCF in the beverages industry in 1995 and 1996, and the ultimate removal of these industries. To some extent, the structural transformation in the manufacturing industries in Hong Kong also contributed to this outcome.[5]

In terms of the magnitudes of the frontier coefficients, the labour coefficients exceeded capital coefficients throughout the entire period. Sizeable variations in the labour coefficients have been identified across industries during the sample period, except in 1994 and 1996; for instance, the range of the labour coefficients in 1976 was between 0.493 and 0.571. One of the objectives of this study is to take industry-specific characteristics into account; in relation to this, it should be noted that the result for Hong Kong has corresponded to the earlier expectation that industries applied their production technology and labour input (or human resources) differently because different industries require various types of skills in the production process. On the other hand, the variations in capital coefficients appeared to be small, indicating that the application of capital inputs across the 21 manufacturing industries was reasonably similar.

With respect to returns to scale, it is possible that the sum of frontier labour and capital coefficients will exceed one, as estimated frontier coefficients are selected from the largest coefficients among various actual response coefficients. Put differently, if industry A utilises labour input most efficiently and industry C applies capital input most productively, then the frontier labour and capital coefficients will be chosen from industries A (labour coefficient) and C (capital coefficient) respectively.[6] Building on estimated frontier coefficients, the returns to scale for Hong Kong's manufacturing industries ranged from 0.923 in 1977 to 1.102 in 1991, as shown in Table 4.3. The estimated frontier coefficients for the other four East Asian manufacturing sectors are briefly described below.

Table 4.4 presents the estimates of frontier and mean coefficients of production function for Japan's manufacturing sector over the period 1965–98. The estimated frontier capital coefficients in Japan were generally larger than the frontier labour coefficients. The extent of variations in labour coefficients ranged from 0.031 in 1981 to 0.095 in 1988 and the returns to scale ranged from 0.948 in 1975 to 1.053 in 1990. Yet the variations in capital coefficients appeared to be zero.

Table 4.5 shows the estimates of frontier and mean coefficients of production function for Korea's manufacturing sector for the period 1970–97. In the early years of the sample period, the application of labour inputs differed considerably across industries due to the significant variation in labour coefficients, but these differences were reduced in the later years. This implies that a number of Korean manufacturing industries that used to apply labour inputs less efficiently caught up with the most efficient industry. In line with Hong Kong's and Japan's manufacturing industries, the degree of variation in capital coefficients seemed small in Korea. The returns to scale according to the estimated frontier coefficients varied from 0.936 in 1979 to 1.193 in 1972.

Table 4.6 presents the estimates of frontier and mean coefficients of production function for Singapore's manufacturing sector during the 1970–97 period. It is interesting to note that certain variations in the labour coefficients occurred from the start of the sample period until the late 1980s. By contrast, there were some variations in the capital coefficients from the mid-1980s. A likely explanation of these estimation outcomes is that on the one hand, different manufacturing industries in Singapore applied labour inputs in different ways in the early 1970s but similarly since the late 1980s. On the other hand, the applications of capital inputs were increasingly diverse after the mid-1980s.[7]

It is worth mentioning that the estimated mean labour coefficient fell sharply from 0.546 in 1976 to 0.271 in 1979. The falling labour share $(=MP_L*L/Y)$ was attributable to the changes in marginal product of labour or labour–output ratio or both. Yet further analysis cannot be undertaken due to the focus of this study and the limited data set. Furthermore, the returns to scale on the basis of estimated frontier coefficients were between 0.974 in 1979 and 1.122 in 1985.

Table 4.7 presents the estimates of frontier and mean coefficients of production function for the Taiwanese manufacturing sector during 1981–99. In contrast to Singapore, Taiwan's manufacturing industries utilised their capital inputs in different ways in the early 1980s but in a similar manner after the mid-1980s. The application of labour inputs became diverse after 1992. Also, there was little variation in capital and labour coefficients between 1987 and 1991. The returns to scale dependent on the estimated frontier coefficients were rising over time, from 0.972 in 1981 to 1.242 in 1996. It should be mentioned that several industries had negative intercepts in 1991 and 1992. As the production function is measured in logarithmic form in the estimation, negative constant terms are caused by logarithmic transformation if the parameter is less than one. To ensure the convergence of the estimation, and positive mean value of intercepts, manufacturing value added was scaled up by 'ln (2)' during the 1993–99 period. This also helps illustrate the sudden increase in intercepts since 1993. However, while calculating the components of output growth, the augmented intercepts were scaled down by 'ln (2)' to restore the originals.

Finally, the averages of labour and capital shares (coefficients) on the basis of estimated frontier and mean coefficients are compared with Young (1995). As Young only gives estimates of labour and capital shares at the manufacturing level for Korea, Singapore and Taiwan, this comparison excludes Hong Kong and Japan. As shown in Table 4.8, except for the Korean manufacturing sector during the 1970–75 period, the average estimates of labour and capital shares, as indicated by the estimated frontier coefficients, are in general comparable with Young's. Additionally, it should again be stressed that the empirical model of this study does not impose the strict assumption of constant returns to scale as in Young (1995). The average returns to scale derived from the estimated frontier coefficients for the Hong Kong, Japanese, Korean, Singaporean and Taiwanese manufacturing sectors were 1.002, 1.00, 1.039, 1063 and 1.117 respectively.

Table 4.3   Estimates of frontier and mean coefficients of production
function for Hong Kong's manufacturing, 1976–97

Year	Range of actual response coefficients								
	Minimal varying coefficients			Frontier coefficients (maximal)			Mean coefficients		
	Const	Lab	Cap	Const	Lab	Cap	Const	Lab	Cap
1976	7.915	0.493	0.374	8.202	0.571	0.374	8.045	0.528	0.374
1977	7.563	0.417	0.432	7.813	0.491	0.432	7.665	0.448	0.432
1978	8.416	0.530	0.337	8.785	0.597	0.337	8.627	0.567	0.337
1979	8.142	0.491	0.382	8.142	0.554	0.382	8.142	0.525	0.382
1980	7.600	0.462	0.409	7.662	0.541	0.409	7.637	0.509	0.409
1981	7.957	0.574	0.344	8.393	0.597	0.351	8.224	0.588	0.348
1982	7.489	0.543	0.384	7.850	0.583	0.384	7.668	0.562	0.384
1983	7.767	0.540	0.369	7.806	0.640	0.369	7.789	0.596	0.369
1984	7.524	0.645	0.334	7.805	0.682	0.334	7.681	0.664	0.334
1985	6.883	0.547	0.408	7.252	0.596	0.408	7.024	0.565	0.408
1986	6.476	0.535	0.426	6.867	0.613	0.426	6.686	0.574	0.426
1987	8.204	0.617	0.314	8.765	0.621	0.335	8.491	0.619	0.325
1988	5.994	0.478	0.482	6.466	0.536	0.482	6.238	0.506	0.482
1989	7.250	0.495	0.413	7.436	0.592	0.413	7.350	0.545	0.413
1990	7.704	0.609	0.335	7.909	0.730	0.335	7.805	0.668	0.335
1991	6.540	0.592	0.397	6.708	0.705	0.397	6.626	0.649	0.397
1992	8.904	0.812	0.188	9.658	0.856	0.199	9.288	0.833	0.193
1993	10.02	0.836	0.137	10.62	0.858	0.153	10.27	0.845	0.144
1994	10.71	0.903	0.068	11.39	0.903	0.099	11.05	0.903	0.082
1995	10.91	0.904	0.064	11.41	0.991	0.064	11.16	0.942	0.064
1996	9.450	0.860	0.157	9.703	0.860	0.185	9.558	0.860	0.169
1997	9.244	0.799	0.193	9.452	0.870	0.193	9.360	0.837	0.193
Ave.	8.121	0.622	0.316	8.459	0.681	0.321	8.290	0.652	0.318

Notes:
1. The minimal varying coefficients denote the lowest estimated coefficients among industries and the frontier coefficients are the largest ones among industries according to the specification of the model.
2. All varying coefficients are averaged to obtain mean coefficients.
3. The abbreviations 'Const' 'Lab' and 'Cap' represent constant, labour and capital respectively.

Source: Author's calculations using the computer program TERAN.

Table 4.4   Estimates of frontier and mean coefficients of production function for Japan's manufacturing, 1965–98

Year	Range of actual response coefficients								
	Minimal varying coefficients			Frontier coefficients (maximal)			Mean coefficients		
	Const	Lab	Cap	Const	Lab	Cap	Const	Lab	Cap
1965	8.060	0.442	0.490	8.414	0.478	0.490	8.190	0.455	0.490
1966	7.954	0.487	0.473	8.243	0.535	0.473	8.087	0.506	0.473
1967	7.499	0.459	0.505	7.754	0.513	0.505	7.630	0.484	0.505
1968	7.478	0.477	0.497	7.888	0.525	0.497	7.695	0.499	0.497
1969	8.007	0.483	0.483	8.437	0.523	0.483	8.197	0.499	0.483
1970	8.380	0.495	0.466	8.830	0.533	0.466	8.576	0.510	0.466
1971	8.740	0.481	0.461	9.219	0.518	0.461	8.911	0.494	0.461
1972	9.544	0.522	0.412	9.809	0.579	0.412	9.667	0.545	0.412
1973	9.197	0.506	0.434	9.309	0.575	0.434	9.257	0.538	0.434
1974	9.071	0.460	0.466	9.409	0.496	0.466	9.199	0.472	0.466
1975	10.11	0.518	0.398	10.64	0.550	0.398	10.29	0.529	0.398
1976	10.35	0.527	0.382	10.67	0.589	0.382	10.50	0.553	0.382
1977	10.31	0.532	0.387	10.76	0.575	0.387	10.49	0.547	0.387
1978	10.24	0.558	0.381	10.67	0.600	0.381	10.37	0.570	0.381
1979	9.613	0.486	0.437	9.890	0.543	0.437	9.729	0.507	0.437
1980	9.134	0.454	0.468	9.565	0.502	0.468	9.318	0.473	0.468
1981	9.192	0.458	0.467	9.737	0.489	0.467	9.379	0.469	0.467
1982	8.966	0.471	0.468	9.418	0.515	0.468	9.149	0.486	0.468
1983	9.113	0.494	0.450	9.603	0.546	0.450	9.325	0.513	0.450
1984	8.633	0.501	0.461	9.021	0.563	0.461	8.831	0.529	0.461
1985	8.897	0.514	0.446	9.060	0.598	0.446	8.984	0.553	0.446
1986	9.364	0.534	0.426	9.694	0.596	0.426	9.494	0.555	0.426
1987	9.079	0.497	0.450	9.398	0.571	0.450	9.227	0.526	0.450
1988	8.887	0.492	0.460	8.950	0.587	0.460	8.920	0.535	0.460
1989	8.942	0.508	0.459	9.051	0.584	0.459	8.984	0.534	0.459
1990	8.971	0.548	0.440	9.229	0.613	0.440	9.066	0.570	0.440
1991	8.772	0.499	0.469	8.924	0.569	0.469	8.835	0.525	0.469
1992	8.640	0.471	0.485	8.944	0.528	0.485	8.759	0.491	0.485
1993	8.216	0.438	0.512	8.630	0.489	0.512	8.372	0.456	0.512
1994	9.033	0.427	0.487	9.370	0.488	0.487	9.183	0.451	0.487
1995	9.449	0.494	0.445	9.833	0.551	0.445	9.590	0.514	0.445
1996	9.362	0.516	0.440	9.896	0.559	0.440	9.550	0.531	0.440
1997	9.162	0.546	0.434	9.706	0.589	0.434	9.346	0.561	0.434
1998	9.625	0.547	0.420	10.03	0.592	0.420	9.752	0.560	0.420
Ave.	8.920	0.493	0.455	9.279	0.545	0.455	9.065	0.513	0.455

Notes and source: As in Table 4.3.

Table 4.5   *Estimates of frontier and mean coefficients of production function for Korea's manufacturing, 1970–97*

Year	Range of actual response coefficients								
	Minimal varying coefficients			Frontier coefficients (maximal)			Mean coefficients		
	Const	Lab	Cap	Const	Lab	Cap	Const	Lab	Cap
1970	9.514	0.859	0.232	10.65	0.930	0.232	10.21	0.900	0.232
1971	8.115	0.772	0.322	9.169	0.868	0.322	8.774	0.830	0.322
1972	8.138	0.630	0.379	8.187	0.814	0.379	8.171	0.744	0.379
1973	8.417	0.616	0.388	9.437	0.687	0.396	8.968	0.653	0.392
1974	7.858	0.567	0.419	8.246	0.709	0.419	8.110	0.657	0.419
1975	7.849	0.622	0.406	8.769	0.672	0.418	8.377	0.649	0.413
1976	7.970	0.584	0.425	8.797	0.638	0.433	8.398	0.610	0.429
1977	7.854	0.418	0.511	8.565	0.479	0.511	8.160	0.442	0.511
1978	9.223	0.463	0.452	9.833	0.467	0.473	9.473	0.465	0.460
1979	9.052	0.376	0.492	9.409	0.444	0.492	9.184	0.402	0.492
1980	8.489	0.316	0.523	8.733	0.428	0.523	8.605	0.368	0.523
1981	8.507	0.399	0.491	9.187	0.469	0.491	8.849	0.436	0.491
1982	8.452	0.452	0.482	8.916	0.514	0.482	8.611	0.472	0.482
1983	8.648	0.436	0.481	9.269	0.483	0.484	8.895	0.454	0.482
1984	8.233	0.424	0.500	8.694	0.498	0.500	8.454	0.459	0.500
1985	7.984	0.395	0.519	8.476	0.466	0.519	8.233	0.430	0.519
1986	8.117	0.444	0.497	8.719	0.499	0.497	8.436	0.474	0.497
1987	8.200	0.476	0.487	8.817	0.521	0.490	8.503	0.497	0.489
1988	8.626	0.471	0.479	9.080	0.521	0.479	8.837	0.494	0.479
1989	8.676	0.466	0.484	9.018	0.522	0.484	8.811	0.487	0.484
1990	8.500	0.456	0.497	8.534	0.456	0.531	8.515	0.456	0.513
1991	9.524	0.598	0.406	9.900	0.598	0.425	9.710	0.598	0.415
1992	8.971	0.562	0.438	9.384	0.603	0.438	9.198	0.584	0.438
1993	9.356	0.548	0.429	9.413	0.633	0.429	9.386	0.591	0.429
1994	8.767	0.610	0.431	9.190	0.613	0.445	8.973	0.611	0.438
1995	7.716	0.610	0.467	8.156	0.610	0.480	7.989	0.610	0.476
1996	7.992	0.642	0.447	8.841	0.642	0.447	8.492	0.642	0.447
1997	7.524	0.637	0.465	8.425	0.637	0.465	8.014	0.637	0.465
Ave.	8.438	0.530	0.448	8.994	0.586	0.453	8.726	0.559	0.451

Notes and source: As in Table 4.3.

Table 4.6   Estimates of frontier and mean coefficients of production function for Singapore's manufacturing, 1970–97

Year	Range of actual response coefficients								
	Minimal varying coefficients			Frontier coefficients (maximal)			Mean coefficients		
	Const	Lab	Cap	Const	Lab	Cap	Const	Lab	Cap
1970	3.469	0.420	0.596	4.408	0.496	0.596	3.960	0.458	0.596
1971	4.173	0.493	0.529	5.364	0.507	0.529	4.726	0.500	0.529
1972	4.789	0.561	0.464	5.499	0.611	0.464	5.136	0.585	0.464
1973	4.795	0.537	0.478	5.234	0.537	0.518	5.008	0.537	0.498
1974	4.381	0.509	0.503	5.203	0.509	0.522	4.804	0.509	0.513
1975	3.809	0.490	0.532	5.217	0.490	0.532	4.565	0.490	0.532
1976	5.189	0.537	0.455	6.156	0.555	0.455	5.626	0.546	0.455
1977	4.764	0.397	0.542	5.476	0.455	0.542	5.125	0.429	0.542
1978	4.319	0.319	0.610	4.788	0.395	0.610	4.540	0.359	0.610
1979	3.708	0.244	0.680	4.452	0.294	0.680	4.099	0.271	0.680
1980	3.393	0.340	0.653	3.978	0.390	0.653	3.646	0.364	0.653
1981	3.418	0.325	0.644	4.118	0.407	0.644	3.771	0.369	0.644
1982	3.726	0.473	0.544	4.307	0.576	0.544	3.975	0.519	0.544
1983	3.540	0.366	0.617	3.791	0.482	0.617	3.649	0.418	0.617
1984	2.634	0.296	0.696	2.860	0.412	0.696	2.741	0.353	0.696
1985	1.605	0.335	0.728	2.235	0.387	0.735	1.912	0.361	0.732
1986	1.602	0.280	0.761	2.134	0.343	0.761	1.860	0.309	0.761
1987	2.032	0.278	0.746	2.585	0.318	0.753	2.319	0.298	0.750
1988	2.486	0.298	0.711	3.085	0.310	0.734	2.817	0.304	0.723
1989	3.078	0.328	0.674	3.600	0.341	0.691	3.316	0.335	0.682
1990	3.654	0.398	0.618	3.748	0.398	0.660	3.695	0.398	0.634
1991	2.205	0.339	0.716	3.084	0.339	0.716	2.591	0.339	0.716
1992	3.042	0.404	0.643	3.332	0.404	0.672	3.181	0.404	0.657
1993	2.595	0.388	0.670	2.906	0.388	0.703	2.755	0.388	0.686
1994	2.224	0.358	0.704	2.379	0.358	0.745	2.304	0.358	0.725
1995	2.811	0.415	0.649	3.069	0.415	0.686	2.923	0.415	0.665
1996	3.986	0.521	0.532	4.254	0.521	0.573	4.122	0.521	0.553
1997	4.215	0.534	0.515	4.503	0.534	0.555	4.360	0.534	0.536
Ave.	3.416	0.399	0.615	3.992	0.435	0.628	3.697	0.417	0.621

Notes and source: As in Table 4.3.

Table 4.7   *Estimates of frontier and mean coefficients of production function for Taiwan's manufacturing, 1981–99*

Year	Range of actual response coefficients								
	Minimal varying coefficients			Frontier coefficients (maximal)			Mean coefficients		
	Const	Lab	Cap	Const	Lab	Cap	Const	Lab	Cap
1981	1.737	0.577	0.368	2.573	0.577	0.395	2.131	0.577	0.380
1982	1.548	0.594	0.365	2.314	0.594	0.402	1.913	0.594	0.381
1983	1.699	0.547	0.411	2.509	0.547	0.444	2.074	0.547	0.425
1984	1.496	0.560	0.430	2.217	0.560	0.458	1.811	0.560	0.442
1985	1.295	0.540	0.477	2.065	0.540	0.494	1.591	0.540	0.484
1986	1.312	0.545	0.490	2.025	0.545	0.493	1.575	0.545	0.491
1987	1.022	0.574	0.488	1.808	0.574	0.488	1.308	0.574	0.488
1988	0.936	0.570	0.493	1.807	0.570	0.493	1.301	0.570	0.493
1989	0.633	0.605	0.486	1.449	0.605	0.486	0.957	0.605	0.486
1990	0.233	0.626	0.496	1.060	0.626	0.496	0.579	0.626	0.496
1991	−0.123	0.667	0.490	0.629	0.667	0.490	0.206	0.667	0.490
1992	−0.071	0.646	0.504	0.521	0.664	0.504	0.204	0.654	0.504
1993	0.650	0.608	0.529	0.960	0.658	0.529	0.822	0.635	0.529
1994	0.580	0.554	0.588	0.693	0.622	0.588	0.643	0.592	0.588
1995	0.240	0.579	0.592	0.386	0.645	0.592	0.319	0.615	0.592
1996	0.296	0.609	0.552	0.375	0.690	0.552	0.336	0.651	0.552
1997	0.326	0.584	0.573	0.610	0.652	0.573	0.465	0.618	0.573
1998	0.501	0.540	0.596	0.782	0.612	0.596	0.639	0.576	0.596
1999	0.530	0.501	0.629	0.883	0.574	0.629	0.685	0.535	0.629
Ave.	0.781	0.580	0.503	1.351	0.606	0.511	1.029	0.594	0.506

Notes and source: As in Table 4.3.

Table 4.8   Comparison of the average labour and capital shares between
Young (1995) and this study for the Korean, Singaporean and
Taiwanese manufacturing sectors

Country	Period	Young (1995)	Frontier coefficients (maximal)		Mean coefficients	
		Labour share	Labour share	Capital share	Labour share	Capital share
Korea	1970–75	0.477	0.802	0.350	0.757	0.349
	1975–80	0.503	0.540	0.465	0.514	0.461
	1980–85	0.547	0.478	0.496	0.438	0.496
	1985–90	0.572	0.506	0.494	0.476	0.494
Singapore	1970–80	0.423	0.485	0.545	0.468	0.542
	1980–90	0.385	0.397	0.683	0.363	0.680
Taiwan	1970–80	0.566	NA	NA	NA	NA
	1980–90	0.613	0.568	0.461	0.568	0.452

Notes:
1. For Hong Kong, the labour shares at the manufacturing level are not available and Japan is
   not included in Young (1995). Young uses growth accounting with the assumption of
   constant returns to scale, hence the capital shares can be simply obtained by one minus
   labour shares.
2. The calculation of the average frontier coefficients of labour and capital, for example for the
   period 1970–75, begins in 1970 and ends in 1974.
3. NA: not available.

4.4   TECHNICAL EFFICIENCY IN EAST ASIAN
MANUFACTURING INDUSTRIES

This section examines carefully whether manufacturing industries in East
Asia have reached their output potential; that is, whether they utilise the
given resources efficiently, using the concept of technical efficiency. The
importance of this issue is evident. If the actual output of manufacturing
industries is found to be far below output potential, this may stem from lack
of a learning-by-doing effect due to poor management and coordination
problems and so on. In addition, introduction of up-to-date technology may
initially contribute to the low level of technical efficiency.[8] According to the
model described in Chapter 3, the potential (best practice) production frontier
is constructed using the estimated frontier coefficients. Then the actual
output of each industry is compared with the potential frontier output. In the

context of the varying coefficients frontier model, technical efficiency is defined as 'actual output over potential output'. Given the same level of inputs, the closer the actual output is to frontier output, the higher the level of technical efficiency, and vice versa.

Table 4.9   Technical efficiency in the East Asian manufacturing sectors

Country	1965	1966	1967	1968	1969	1970	1971	1972	1973	1974	1975	1976
Hong Kong	–	–	–	–	–	–	–	–	–	–	–	58.0
Japan	61.5	60.8	62.6	61.7	59.3	59.0	55.2	58.1	60.9	60.7	54.8	56.2
Korea	–	–	–	–	–	50.9	49.8	52.3	44.1	54.1	49.2	46.6
Singapore	–	–	–	–	–	50.9	52.8	59.1	50.8	38.3	55.7	56.8
Taiwan	–	–	–	–	–	–	–	–	–	–	–	–

	1977	1978	1979	1980	1981	1982	1983	1984	1985	1986	1987	1988
Hong Kong	58.2	70.0	80.4	72.2	73.7	69.2	65.1	75.1	59.4	58.1	61.1	53.9
Japan	54.9	52.5	55.6	56.1	55.7	55.1	52.3	55.9	54.9	51.3	50.3	52.3
Korea	46.6	49.8	51.7	47.8	51.5	48.4	49.2	52.5	54.2	58.6	54.8	58.4
Singapore	58.7	59.3	60.1	51.4	54.0	44.6	52.6	55.2	51.0	50.9	42.6	34.3
Taiwan	–	–	–	–	57.7	56.9	55.7	59.0	57.5	64.0	62.2	61.7

	1989	1990	1991	1992	1993	1994	1995	1996	1997	1998	1999
Hong Kong	59.9	52.0	56.7	51.6	53.1	52.6	52.2	61.6	69.6	–	–
Japan	51.8	51.1	54.4	54.5	53.3	54.2	51.6	51.8	51.1	52.9	
Korea	56.1	59.5	64.2	68.3	61.6	65.5	75.2	71.9	67.3	–	–
Singapore	48.6	51.7	58.9	66.1	63.8	64.6	59.8	61.2	61.3	–	–
Taiwan	62.8	63.5	67.2	66.9	68.6	69.1	68.5	63.8	60.5	60.1	54.9

Source: Author's calculations.

Table 4.9 shows the level of technical efficiency (simple average) for the entire manufacturing sector. The average technical efficiency of Hong Kong's manufacturing sector ranged from 51.6 per cent in 1992 to 80.4 per cent in 1979. Technical efficiency was relatively higher (over 65 per cent) over the period 1978–84. Except for 1987, technical efficiency fell below 60 per cent from 1985 to 1995. Recently, there has been considerable improvement in technical efficiency, from 52.2 per cent in 1995 to 69.6 per cent in 1997. On average, the technical efficiency of Japan's manufacturing sector varied from 50.3 per cent in 1987 to 62.6 per cent in 1967. Unlike Hong Kong, the variation in technical efficiency in Japan's manufacturing sector was comparatively small, but it has gradually fallen since the early 1970s. This suggests that manufacturers in Japan did not apply the best practice technology efficiently, because actual output was falling short of output potential.

Unlike Hong Kong and Japan, technical efficiency in Korea improved, from 44.1 per cent in 1973 to 75.2 per cent in 1995. More specifically, in the first phase (1970–85) technical efficiency was below 55 per cent and fluctuated at around 50 per cent. During the second phase (1986–90), technical efficiency increased to above 55 per cent except for 1987, and in the third phase (since 1991) it even exceeded 60 per cent. Technical efficiency for Singapore's manufacturing sector varied significantly from 34.3 per cent in 1988 to 66.1 per cent in 1992. Despite the large fluctuation, Singapore's industries became more technically efficient in the 1990s. The highest technical efficiency for Taiwan's manufacturing sector occurred in 1994 at 69.1 per cent and the lowest in 1999 at 54.9 per cent. Technical efficiency from 1981 to 1985 was below 60 per cent but above 60 per cent between 1986 and 1998. More specifically, technical efficiency was at an all-time high during the 1991–95 period.

Table 4.10 presents the technical efficiency of individual manufacturing industries in Hong Kong in selected years. On average, the beverages industry had the highest technical efficiency, followed by basic metals and chemical products. Interestingly, a number of industries also reached their full potential during this period, for example the wood industry in 1981 and the non-metal mineral industry in 1995.

Table 4.11 presents the technical efficiency of individual manufacturing industries in Japan in selected years. Except for 1980, the chemicals industry (ISIC 352) always utilised labour and capital inputs efficiently. The second most efficient industry was petroleum refineries, followed by printing and publishing, and leather. On the other hand, the paper products, miscellaneous petroleum and iron and steel industries were the least efficient industries over the sample period. Although many industries suffered a slight deterioration in technical efficiency, this increasingly improved in the beverages industry.

Table 4.12 presents the technical efficiency of individual manufacturing industries in Korea in selected years. Like Japan, the Korean chemicals industry was the most efficient in terms of applying the best practice technology by reaching full output potential from 1976, except for 1981, 1986 and 1995. The second most efficient industry was miscellaneous petroleum, which also achieved its full potential over the 1971–73 period, as well as in 1981 and 1986. Besides theses two, the industrial chemicals, leather, and printing and publishing industries reached full potential in 1970, 1974 and 1995 respectively. Although there has been a substantial technical efficiency improvement in recent years, the pottery industry was the least efficient industry in the 1970s. Similarly, the textile industry in general experienced the lowest technical efficiency in the 1980s and 1990s.

Table 4.10 Technical efficiency of individual industries in Hong Kong, selected years

Industry	1976	1980	1981	1985	1990	1995	1997
311 Food products	58.2	70.9	80.4	57.5	61.7	77.8	58.2
313 Beverages	100	95.9	100	100	100	#	100
321 Textiles	39.8	53.6	49.9	51.3	37.1	45.1	39.8
322 Wearing apparel	66.0	72.8	67.3	47.9	35.2	41.1	66.0
323 Leather products	51.9	59.2	58.7	59.8	51.7	59.1	51.9
324 Footwear	48.8	69.8	65.1	61.9	34.6	#	48.8
331 Wood products	80.0	100	82.9	73.1	52.0	55.0	80.0
332 Furniture	59.2	82.8	76.3	59.7	56.7	61.5	59.2
341 Paper and paper products	49.1	66.7	66.5	65.5	52.8	55.9	49.1
342 Printing, publishing	55.4	84.9	75.2	54.4	53.5	64.8	55.4
351 +352 Chemical products	54.2	79.8	71.8	63.0	96.6	100	54.2
355 Rubber products	41.6	46.4	49.7	38.1	45.1	58.3	41.6
356 Plastic products	46.2	58.8	53.8	47.0	35.3	46.6	46.2
36 Non-metal mineral	48.2	76.0	54.3	55.2	78.3	42.4	48.2
371 +372 (Basic metals)	80.7	70.9	69.0	55.9	84.9	86.2	80.7
381 Fabricated metal prod.	52.6	65.0	57.0	47.2	42.5	49.6	52.6
382 Non-electrical mach.	45.4	89.5	82.5	60.8	62.0	76.0	45.4
383 Electric machinery	58.7	84.0	77.1	45.4	37.6	70.4	58.7
384 Transport equipment	71.3	73.5	80.6	61.7	76.1	71.5	71.3
385 Professional equip.	52.6	69.9	62.2	51.2	47.7	54.3	52.6
390 Other manufactured	61.8	78.0	74.0	63.8	49.8	55.4	61.8

Notes:
1. # denotes the removal of industry in the estimation; see Appendix for details.
2. Non-metal mineral products (36) industry includes pottery, china, earthenware (361), glass and glass products (362) and other non-metallic mineral (369) industries.

Source: Author's calculations.

Table 4.11   Technical efficiency of individual industries in Japan, selected years

Industry	1965	1970	1975	1980	1985	1990	1995	1998
311 Food products	62.0	49.4	58.0	51.5	47.4	41.1	44.4	42.8
313 Beverages	57.2	61.0	63.8	55.7	67.9	61.7	81.7	88.3
321 Textiles	50.8	44.2	41.3	40.9	37.6	33.4	33.5	44.1
322 Wearing apparel	57.0	52.8	48.9	48.5	42.8	38.3	38.9	38.7
323 Leather products	82.2	71.8	63.3	64.9	75.8	68.1	59.2	70.3
324 Footwear	59.9	66.7	55.0	62.3	61.9	61.0	66.4	60.0
331 Wood products	57.0	52.6	46.5	51.4	44.0	45.2	50.8	46.8
332 Furniture	60.9	57.1	53.2	57.0	54.9	54.8	56.4	53.6
341 Paper and paper products	56.8	49.8	44.8	39.5	40.6	39.8	40.6	42.2
342 Printing and publishing	73.2	68.9	74.5	75.6	68.4	60.0	61.8	62.5
351 Industrial chemicals	61.2	63.6	50.4	45.6	57.2	65.2	60.0	63.5
352 Other chemicals	100	100	100	97.4	100	100	100	100
353 Petroleum refineries	76.8	76.9	74.1	98.3	87.0	52.3	70.9	46.2
354 Miscellaneous petroleum	53.2	44.2	48.5	40.5	37.8	46.4	42.2	50.6
355 Rubber products	56.6	47.7	45.4	46.0	47.0	45.9	42.0	46.2
356 Plastic products	45.8	52.7	51.5	52.7	51.9	44.2	42.1	43.3
361 Pottery, china, earthenware	57.7	53.1	49.5	49.4	43.7	37.2	39.2	40.6
362 Glass and glass products	68.0	67.4	49.9	54.0	67.2	58.8	44.2	51.3
369 Other non-metallic mineral	47.1	48.1	48.7	50.0	47.3	50.3	51.2	48.8
371 Iron and steel	45.1	45.7	42.3	48.0	44.7	48.2	39.2	43.7
372 Non-ferrous metals	55.3	51.1	40.3	51.2	39.2	41.8	35.1	40.9
381 Fabricated metal products	64.6	66.2	55.5	57.4	54.1	52.2	54.2	52.1
382 Non-electrical machinery	60.6	69.2	63.0	63.0	57.3	54.8	52.3	54.4
383 Electric machinery	66.3	65.8	50.9	58.6	50.0	40.4	40.9	42.4
384 Transport equipment	70.8	56.9	54.9	49.2	49.1	45.8	44.0	49.4
385 Professional equipment	50.0	51.3	50.6	50.4	48.7	39.2	47.2	53.7
390 Other manufactured	64.3	59.4	55.1	55.9	59.8	54.9	54.7	52.1

Source: Author's calculations.

Table 4.13 shows the technical efficiency of individual manufacturing industries in Singapore in selected years. There were six industries at different stages achieving full efficiency, including beverages, iron and steel and industrial chemicals. In addition to those industries, rubber, other non-metallic mineral and non-electrical machinery occasionally reached full efficiency. The beverages industry was the most efficient, followed by iron and steel. The three industries regarded as the least efficient in Singapore were textiles, plastics and other manufactured products. It remains unclear why technical efficiency fluctuated so drastically in several industries, such as non-electrical machinery, electrical machinery and other non-metallic minerals.

Table 4.12   Technical efficiency of individual industries in Korea, selected years

Industry	1970	1974	1975	1980	1981	1986	1990	1995	1997
311 Food products	55.4	33.2	45.3	57.6	59.6	55.7	57.6	70.9	66.2
321 Textiles	23.3	25.6	28.4	35.0	38.8	43.8	34.6	43.9	40.4
322 Wearing apparel	34.3	40.7	36.4	53.9	61.4	58.4	61.0	88.5	76.1
323 Leather products	48.2	100	98.6	39.8	61.3	67.8	70.6	83.3	73.5
324 Footwear	55.6	51.4	42.5	38.7	42.0	56.5	62.6	61.6	61.3
331 Wood products	39.4	46.0	36.5	23.2	23.7	30.5	45.3	71.5	67.0
332 Furniture	35.3	43.2	35.4	40.7	41.7	51.0	71.1	48.3	48.2
341 Paper, paper products	54.7	55.0	42.2	43.4	48.1	57.5	49.7	72.9	65.9
342 Printing, publishing	50.9	54.1	50.2	59.9	60.4	69.5	82.5	100	86.4
351 Industrial chemicals	100	69.9	67.8	60.0	60.7	63.1	62.0	80.7	93.8
352 Other chemicals	93.9	98.5	98.8	100	97.2	96.6	100	98.1	100
354 Miscellaneous petrol.	65.3	75.7	69.3	83.1	98.1	99.4	69.1	78.6	63.2
355 Rubber products	38.1	35.6	33.4	42.2	38.8	47.7	45.3	62.3	58.5
356 Plastic products	65.2	56.7	30.3	48.2	49.4	55.8	53.4	86.3	47.1
361 Pottery, china, earth.	17.1	19.5	18.8	38.3	40.9	44.0	42.1	60.1	56.4
362 Glass and glass prod.	73.7	64.5	68.0	48.0	44.2	55.1	54.2	88.8	72.6
369 Other non-metallic	44.4	44.8	52.3	45.9	46.8	50.7	59.9	72.3	68.3
371 Iron and steel	61.5	78.0	58.7	37.3	50.7	53.4	53.3	78.5	66.5
372 Non-ferrous metals	44.6	55.6	43.6	49.9	39.7	49.7	48.9	77.1	66.7
381 Fabricated metal prod.	39.6	56.6	42.2	40.3	50.3	56.5	64.8	70.4	64.1
382 Non-electrical mach.	39.6	52.8	46.5	34.3	38.7	58.3	65.5	73.4	70.6
383 Electric machinery	48.4	58.7	47.3	42.8	49.9	64.1	59.5	90.4	65.8
382 Transport equipment	62.7	48.5	40.2	39.1	48.5	58.0	59.6	65.9	65.5
385 Professional equip.	41.1	49.1	57.3	47.4	42.9	58.6	59.3	85.0	79.3
390 Other manufactured	39.1	38.7	39.6	45.6	53.1	61.9	56.2	72.4	60.7

Source: Author's calculations.

Table 4.13   *Technical efficiency of individual industries in Singapore,*
              selected years

Industry	1970	1975	1980	1985	1990	1995	1997
311 Food products	42.1	60.5	42.0	45.7	49.0	49.5	59.1
313 Beverages	100	100	83.3	100	51.8	74.8	100
321 Textiles	21.8	24.4	30.1	30.5	40.2	44.0	48.1
322 Wearing apparel	31.7	32.3	44.6	40.1	40.4	38.5	35.1
323 Leather products	48.5	52.5	60.5	75.8	72.4	83.7	94.6
324 Footwear	39.9	50.8	35.8	37.0	43.0	63.0	62.6
331 Wood products	45.3	31.5	32.0	34.1	41.8	58.8	56.3
332 Furniture	60.9	44.9	41.6	49.7	38.2	58.5	50.4
341 Paper and paper products	34.6	42.3	53.4	60.9	60.5	57.9	58.7
342 Printing and publishing	42.8	63.8	50.8	51.3	52.5	70.1	71.9
351 Industrial chemicals	49.4	56.4	47.8	71.9	100	48.9	62.5
355 Rubber products	70.6	57.7	55.6	39.1	38.4	60.5	57.5
356 Plastic products	35.5	32.8	35.6	36.3	38.3	44.6	39.9
361 +362 Pottery, glass	29.4	46.8	39.0	35.1	28.3	63.3	51.7
369 Other non-metallic	51.5	95.1	71.5	53.9	52.6	100	81.7
371 Iron and steel	81.7	72.0	100	67.0	70.8	50.2	59.1
372 Non-ferrous metals	72.6	49.0	53.3	84.9	84.1	49.5	49.4
381 Fabricated metal products	54.1	64.7	48.5	35.4	40.8	48.4	43.2
382 Non-electrical machinery	67.6	95.0	55.9	41.4	75.1	94.5	90.8
383 Electric machinery	76.9	70.1	56.2	41.1	29.9	48.9	42.5
384 Transport equipment	64.4	64.8	66.5	49.3	60.0	54.5	69.6
385 Professional equipment	23.5	35.3	28.9	50.9	46.9	72.7	81.2
390 Other manufactured prod.	24.6	38.4	50.1	41.1	34.9	40.4	43.8

Source: Author's calculations.

Table 4.14 shows the technical efficiency of individual manufacturing industries in Taiwan in selected years. The combined industry of food, beverages and tobacco experienced full efficiency over the period 1981–93, and full efficiency occurred in the chemical materials industry during the 1994–95 period. Interestingly, from 1996 to 1999 the furniture industry utilised its inputs most efficiently. Despite being the most efficient industry over the period 1981–93, technical efficiency in the food industry has dropped gradually after 1993. By contrast, technical efficiency improved in the furniture industry from about 40 per cent in the early 1980s to 100 per cent in 1999. The textiles industry experienced the lowest rate of technical efficiency.

Table 4.14   Technical efficiency of individual industries in Taiwan, selected years

Industry	1981	1985	1990	1993	1995	1999
Food, beverages and tobacco	100	100	100	100	96.7	79.7
Textile mill products	49.3	41.9	43.7	42.5	39.9	29.1
Wearing app., accessories	82.3	87.4	88.7	83.7	70.5	49.1
Leather, fur and products	65.5	71.8	64.5	59.6	57.8	40.3
Wood and bamboo products	33.1	43.1	45.0	68.2	61.4	49.2
Furniture and fixtures	46.5	40.7	59.0	82.6	97.5	100
Pulp, paper and paper prod.	70.2	61.8	54.3	42.0	41.9	32.0
Printing processings	76.2	55.2	53.8	55.6	53.8	47.5
Chemical materials	52.9	67.4	79.0	94.8	100	76.5
Chemical products	34.3	45.6	49.5	62.6	69.5	69.7
Rubber products	48.4	49.4	56.6	65.8	64.4	41.7
Plastic products	33.3	38.0	45.0	48.4	46.2	36.4
Non-metallic mineral products	49.4	46.4	64.5	74.8	80.2	63.2
Basic metal industries	54.7	57.0	73.1	79.4	65.2	59.3
Fabricated metal products	50.4	46.9	50.5	52.5	52.2	41.0
Machinery and equipment	50.4	51.4	65.9	72.5	77.7	59.1
Electrical, electronic mach.	47.6	47.7	54.0	59.7	66.8	55.3
Transport equipment	80.0	65.3	87.9	86.7	78.6	50.2
Precision instruments	54.5	57.9	62.1	62.3	67.6	52.5
Other industrial products	75.0	75.2	73.7	77.5	82.3	66.4

Source: Author's calculations.

NOTES

1. For consistency, the manufacturing shares in GDP are calculated by using manufacturing GDP from national accounts and not UNIDO's value added. However, there is no reason why UNIDO's value added cannot be adopted because the difference is insignificant.
2. Mr Tetsuo Yamada of the Statistics and Information Networks Branch at the UNIDO clarified the puzzle on this matter.

3. This ongoing structural transformation in Hong Kong's manufacturing industries had a significant impact on productivity growth; see Imai (2001), Kwong *et al.* (2000) and Tuan and Ng (1995).

4. Because there were difficulties with the estimations for Hong Kong and Singapore manufacturing industries, some industries were removed temporarily in order to maintain the consistency of the frontier coefficients throughout the entire sample period.

5. This refers to the rapid relocation of Hong Kong's manufacturing industries to mainland China since the mid-1980s; see Tuan and Ng (1995) for details.

6. The possibility of estimated labour and capital coefficients chosen from the same industry cannot be completely ruled out.

7. As mentioned earlier, one or two industries were removed temporarily for Singapore; this elucidates why there were inconsistencies in 1991 between Table 4.2 and Table 4.6. According to Table 4.6, no variations were found in estimated labour and capital coefficients, but the heterogeneity of manufacturing industries was statistically significant in Singapore, as shown in Table 4.2. This problem arose due to the temporary removal of an industry.

8. In general, if a firm continues to update production technology without ever completely mastering its old technology, technical efficiency is unlikely to improve over time.

5. Sources of output growth

The use of the varying coefficients frontier model is strengthened by the Breusch–Pagan LM test discussed in Chapter 4. Therefore, the main objective of this chapter is to identify the sources of output growth and to analyse the importance of TFP growth in different stages of economic growth in the East Asian manufacturing sectors. Section 5.1 decomposes output growth into input growth and TFP growth on the basis of five-year intervals for individual manufacturing industries. The average share of industries in each manufacturing sector is briefly discussed prior to presenting the sources of long-term output growth in section 5.2. The estimates and trends in annual TFP growth for the five manufacturing sectors are shown in section 5.3, and detailed annual TFP growth estimates for individual manufacturing industries are presented in Tables A5.1 to A5.5. Chapter 6 will analyse the components of TFP growth and compare the results of the current study with earlier studies on the subject.

It should be noted that TFP growth rates at the manufacturing level throughout this study are derived by aggregating the contribution made by individual industry TFP growth estimates, that is, the TFP growth estimate for the manufacturing sector is a weighted average.[1] Thus, the weighted TFP growth for the manufacturing sector over a five-year period is obtained by the summation of the TFP growth of individual industries multiplied by the average shares of individual industries over the endpoints, say, 1970 and 1975. For instance, if the textiles industry had 10 per cent TFP growth over the period 1970–75 and 8 per cent and 4 per cent shares in the overall manufacturing sector in 1970 and 1975 respectively, it contributed 0.6 per cent TFP growth to final weighted TFP growth for the manufacturing sector. Unless otherwise indicated, the discussion in general focuses on the overall manufacturing sector. Due to rounding, the figures may not add up precisely in the following discussion.

5.1   DECOMPOSITION OF OUTPUT GROWTH: FIVE-YEAR SPAN

This section examines the components of output growth during five-year intervals and Tables 5.1 to 5.5 present the results of decomposing output growth into input growth and TFP growth. As several industries are not included in the estimation, the weighted TFP growth and output growth for the manufacturing sectors exclude these industries. Thus, the weighted output growth rates in this study may differ slightly from those in official publications. Technical efficiency change and technological progress of individual industries over a five-year span are obtained using the frontier coefficients at the endpoints, say 1970 and 1975, and input and output data.

5.1.1   Hong Kong

Table 5.1 shows the decomposition of output growth into input growth and TFP growth for manufacturing industries in Hong Kong over the 1976–97 period. Output growth over the period 1976–80 was positive across industries with the exception of the rubber industry (–3.7 per cent) while only two industries, namely textiles and rubber, experienced negative input growth during this period. Despite five industries having negative TFP growth, the TFP growth for the entire manufacturing sector remained promising and, in particular, the non-metal mineral industry experienced the highest average annual TFP growth of 12.8 per cent, followed by footwear with 9.8 per cent. On average, the annual output growth rate for the entire manufacturing sector was 8.2 per cent, resulting from 3.8 per cent TFP growth and 4.5 per cent input growth.

Because 12 out of 21 industries experienced negative output growth between 1980 and 1985, the average annual output growth of the manufacturing sector fell sharply, from 8.2 to –1.0 per cent. The worst result of –10.5 per cent occurred in the basic metals industry; in contrast, the beverages industry had the highest average annual output growth rate of 6.0 per cent. On average, input growth grew by only 0.3 per cent a year and TFP growth fell sharply, from 3.8 to –1.3 per cent. Over the 1985–90 period, six out of 21 industries underwent negative output growth, with the footwear industry recording the worst result of –19.6 per cent, while the non-electrical machinery industry recorded the best result at 22.3 per cent. The annual output growth rate for the manufacturing sector remained positive at 3.8 per cent a year along with 4.1 per cent annual TFP growth, indicating that annual input growth of –0.3 per cent played no role over this period.

Over the period 1990–95, output growth and input growth declined sharply by 8.8 per cent and 12.5 per cent a year respectively. Yet average annual

TFP growth was maintained at a similar rate (3.8 per cent) to the previous period. As discussed in Chapter 2, the fall in output growth was due mainly to a rapid reallocation of manufacturing industries to mainland China from the mid-1980s. In 1995–97, output growth and input growth did not improve. There was a negative annual output growth rate of –4.8 per cent, and input growth fell even more, by 8.3 per cent a year, suggesting an average annual TFP growth rate of 3.6 per cent for the manufacturing sector.

5.1.2 Japan

Table 5.2 presents the decomposition of output growth into input growth and TFP growth for manufacturing industries at the 3-digit level in Japan over the period 1965–98. Over the 1965–70 period, the Japanese manufacturing sector made significant progress in TFP at an annual rate of 6.6 per cent. With this impressive TFP growth together with substantial input growth of 6.1 per cent, manufacturing output grew remarkably, by 12.7 per cent a year. Also, all industries gained positive output, input and TFP growth.

In spite of 3.5 per cent annual input growth, the average annual output growth over the 1970–75 period fell to 3.7 per cent, suggesting that it was predominantly input-driven. In the wake of the oil crises in the early 1970s, TFP growth for the entire manufacturing sector only increased by 0.2 per cent a year. Output growth during the 1975–80 period recovered to 6.2 per cent a year but zero input growth implied substantial average annual TFP growth of 6.2 per cent. In contrast to the first half of the 1970s, manufacturing output growth was entirely driven by TFP growth during this period.

Notwithstanding the sharp slowdown of annual TFP growth to 1.7 per cent over the period 1980–85, manufacturing output still grew by 3.8 per cent a year, due partly to 2.1 per cent annual input growth. Similarly, between 1985 and 1990 average annual output, input and TFP growth improved slightly to 5.2 per cent, 3.0 per cent and 2.2 per cent respectively. The decomposition of output growth in the 1980s suggests that input growth and TFP growth were both crucial to the output growth of the manufacturing sector.

During the first half of the 1990s, and unprecedented in post-war Japan, output growth for the entire manufacturing sector declined by 0.8 per cent a year due to the domestic economic downturn. The average annual input growth of 1.3 per cent with negative output growth implicitly indicates that TFP growth fell by 2.2 per cent per annum. During the 1995–98 period, manufacturing average annual output growth recovered slightly to 1.1 per cent, which was mostly attributed to annual TFP growth of 0.9 per cent because there was little input growth at 0.2 per cent a year.

5.1.3 Korea

Table 5.3 exhibits the decomposition of output growth into input growth and TFP growth for manufacturing industries at the 3-digit level in Korea over the period 1970–97.   During the period 1970–75 Korean manufacturing output grew spectacularly by 20.4 per cent a year, mainly attributable to 17.6 per cent input growth. Yet during this period TFP growth was moderate at 2.8 per cent per annum. All industries enjoyed positive and considerable output and input growth. The highest average annual output growth of 58.2 per cent, input growth of 39.4 per cent and TFP growth of 18.8 per cent came from the leather industry. In contrast, the plastics industry had the worst average annual TFP growth of –10.5 per cent. Likewise, the average annual output growth rate of 15.2 per cent between 1975 and 1980 was mainly due to the 13.6 per cent input growth, indicating a small TFP growth rate of 1.5 per cent.   Suddenly, the leather industry experienced the worst average annual output growth of –0.4 per cent and TFP growth of –16.2 per cent.

The average annual output growth of 11 per cent over the 1980–85 period was due to 4.3 per cent TFP growth and 6.7 per cent input growth respectively.   Compared with the previous decade, TFP growth played a greater role in the process of output growth. On examining the contribution of the components to the average annual output growth of 17.1 per cent for the period 1985–90, it was attributed to 9.8 per cent input growth and 7.3 per cent TFP growth. In the 1980s, except for the wood industry with negative input growth (1980–85) and miscellaneous petroleum with negative TFP growth (1985–90), all industries experienced positive output growth and input growth, and impressive TFP growth.

TFP growth in the 1990–95 period continued rising by 5.4 per cent a year. Due to the sizeable TFP growth along with 7.0 per cent input growth, manufacturing output grew strongly by 12.4 per cent a year. In 1995–97, the 5.6 per cent output growth was attributable to 3.7 per cent input growth and 1.9 per cent TFP growth. Overall, it is suggested that TFP growth played a minor role in the 1970s but a relatively important one since 1980.

5.1.4 Singapore

Table 5.4 displays the decomposition of output growth into input growth and TFP growth for manufacturing industries in Singapore between 1970 and 1997. Singapore's manufacturing sector started with a remarkable average annual output growth of 12.6 per cent over the 1970–75 period. Nevertheless, such an impressive output performance was the result of even higher input growth of 18.4 per cent. As a result, TFP growth turned out to be negative for most industries and average annual TFP growth was –5.8 per cent. In terms of individual industries, the professional equipment industry especially had a significant 54.2 per cent annual output growth, followed by non-electrical machinery with 39 per cent. Likewise, the strong output growth in those two industries was mainly driven by massive factor accumulation with little TFP growth. Output growth during the 1975–80 period remained strong at 12.7 per cent per annum, but average annual input growth dropped considerably from 18.4 per cent to 9.5 per cent. Therefore, part of the output growth was due to 3.2 per cent TFP growth.

Unlike the 1970s, average annual output growth over the 1980–85 period fell drastically, from 12.7 per cent to only 3.2 per cent. However, input growth on average stayed at a high level of 7.9 per cent, suggesting a substantial negative TFP growth of –4.7 per cent. In fact, except for the professional equipment industry, all industries experienced negative TFP growth. On average, manufacturing output and factor inputs over the 1985–90 period grew by 12.7 per cent and 9.8 per cent respectively, implying 2.8 per cent TFP growth. In addition, apart from the beverages, furniture and electric machinery industries, all industries achieved TFP growth.

The average annual output growth of 7.6 per cent for the period 1990–95 was close to the input growth of 6.6 per cent. Consequently, TFP growth for the entire manufacturing sector was insignificant at 1.0 per cent per annum. The moderate 4.3 per cent annual output growth in the period 1995–97 was achieved as a result of the intensive 8.5 per cent input growth. Despite some industries gaining TFP growth, on average it was –4.3 per cent per annum for the manufacturing sector.

5.1.5 Taiwan

Table 5.5 shows the decomposition of output growth into input growth and TFP growth for 20 manufacturing industries in Taiwan. Due to the change of industrial classification in Taiwan in 1981, the sample period is from 1981 to 1999. Despite output growth and input growth over the 1981–85 period being significant and positive for all industries, seven industries, including printing, furniture and transport, experienced negative TFP growth. Yet some industries, such as chemical materials and chemical products, enjoyed sizeable TFP growth of 12.2 per cent and 9.3 per cent respectively. On average, the annual output growth of 8.2 per cent for the manufacturing sector together with 5.7 per cent input growth indicates TFP growth at an annual rate of 2.5 per cent.

Output growth over the period 1985–90 remained significant and positive except for the wearing apparel (2.2 per cent) and leather (0.9 per cent) industries. Apart from the textile, wearing apparel and wood industries, input growth was positive across all industries. In comparison with the last period,

Table 5.1   Sources of output growth: average annual growth rates of output, input and TFP in Hong Kong's manufacturing industries

Industry	1976–80			1980–85			1985–90			1990–95			1995–97		
	Output	Input	TFP	Output	Input	TFP	Output	Input	TFP	Output	Input	TFP	Output	Input	TFP
311 Food products	8.2	5.8	2.4	2.5	1.8	0.7	8.9	2.8	6.0	2.2	−1.4	3.5	−4.5	−6.4	1.9
313 Beverages	5.6	6.9	−1.3	6.0	5.4	0.6	1.3	−3.0	4.3	−1.1	−1.9	0.8	#	#	#
321 Textiles	0.3	−1.0	1.3	0.1	−2.6	2.7	4.5	1.1	3.4	−13.6	−14.9	1.4	−3.8	−8.6	4.8
322 Wearing apparel	6.2	2.5	3.8	−2.4	0.3	−2.7	0.6	−2.2	2.8	−15.9	−19.4	3.6	−4.5	−9.3	4.8
323 Leather products	20.8	13.6	7.2	−9.3	−3.7	−5.5	−0.3	−7.0	6.7	−14.0	−20.5	6.5	−7.9	−14.0	6.1
324 Footwear	14.1	4.4	9.8	2.3	6.5	−4.2	−19.6	−12.0	−7.5	−50.4	−48.1	−2.4	−1.4	−7.7	6.3
331 Wood products	1.3	4.8	−3.5	−5.2	−5.2	−0.1	−4.5	−4.5	0.0	−11.5	−18.6	7.1	−7.6	−9.4	1.8
332 Furniture	7.1	2.6	4.6	−1.4	0.7	−2.1	−3.9	−6.8	2.9	−37.1	−35.7	−1.4	2.4	−6.8	9.1
341 Paper and paper products	14.4	10.1	4.3	−2.6	−0.9	−1.7	14.3	11.6	2.6	−10.3	−12.6	2.3	−4.4	−9.3	4.9
342 Printing and publishing	13.7	8.5	5.1	5.2	3.4	1.7	10.3	6.1	4.2	0.5	3.7	−3.2	−1.9	−9.2	7.3
351+352 Chemical products	10.1	3.7	6.4	−0.4	0.9	−1.2	6.2	−0.1	6.3	−4.8	−7.2	2.3	0.3	−6.7	7.0
355 Rubber products	−3.7	−1.6	−2.1	−8.9	−9.3	0.3	−9.1	−13.7	4.5	−17.6	−21.5	3.9	0.4	−1.2	1.6
356 Plastic products	6.2	2.7	3.5	3.0	1.4	1.6	−3.8	−6.3	2.5	−25.3	−30.1	4.8	−4.5	−6.6	2.1
36 Non-metal mineral product	17.8	5.1	12.8	0.3	6.0	−5.7	3.8	−8.0	11.8	7.5	−1.1	8.6	−24.1	−9.6	−14.5
371+372 (Basic metals)	1.8	5.4	−3.6	−10.5	−0.2	−10.3	8.4	−4.7	13.1	1.8	−6.3	8.1	−14.4	−8.0	−6.4
381 Fabricated metal products	13.7	8.8	4.9	−5.2	−2.6	−2.6	0.8	−3.8	4.6	−11.8	−15.8	4.0	−5.7	−10.4	4.7
382 Non-electrical machinery	12.4	5.1	7.3	5.9	5.8	0.2	22.3	14.6	7.7	−7.6	−11.1	3.4	−6.8	−9.2	2.4
383 Electric machinery	14.8	7.5	7.3	−4.1	1.5	−5.6	0.5	−3.6	4.1	−1.8	−14.2	12.4	−4.9	−7.5	2.7

Table 5.1 (continued)

Industry	1976–80			1980–85			1985–90			1990–95			1995–97		
	Output	Input	TFP	Output	Input	TFP	Output	Input	TFP	Output	Input	TFP	Output	Input	TFP
384 Transport equipment	4.6	8.7	–4.1	–0.9	–1.3	0.4	7.1	–2.1	9.1	–1.2	–2.8	1.6	–6.4	–7.4	1.0
385 Professional equipment	24.4	17.0	7.4	–3.2	0.1	–3.3	4.3	–1.8	6.1	–12.1	–17.8	5.7	–6.6	–9.9	3.3
390 Other manufactured	6.6	4.5	2.1	1.5	0.6	0.9	2.7	1.4	1.3	–9.2	–13.2	3.9	–2.4	–7.6	5.3
300 Manufacturing	8.2	4.5	3.8	–1.0	0.3	–1.3	3.8	–0.3	4.1	–8.8	–12.5	3.8	–4.8	–8.3	3.6

Notes:
1. Due to rounding, figures may not add up precisely.
2. # denotes the removal of industry due to negative capital stock in 1995 and 1996.
3. The period covered for the beverages industry is from 1976 to 1994, so the result of the 1990–95 period for the beverages industry represents the 1990–94 period.
4. The non-metal mineral products industry (36) includes pottery, china, earthenware (361), glass and glass products (362) and other non-metallic mineral industries (369).

Source: Author's calculations.

Table 5.2   Sources of output growth: average annual growth rates of output, input and TFP in Japan's manufacturing industries

Industry	1965–70			1970–75			1975–80			1980–85			1985–90			1990–95			1995–98		
	Output	Input	TFP	Output	Input	TFP	Output	Input	TFP	Output	Input	TFP	Output	Input	TFP	Output	Input	TFP	Output	Input	TFP
311	7.9	4.5	3.4	9.4	4.3	5.0	5.1	1.9	3.3	4.1	1.9	2.2	4.5	3.5	1.0	2.3	1.1	-1.2	0.6	0.5	0.1
313	10.0	2.3	7.7	5.3	2.0	3.3	1.7	-2.0	3.7	1.0	-3.0	4.0	3.0	1.7	1.3	4.0	10.1	6.1	1.5	0.7	0.9
321	7.6	2.0	5.6	1.2	0.7	0.5	2.0	-3.4	5.4	-0.4	-2.3	1.9	1.3	-0.2	1.4	-2.5	-4.6	-2.1	3.6	-2.4	6.0
322	12.4	6.3	6.1	10.7	7.3	3.4	3.3	0.5	2.9	1.5	0.5	1.0	4.9	3.2	1.7	-2.0	-3.6	-1.6	-1.7	-2.8	1.1
323	6.9	3.3	3.6	5.9	2.2	3.7	4.0	0.8	3.2	1.8	-1.1	2.8	2.7	1.3	1.4	0.4	-1.5	-1.9	1.8	-1.7	3.5
324	10.8	2.8	8.0	4.9	2.3	2.6	7.3	2.2	5.1	-1.3	-0.5	-0.8	6.0	2.8	3.2	5.6	8.5	2.8	-3.2	-1.8	-1.5
331	10.1	3.8	6.3	2.5	1.9	0.7	4.0	-2.7	6.8	-5.6	-5.3	-0.3	4.0	-0.3	4.3	-1.4	-0.3	1.1	-0.8	0.2	-1.0
332	11.6	5.7	5.9	9.5	6.2	3.3	5.1	-0.3	5.3	-0.1	-1.0	0.8	6.4	2.7	3.7	1.0	0.9	-0.2	-0.6	0.0	-0.5
341	9.4	5.1	4.3	4.0	4.1	-0.1	3.6	-0.2	3.8	0.8	-1.4	2.1	6.3	3.2	3.1	1.6	1.1	-0.6	0.6	0.0	0.6
342	10.6	4.3	6.3	7.7	3.5	4.2	6.2	0.8	5.4	3.7	2.8	0.9	6.5	5.3	1.2	2.0	0.6	-1.4	1.3	0.6	0.7
351	11.2	4.0	7.2	-3.0	1.4	-4.4	3.7	-2.2	5.9	3.8	-1.5	5.2	6.1	0.2	5.9	-0.4	-2.5	-2.1	-0.2	-0.3	0.1
352	11.5	4.7	6.8	6.0	3.5	2.5	6.5	1.1	5.4	4.7	2.9	1.7	7.0	3.5	3.5	3.9	3.1	-0.8	0.3	0.6	-0.3
353	10.9	6.6	4.3	8.2	7.6	0.6	14.2	0.1	14.1	-7.4	-2.4	-5.1	-9.2	-1.8	-7.4	2.9	11.1	8.2	0.2	-10.3	-10.6
354	14.0	12.7	1.4	12.2	7.0	5.2	3.4	0.1	3.3	-8.2	-3.6	-4.5	5.2	-1.8	7.0	-3.4	-2.5	0.8	0.8	-1.0	1.8
355	7.7	4.3	3.4	4.9	2.7	2.2	6.0	0.2	5.8	3.8	2.7	1.1	6.0	3.0	3.0	0.2	-2.1	-2.3	1.1	-0.5	1.6
356	18.9	9.4	9.5	8.5	6.0	2.4	7.9	1.9	6.0	7.0	5.1	1.9	6.2	5.6	0.6	2.5	-0.2	-2.7	1.4	0.6	0.8
361	10.1	4.8	5.3	6.5	2.8	3.7	3.6	-0.3	3.8	-0.1	1.9	-2.0	1.9	1.7	0.3	0.6	2.1	1.4	1.9	1.4	0.5
362	11.5	5.6	5.9	-0.3	2.4	-2.7	6.5	-0.9	7.4	6.6	2.8	3.7	4.7	4.1	0.6	-1.2	-6.4	-5.2	1.2	-0.8	2.1

Table 5.2   *(continued)*

Industry	1965–70			1970–75			1975–80			1980–85			1985–90			1990–95			1995–98		
	Output	Input	TFP	Output	Input	TFP	Output	Input	TFP	Output	Input	TFP	Output	Input	TFP	Output	Input	TFP	Output	Input	TFP
369	13.3	6.1	7.2	5.9	3.7	2.2	6.4	−0.3	6.7	−0.6	−1.6	1.0	5.2	0.4	4.8	0.1	1.0	−0.9	−0.8	0.1	−0.9
371	13.5	6.3	7.2	1.4	2.8	−1.4	9.6	−0.8	10.3	−1.1	−1.6	0.4	2.9	−2.1	5.0	−7.2	−1.7	−5.4	−0.1	−1.7	1.6
372	13.5	8.9	4.6	1.8	4.6	−2.7	10.7	−0.9	11.6	−7.2	−2.4	−4.9	6.3	1.7	4.5	−3.9	−0.4	−3.5	1.8	−0.4	2.2
381	15.6	7.3	8.4	3.5	4.8	−1.3	5.4	−0.9	6.3	3.1	0.7	2.4	7.2	4.0	3.2	1.1	2.8	−1.8	0.1	0.3	−0.1
382	18.2	7.6	10.5	3.1	3.6	−0.5	5.8	−0.3	6.1	6.1	3.9	2.2	6.9	4.0	2.9	−1.8	2.2	−4.0	1.9	0.5	1.5
383	16.6	8.9	7.8	−1.1	2.5	−3.6	10.5	1.8	8.7	9.6	8.5	1.1	4.8	5.0	−0.2	−3.2	−0.1	−3.1	2.1	0.8	1.3
384	12.2	9.0	3.2	5.2	5.0	0.3	4.8	0.4	4.5	6.7	3.3	3.4	4.7	2.3	2.3	−1.3	1.9	−3.1	2.2	−0.1	2.3
385	12.9	5.6	7.3	7.5	4.1	3.4	8.1	3.5	4.6	3.8	2.6	1.2	1.9	2.6	−0.7	5.5	2.7	2.8	2.7	−0.1	2.8
390	10.0	4.3	5.7	4.5	2.1	2.4	4.3	−0.2	4.5	4.4	1.3	3.2	4.8	2.8	2.0	0.7	1.7	−1.1	−1.1	−0.5	−0.6
300	12.7	6.1	6.6	3.7	3.5	0.2	6.2	0.0	6.2	3.8	2.1	1.7	5.2	3.0	2.2	−0.8	1.3	−2.2	1.1	0.2	0.9

Note: Due to rounding, figures may not add up precisely.

Source: Author's calculations.

Table 5.3   Sources of output growth: average annual growth rates of output, input and TFP in Korea's manufacturing industries

Industry	1970–75			1975–80			1980–85			1985–90			1990–95			1995–97		
	Output	Input	TFP	Output	Input	TFP	Output	Input	TFP	Output	Input	TFP	Output	Input	TFP	Output	Input	TFP
311 Food products	15.0	18.0	-3.1	15.8	10.9	4.9	7.3	7.1	0.3	14.4	7.3	7.1	10.3	5.5	4.8	6.2	1.3	5.0
321 Textiles	22.1	16.7	5.4	10.0	8.5	1.6	5.8	1.0	4.8	7.3	4.3	3.0	8.0	1.2	6.8	0.3	-4.3	4.6
322 Wearing apparel	27.4	28.1	-0.7	15.6	12.1	3.5	8.5	6.1	2.4	12.2	4.8	7.4	11.0	0.7	10.3	-1.7	-3.8	2.1
323 Leather products	58.2	39.4	18.8	-0.4	15.7	-16.2	14.9	7.4	7.4	21.6	11.7	9.9	1.7	0.1	1.7	-5.2	-6.5	1.4
324 Footwear	22.3	23.6	-1.3	23.8	21.9	1.9	14.2	7.5	6.6	13.4	4.5	8.8	15.9	18.3	-2.3	-2.9	-11.1	8.2
331 Wood products	13.2	9.6	3.6	0.2	5.9	-5.6	3.3	-1.6	4.9	16.9	1.9	15.0	10.8	3.6	7.2	1.4	-3.2	4.6
332 Furniture	11.6	10.0	1.6	27.8	20.6	7.2	15.6	10.3	5.3	24.0	12.4	11.6	13.5	22.4	-8.9	1.7	-5.7	7.4
341 Paper and products	15.8	13.5	2.3	15.7	10.9	4.7	10.8	6.4	4.4	15.4	10.6	4.8	13.3	7.6	5.7	6.8	4.4	2.4
342 Printing, publishing	12.3	10.3	2.0	16.3	11.3	5.0	11.7	8.4	3.3	17.5	8.0	9.5	12.6	9.4	3.2	3.5	2.3	1.2
351 Industrial chemicals	18.2	17.6	0.5	11.3	7.5	3.8	6.4	6.4	0.0	16.5	9.0	7.5	10.6	8.7	1.9	26.1	12.0	14.1
352 Other chemicals	18.3	13.7	4.6	15.8	14.0	1.8	8.2	7.4	0.9	17.6	11.7	5.9	5.7	7.4	-1.7	13.7	5.2	8.5
354 Misc. petroleum	13.5	8.0	5.5	15.1	6.0	9.2	7.9	5.3	2.6	4.2	5.1	-0.9	-4.5	-1.7	-2.8	-15.8	-10.5	-5.3
355 Rubber products	23.7	23.7	0.0	19.8	14.8	5.0	8.0	5.8	2.1	17.0	10.8	6.3	-9.3	-17.1	7.8	6.3	2.4	3.9
356 Plastic products	18.6	29.2	-10.5	27.6	14.4	13.1	15.1	11.2	3.9	19.8	15.0	4.7	23.5	14.2	9.3	-24.7	-2.5	-22.2
361 Pottery, china	11.1	-1.2	12.3	34.5	12.6	21.9	5.2	3.6	1.6	11.5	5.6	5.8	7.9	4.4	3.5	-2.1	-6.2	4.1
362 Glass and products	17.5	14.6	2.9	14.9	16.0	-1.1	10.3	9.0	1.3	16.2	9.0	7.2	13.1	6.9	6.2	1.1	4.4	-3.4
369 Other non-metallic	18.0	4.1	13.9	12.7	10.4	2.4	6.3	5.2	1.1	17.6	6.6	11.1	10.8	8.4	2.4	3.9	-0.7	4.5
371 Iron and steel	28.3	24.2	4.1	16.4	19.3	-2.9	11.1	5.3	5.8	15.0	6.6	8.4	9.9	4.5	5.4	2.4	3.8	-1.4

Table 5.3   (continued)

Industry	1970–75			1975–80			1980–85			1985–90			1990–95			1995–97		
	Output	Input	TFP	Output	Input	TFP	Output	Input	TFP	Output	Input	TFP	Output	Input	TFP	Output	Input	TFP
372 Non-ferrous metals	28.0	15.0	12.9	24.2	13.2	11.0	6.1	9.2	-3.1	18.3	9.5	8.8	14.3	8.4	5.8	-3.1	-2.6	-0.6
381 Fabricated metals	19.0	17.0	2.1	20.0	20.1	-0.1	14.9	9.5	5.3	21.2	10.0	11.2	12.2	9.4	2.7	4.6	0.4	4.2
382 Non-electrical mach.	23.4	18.3	5.1	22.5	27.9	-5.4	16.8	8.4	8.4	24.3	12.8	11.5	16.1	12.6	3.5	16.6	9.8	6.8
383 Electric machinery	30.5	28.0	2.6	16.4	20.0	-3.7	18.0	9.9	8.0	21.3	15.1	6.2	17.2	6.3	10.9	-2.8	4.2	-7.0
384 Transport equip.	14.2	18.9	-4.7	21.5	18.3	3.1	19.2	10.5	8.7	18.7	11.7	7.0	14.0	11.1	3.0	16.6	8.6	8.0
385 Professional equip.	32.4	18.3	14.0	21.3	22.6	-1.3	7.5	5.9	1.6	20.2	11.2	9.0	6.8	1.2	5.6	19.3	14.8	4.5
390 Other manufactured	10.5	13.2	-2.7	13.5	11.5	2.0	11.2	7.9	3.3	14.4	6.9	7.5	2.6	-2.8	5.4	-4.7	-3.7	-1.0
300 Manufacturing	20.4	17.6	2.8	15.2	13.6	1.5	11.0	6.7	4.3	17.1	9.8	7.3	12.4	7.0	5.4	5.6	3.7	1.9

Note: Due to rounding, figures may not add up precisely.

Source: Author's calculations.

Table 5.4 Sources of output growth: average annual growth rates of output, input and TFP in Singapore's manufacturing industries

Industry	1970–75			1975–80			1980–85			1985–90			1990–95			1995–97		
	Output	Input	TFP	Output	Input	TFP	Output	Input	TFP	Output	Input	TFP	Output	Input	TFP	Output	Input	TFP
311 Food products	3.3	4.8	-1.5	5.0	5.2	-0.2	5.7	8.1	-2.4	5.8	1.0	4.8	4.2	7.5	-3.3	13.8	8.2	5.6
313 Beverages	-0.6	5.8	-6.4	7.5	5.8	1.7	5.3	9.7	-4.3	6.3	14.8	-8.5	0.9	-5.2	6.1	0.9	-4.9	5.8
321 Textiles	13.5	19.1	-5.5	7.0	-4.3	11.2	-20.4	-16.3	-4.1	12.7	0.9	11.8	-8.9	-6.9	-2.0	-3.2	-7.6	4.5
322 Wearing apparel	16.6	22.3	-5.8	15.8	5.9	9.9	2.0	3.5	-1.5	6.7	3.4	3.3	-13.3	-5.7	-7.6	-16.7	-18.0	1.3
323 Leather products	-0.1	2.2	-2.3	14.7	11.0	3.7	-6.9	-2.4	-4.4	9.0	-0.2	9.3	7.1	10.5	-3.3	11.4	0.3	11.1
324 Footwear	3.6	3.4	0.1	3.3	7.9	-4.6	-11.9	-3.2	-8.7	4.2	-8.2	12.3	-5.1	-7.1	2.0	-11.6	-14.7	3.1
331 Wood products	-4.3	11.0	-15.3	10.1	3.0	7.1	-15.7	-13.1	-2.6	-1.1	-9.9	8.9	-5.5	-8.5	3.0	4.4	6.1	-1.7
332 Furniture	2.6	13.9	-11.3	22.1	19.7	2.4	6.3	7.5	-1.2	1.8	2.5	-0.6	4.2	0.8	3.3	4.1	8.2	-4.1
341 Paper and products	9.3	11.7	-2.4	16.3	6.3	10.0	9.4	13.0	-3.6	11.1	5.7	5.3	4.3	8.2	-3.9	-2.3	0.7	-3.0
342 Printing, publishing	7.6	7.5	0.1	9.9	8.7	1.2	9.3	12.2	-3.0	10.4	7.1	3.3	8.4	6.2	2.2	3.4	3.9	-0.5
351 Industrial chemicals	10.4	14.6	-4.2	12.2	5.6	6.6	17.3	19.0	-1.7	23.0	12.0	11.1	-11.3	4.0	-15.3	-0.2	1.2	-1.4
355 Rubber products	-10.7	0.6	-11.2	4.9	0.3	4.6	-17.2	-3.8	-13.5	4.4	-1.9	6.3	8.6	2.9	5.7	5.1	7.9	-2.7
356 Plastic products	14.3	21.9	-7.6	23.7	15.8	7.9	1.6	5.2	-3.5	17.4	12.1	5.3	6.5	7.3	-0.8	0.2	6.4	-6.3
361 +362 Pottery, glass	-4.6	-7.8	3.2	9.5	5.3	4.2	-18.5	-4.1	-14.4	31.6	27.5	4.1	16.8	0.7	16.2	6.6	24.0	-17.4
369 Other non-metallic	21.2	14.1	7.1	3.2	2.0	1.3	8.5	21.3	-12.8	-4.7	-7.5	2.9	11.2	1.4	9.7	5.1	17.5	-12.5
371 Iron and steel	12.1	20.7	-8.7	12.9	-2.6	15.6	-7.4	10.2	-17.6	8.2	0.6	7.6	-4.7	4.4	-9.1	-4.5	-6.6	2.2
372 Non-ferrous metals	5.5	14.6	-9.2	6.1	-5.1	11.2	10.0	15.6	-5.6	11.3	3.0	8.3	-15.5	-1.9	-13.6	-12.2	-5.8	-6.4
381 Fabricated metals	7.2	11.6	-4.4	12.8	12.5	0.3	5.2	13.3	-8.1	12.0	6.8	5.2	8.2	8.5	-0.3	-0.6	7.7	-8.2

Table 5.4   (continued)

Industry	1970–75			1975–80			1980–85			1985–90			1990–95			1995–97		
	Output	Input	TFP	Output	Input	TFP	Output	Input	TFP	Output	Input	TFP	Output	Input	TFP	Output	Input	TFP
382 Non-electrical mach.	39.0	38.6	0.5	8.7	13.5	–4.8	0.7	9.1	–8.4	34.2	18.6	15.6	11.4	11.3	0.2	10.8	14.0	–3.3
383 Electric machinery	19.1	29.1	–10.0	20.2	19.0	1.2	7.4	10.2	–2.8	5.5	13.3	–7.8	9.9	2.9	7.0	–5.6	6.8	–12.4
384 Transport equipment	12.7	21.4	–8.7	9.3	2.0	7.3	–3.6	3.2	–6.7	7.0	0.8	6.2	5.2	11.2	–6.0	16.0	4.8	11.2
385 Professional equip.	54.2	51.3	2.9	7.5	3.6	4.0	–0.2	–7.7	7.5	10.4	6.6	3.8	11.1	6.5	4.7	7.7	2.7	5.0
390 Other manufactured	–4.9	–7.3	2.4	21.2	9.7	11.5	–5.6	2.2	–7.8	7.7	5.8	1.8	–3.2	–2.1	–1.1	–1.0	–4.0	3.1
300 Manufacturing	12.6	18.4	–5.8	12.7	9.5	3.2	3.2	7.9	–4.7	12.7	9.8	2.8	7.6	6.6	1.0	4.3	8.5	–4.3

Note: Due to rounding, figures may not add up precisely.

Source: Author's calculations.

Table 5.5 Sources of output growth: average annual growth rates of output, input and TFP in Taiwan's manufacturing industries

Industry	1981–85			1985–90			1990–95			1995–99		
	Output	Input	TFP	Output	Input	TFP	Output	Input	TFP	Output	Input	TFP
Food	8.9	5.4	3.5	3.2	2.5	0.8	2.4	3.9	-1.5	-1.3	0.7	-2.0
Textiles	5.2	5.3	-0.1	1.7	-0.8	2.5	-1.2	0.5	-1.8	0.9	6.1	-5.3
Wearing apparel*	5.8	4.9	0.9	-2.2	-4.2	2.0	-12.2	-3.4	-8.8	-1.9	6.0	-7.9
Leather	14.8	15.0	-0.3	-0.9	1.8	-2.8	-10.3	-2.7	-7.7	-4.7	1.8	-6.5
Wood	7.7	0.1	7.6	0.3	-0.3	0.5	-6.3	-8.2	1.9	-7.7	-5.6	-2.2
Furniture	4.4	7.9	-3.6	10.5	3.1	7.4	5.2	-0.1	5.3	3.4	0.2	3.2
Pulp, paper	3.7	4.0	-0.4	2.5	5.9	-3.4	-1.7	5.7	-7.4	2.9	6.1	-3.2
Printing	2.6	9.8	-7.2	9.1	10.5	-1.4	1.3	5.4	-4.0	3.4	3.5	-0.1
Chemical materials	13.2	1.0	12.2	6.5	4.0	2.5	8.6	4.2	4.4	5.5	7.9	-2.4
Chemical products	14.8	5.5	9.3	11.6	10.2	1.4	11.3	7.0	4.3	5.9	2.3	3.6
Rubber products	8.6	8.0	0.6	3.3	1.6	1.7	1.3	3.2	-2.0	-0.6	7.1	-7.7
Plastic products	14.0	7.1	6.9	7.7	1.7	6.0	0.1	-0.1	0.2	2.4	6.1	-3.7
Non-metallic	4.3	2.8	1.6	7.8	0.9	7.0	7.4	4.9	2.5	-1.9	1.3	-3.2
Basic metal	10.7	4.5	6.1	8.2	3.4	4.8	6.3	9.1	-2.8	7.7	6.5	1.2
Fabricated metals	9.1	9.4	-0.3	12.7	10.1	2.6	6.2	6.9	-0.6	1.5	6.1	-4.6
Machinery	6.1	4.4	1.6	13.4	8.3	5.1	8.6	7.8	0.7	2.9	8.0	-5.1
Electrical and electronic	10.7	8.0	2.7	14.3	9.2	5.1	12.8	7.9	4.9	15.0	18.5	-3.6
Transport	1.8	4.2	-2.4	11.4	4.9	6.5	3.0	6.9	-3.9	-1.8	7.0	-8.8

Table 5.5 (continued)

Industry	1981–85			1985–90			1990–95			1995–99		
	Output	Input	TFP	Output	Input	TFP	Output	Input	TFP	Output	Input	TFP
Precision instruments	9.2	7.1	2.0	7.2	7.0	0.2	−1.6	1.6	−3.2	−0.3	2.8	−3.0
Other industrial products	8.8	8.4	0.5	2.3	2.0	0.3	−3.9	−2.7	−1.2	−2.7	0.7	−3.4
Manufacturing	8.2	5.7	2.5	7.2	4.0	3.2	5.0	4.8	0.2	5.8	9.1	−3.3

Notes:
1. * denotes wearing apparel, accessories and other textile products.
2. Due to rounding, figures may not add up precisely.

Source: Author's calculations.

the number of industries with negative TFP growth fell to three. These were the leather, paper and printing industries. The average annual output growth of 7.2 per cent for the entire manufacturing sector was a result of 4.0 per cent input growth and a substantial 3.2 per cent TFP growth.

With the exception of the chemical materials industry, the output growth for the 1990–95 period fell moderately for all industries, especially for labour-intensive industries such as wearing apparel, leather and wood. Due to the moderate output growth of 5.0 per cent and relatively high input growth of 4.8 per cent, average annual TFP growth for the manufacturing sector slowed down considerably to just 0.2 per cent. Unlike the 1980s, input growth during this period almost accounted for output growth. Input growth between 1995 and 1999 increased by 9.1 per cent a year but output growth dropped slightly to 5.8 per cent. On average, input growth outweighed output growth by 3.3 per cent, implying a substantial decline of 3.3 per cent in the level of TFP. As opposed to the 1980s, TFP growth played no role in the 1990s as input growth completely accounted for output growth.

5.2   SOURCES OF LONG-TERM OUTPUT GROWTH

The focus of this section is identification of the sources of long-term output growth. Following the decomposition approach described in Chapter 3, long-term output growth across five East Asian manufacturing industries is decomposed into input growth and TFP growth. Special attention will also be paid to several leading industries within each manufacturing sector. The estimates of output, input and TFP growth in the following tables are all presented on an average annual basis. The discussion commences with Hong Kong, followed by Japan, Korea, Singapore and Taiwan.

5.2.1 Hong Kong

To appreciate the development of individual industries over the past few decades, it is informative to examine their respective shares in the overall manufacturing sector prior to further discussion. Table 5.6 presents the average shares of industries in Hong Kong's manufacturing sector over the period 1976–97. The shares of the food, printing and publishing, and non-electrical machinery industries have been increasing over time. Based on shares in the manufacturing sector, three major industries over the period 1976–97 were wearing apparel with 22 per cent, textiles with 14.6 per cent and electric machinery with 12.8 per cent. Overall, these three leading industries accounted for nearly 55 per cent of total manufacturing output in the late 1970s and just over 40 per cent in the 1990s. Even without considering the tobacco industry, the remaining 21 industries still made up over 97 per cent of total manufacturing output between 1976 and 1997. Because the value added data for the petroleum refineries (ISIC 353) and miscellaneous petroleum (ISIC 354) industries are not available until the late 1980s, Table 5.6 does not include these two industries.

Table 5.7 gives the detailed decomposition of output growth across manufacturing industries in Hong Kong during the 1976–97 period.[1] Despite their declining manufacturing share in the overall economy, some industries grew remarkably, for example non-electrical machinery with an average annual rate of 6.6 per cent, printing and publishing with 6.2 per cent and food with 4.3 per cent. Those generally regarded as labour-intensive industries shrank sharply in output growth, such as footwear (–13.5 per cent per annum), rubber (–9.2 per cent) and furniture (–8.5 per cent). Positive input growth occurred in the printing and publishing (3.6 per cent per annum) and non-electrical machinery (2.7 per cent) industries. Yet there were more industries with negative input growth. Out of 21 industries, 16 experienced negative input growth; the worst average annual input growth occurred in the footwear industry with –12.5 per cent, followed by rubber with –12.4 per cent and furniture with –10.3 per cent.

With the exception of the footwear industry with –1.0 per cent, average annual TFP growth for all industries between 1976 and 1997 was positive and ranged from 0.9 per cent in the beverages industry to 4.6 per cent in electric machinery. A number of industries with substantial TFP growth included leather with 4.1 per cent and non-metal mineral products with 4.0 per cent. On the other hand, lower TFP growth tended to take place in labour-intensive industries, such as basic metals with 1.6 per cent and furniture with 1.7 per cent. Overall, the main reason for the output decline in Hong Kong's manufacturing sector over the 1976–97 period was the rapid reallocation of manufacturing production to mainland China since the mid-1980s, resulting in the loss of comparative advantage in its labour-intensive industries. This also explains why Hong Kong's manufacturing share in GDP declined so quickly, from 20 per cent in the mid-1980s to 5.5 per cent in 1997. The overall effect of the considerable reduction in labour and capital inputs by 3.0 per cent per annum was that output growth fell by 0.3 per cent, indicating a considerable TFP growth of 2.7 per cent during 1976–97.

5.2.2 Japan

Table 5.8 shows the average shares of industries in the Japanese manufacturing sector over the period 1965–98. The highest share was electric machinery with 13.2 per cent, followed by non-electrical machinery with 12.7 per cent and transport equipment with 10.3 per cent. The sum of the three major industries' shares exceeded 36 per cent of total manufacturing output. However, a number of industries, including textiles, wood products and iron and steel, experienced declining shares over time. Irrespective of the removal of the tobacco industry due to the incomplete data, the remaining 27 industries still accounted for 99.8 per cent of total manufacturing output.

Table 5.6   The average shares of individual industries in overall manufacturing in Hong Kong, 1976–97

Industry	1976–79	1980–84	1985–89	1990–94	1995–97	1976–97
311 Food products	2.3	2.4	2.5	3.8	6.2	3.1
313 Beverages	1.5	1.4	1.6	1.8	2.4	1.7
314 Tobacco	1.3	1.1	1.8	4.5	2.9	2.3
321 Textiles	16.4	13.4	15.9	14.4	11.9	14.6
322 Wearing apparel	26.5	24.8	22.4	18.6	14.1	22.0
323 Leather products	0.5	0.5	0.4	0.3	0.2	0.4
324 Footwear	0.6	0.7	0.7	0.2	0.0	0.5
331 Wood products	0.9	0.7	0.4	0.3	0.3	0.5
332 Furniture	1.0	0.9	0.7	0.4	0.1	0.7
341 Paper and paper products	1.3	1.4	1.9	2.5	2.1	1.8
342 Printing, publishing	3.6	4.5	5.2	8.4	12.7	6.3
351+352 (Chemical products)	1.6	1.6	1.6	2.0	2.5	1.8
355 Rubber products	0.5	0.3	0.2	0.1	0.1	0.2
356 Plastic products	8.6	8.1	8.4	4.8	2.8	7.0
36 Non-metal minerals	1.0	1.0	1.0	1.1	1.6	1.1
371+372 (Basic metals)	1.1	0.8	0.6	0.8	1.1	0.8
381 Fabricated metal	7.5	7.4	6.8	5.9	4.9	6.6
382 Non-electrical machinery	2.3	3.4	4.5	8.5	9.5	5.3
383 Electric machinery	11.9	14.8	12.9	10.7	13.6	12.8
384 Transport equipment	2.4	2.5	2.3	3.3	3.9	2.7
385 Professional equipment	3.6	4.8	4.3	4.1	3.6	4.2
390 Other manufactured	3.7	3.6	3.8	3.5	3.7	3.6

Notes:
1. Due to rounding, figures may not add up precisely.
2. The average share is calculated by the sum of value added of each industry divided by the sum of manufacturing value added over the period at constant 1990 prices, that is, $(y_i^t + y_i^{t-1})/(Y^t + Y^{t-1})$, not a simple average share.

Source: Author's calculations based on the UNIDO database.

Table 5.7   Decomposition of output growth: average annual growth rates of output, input and TFP by industry in Hong Kong, 1976–97

Industry	Output	Input growth		TFP growth	
311 Food products	4.3	1.4	(33%)	2.9	(67%)
313 Beverages	2.6	1.6	(64%)	0.9	(36%)
321 Textiles	−2.4	−4.8	†	2.3	†
322 Wearing apparel	−3.5	−5.3	†	1.9	†
323 Leather products	−2.4	−6.5	†	4.1	†
324 Footwear	−13.6	−12.5	†	−1.0	†
331 Wood products	−5.5	−7.8	†	2.2	†
332 Furniture	−8.5	−10.3	†	1.7	†
341 Paper and paper products	2.6	0.3	(10%)	2.4	(90%)
342 Printing and publishing	6.2	3.6	(57%)	2.7	(43%)
351+352 (Chemical products)	2.2	−0.5	(−23%)	2.7	(123%)
355 Rubber products	−9.2	−12.4	†	3.3	†
356 Plastic products	−5.4	−8.5	†	3.0	†
36 Non-metal mineral products	3.9	−0.2	(−5%)	4.0	(105%)
371+372 (Basic metals)	−1.1	−2.7	†	1.6	†
381 Fabricated metal products	−1.8	−5.0	†	3.2	†
382 Non-electrical machinery	6.6	2.7	(40%)	4.0	(60%)
383 Electric machinery	1.1	−3.6	(−337%)	4.6	(437%)
384 Transport equipment	1.4	−1.0	(−72%)	2.5	(172%)
385 Professional equipment	1.4	−1.4	(−101%)	2.8	(201%)
390 Other manufactured	−0.2	−2.6	†	2.5	†
300 Manufacturing	−0.3	−3.0	†	2.7	†

Notes:
1. Due to rounding, figures may not add up precisely.
2. Figures in parentheses denote contributions to output growth. The relative contributions are calculated based on the entire period, not annual input and TFP growth estimates.
3. Non-metal mineral products (36) industry includes pottery, china, earthenware (361), glass and glass products (362) and other non-metallic mineral (369) industries.
4. The calculation of percentage contributions to negative output growth is not meaningful so it is denoted by '†'.

Source: Author's calculations.

Table 5.8   The average shares of individual industries in overall manufacturing in Japan, 1965–98

Industry	1965–9	1970–9	1980–4	1985–9	1990–4	1995–8	1965–98
311 Food products	1.9	1.7	1.5	1.3	1.3	2.0	1.6
313 Beverages	—	—	—	0.2	0.3	0.3	0.2
314 Tobacco	7.3	5.8	4.2	3.5	2.9	2.5	4.0
321 Textiles	1.3	1.6	1.5	1.4	1.3	1.1	1.4
322 Wearing apparel	0.3	0.3	0.2	0.2	0.2	0.2	0.2
323 Leather products	0.2	0.2	0.2	0.2	0.2	0.2	0.2
324 Footwear	3.4	3.0	2.1	1.7	1.6	1.5	2.1
331 Wood products	0.9	1.1	1.0	1.0	1.0	1.0	1.0
332 Furniture	3.3	3.1	2.7	2.6	2.5	2.7	2.8
341 Paper and paper products	4.5	4.6	5.1	5.3	5.5	5.8	5.2
342 Printing and publishing	6.9	5.0	4.0	4.4	4.2	3.8	4.5
351 Industrial chemicals	4.1	4.4	4.9	5.2	5.6	6.3	5.2
352 Other chemicals	1.1	1.3	1.6	1.0	1.0	0.7	1.1
353 Petroleum refineries	0.2	0.3	0.3	0.2	0.2	0.2	0.2
354 Miscellaneous petrol.	1.4	1.2	1.2	1.3	1.3	1.2	1.2
355 Rubber products	1.8	2.6	3.0	3.4	3.6	3.6	3.2
356 Plastic products	0.5	0.5	0.4	0.4	0.3	0.4	0.4
361 Pottery, china, earthen.	1.1	1.0	0.9	1.0	0.9	0.7	0.9
362 Glass and glass products	3.3	3.6	3.5	3.1	3.1	3.0	3.3
369 Other non-metallic	7.3	7.3	6.7	5.6	5.0	3.9	5.8
371 Iron and steel	1.9	2.0	1.7	1.3	1.3	1.2	1.5
372 Non-ferrous metals	6.3	6.9	6.4	6.6	7.4	7.6	7.0
381 Fabricated metal prod.	10.5	11.5	12.1	12.8	13.5	13.9	12.7
382 Non-electrical mach.	10.6	10.7	13.5	15.1	14.4	13.6	13.2
383 Electric machinery	9.8	9.8	10.2	10.2	10.5	10.9	10.3
384 Transport equipment	1.3	1.5	1.7	1.5	1.5	2.1	1.6
385 Professional equipment	1.8	1.6	1.6	1.5	1.6	1.6	1.6
390 Other manufactured	1.9	1.7	1.5	1.3	1.3	2.0	1.6

Notes: As in Table 5.6.

Source: Author's calculations.

Table 5.9   Decomposition of output growth: average annual growth rates of output, input and TFP by industry in Japan, 1965–98

Industry	Output growth	Input growth	TFP growth
311 Food products	4.9	2.8 (57%)	2.1 (43%)
313 Beverages	4.9	0.8 (16%)	4.1 (84%)
321 Textiles	1.6	−1.3 (−82%)	2.9 (182%)
322 Wearing apparel	4.2	2.0 (48%)	2.2 (52%)
323 Leather products	3.3	0.8 (23%)	2.5 (77%)
324 Footwear	5.0	2.1 (42%)	2.9 (58%)
331 Wood products	2.1	−0.6 (−28%)	2.7 (128%)
332 Furniture	5.0	2.2 (44%)	2.8 (56%)
341 Paper and paper products	3.9	1.8 (47%)	2.1 (53%)
342 Printing and publishing	5.6	2.9 (52%)	2.7 (48%)
351 Industrial chemicals	2.9	0.1 (2%)	2.8 (98%)
352 Other chemicals	5.9	3.0 (50%)	2.9 (50%)
353 Petroleum refineries	2.6	2.0 (77%)	0.6 (23%)
354 Miscellaneous petroleum	3.8	1.4 (37%)	2.4 (63%)
355 Rubber products	4.2	1.8 (43%)	2.4 (57%)
356 Plastic products	7.5	4.7 (63%)	2.8 (37%)
361 Pottery, china, earthenware	3.9	1.8 (47%)	2.1 (53%)
362 Glass and glass products	3.6	1.7 (46%)	1.9 (54%)
369 Other non-metallic minerals	4.5	1.5 (32%)	3.0 (68%)
371 Iron and steel	2.9	0.1 (4%)	2.8 (96%)
372 Non-ferrous metals	3.5	1.6 (47%)	1.9 (53%)
381 Fabricated metal products	5.5	2.8 (52%)	2.6 (48%)
382 Non-electrical machinery	6.1	3.2 (53%)	2.9 (47%)
383 Electric machinery	6.0	4.1 (69%)	1.9 (31%)
384 Transport equipment	5.2	3.2 (62%)	2.0 (38%)
385 Professional equipment	6.4	3.2 (50%)	3.2 (50%)
390 Other manufactured	4.2	1.7 (40%)	2.5 (60%)
300 Manufacturing (weighted)	4.8	2.3 (48%)	2.5 (52%)

Notes:
1. As in Table 5.7.
2. The final weighted growth rates for manufacturing sector do not include the tobacco industry.

Source: Author's calculations.

Table 5.9 reports the decomposition of output growth for Japanese manufacturing industries during the 1965–98 period. Output growth for all industries was positive; in particular, the plastics industry experienced the highest average annual output growth of 7.5 per cent, followed by professional equipment with 6.4 per cent and non-electrical machinery with 6.1 per cent. On the other hand, two industries with the lowest output growth were textiles with 1.6 per cent and wood with 2.1 per cent, both considered to be traditional and labour-intensive industries. Apart from these two, average annual input growth for all industries was positive, ranging from 0.1 per cent in the industrial chemicals industry to 4.7 per cent in plastics. TFP growth increased substantially in all industries by at least 1.9 per cent a year, with the exception of the petroleum refineries industry, which had only 0.6 per cent. The highest annual TFP growth occurred in the beverages industry with 4.1 per cent, followed by professional equipment with 3.2 per cent.

Due to negative input growth, output growth for the textiles and wood industries was wholly explained by TFP growth.   In contrast, for the industrial chemicals and iron and steel industries, TFP growth accounted for 98 per cent and 96 per cent of output growth respectively. Over the 1965–98 period, the manufacturing sector's output grew by 4.8 per cent a year, stemming from 2.5 per cent TFP growth and 2.3 per cent input growth. TFP growth and input growth have made comparable contributions to output growth, at 52 and 48 per cent respectively.

5.2.3   Korea

Table 5.10 shows the average shares of industries in the Korean manufacturing sector over the period 1970–97. The textiles industry, which had the highest share at 14.6 per cent in the 1970s, experienced a declining share to about 6 per cent in the 1990s. By contrast, a number of industries, such as electric machinery, transport equipment and non-electrical machinery, increased their shares in the manufacturing sector over time. As in Japan's manufacturing sector, the four major industries during the 1970–97 period were electric machinery (14.7 per cent), transport equipment (10.2 per cent), textiles (7.9 per cent) and non-electrical machinery (7.4 per cent). In general, these four dominant industries were responsible for 40 per cent of total manufacturing output. Despite the removal of the tobacco, beverages and petroleum industries, the remaining 25 industries accounted for nearly 92 per cent of total manufacturing output.

Table 5.11 reveals the decomposition of output growth for Korean manufacturing industries during the 1970–97 period.   These industries achieved outstanding performance with regard to output growth. In particular, average annual output growth of the non-electrical machinery and electric

Table 5.10 The average shares of individual industries in overall manufacturing in Korea, 1970–97

Industry	1970–79	1980–84	1985–89	1990–94	1995–97	1970–97
311 Food products	7.3	7.2	6.0	6.2	5.5	6.1
313 Beverages	5.5	2.9	2.2	1.8	1.5	2.2
314 Tobacco	6.1	5.7	3.8	2.2	1.7	2.9
321 Textiles	14.6	11.8	9.8	7.0	5.2	7.9
322 Wearing apparel	4.3	4.6	4.0	3.2	2.9	3.5
323 Leather products	0.9	0.8	1.1	1.0	0.6	0.9
324 Footwear	0.5	0.7	0.6	1.2	0.7	0.9
331 Wood products	2.6	1.1	0.8	0.9	0.8	1.0
332 Furniture	0.4	0.6	0.7	1.2	1.0	0.9
341 Paper and paper products	2.2	2.2	2.3	2.3	2.3	2.3
342 Printing and publishing	2.0	2.3	2.3	2.6	2.6	2.4
351 Industrial chemicals	4.8	4.6	3.7	3.7	5.0	4.3
352 Other chemicals	4.7	4.8	4.8	4.6	3.9	4.4
353 Petroleum refineries	5.0	4.2	2.7	2.9	3.4	3.3
354 Miscellaneous petroleum	1.0	1.0	0.7	0.4	0.2	0.5
355 Rubber products	2.7	2.7	3.1	1.5	1.1	1.8
356 Plastic products	1.4	1.9	2.5	4.0	3.3	3.1
361 Pottery, china, earthen.	0.3	0.4	0.3	0.3	0.2	0.3
362 Glass and glass products	0.9	0.9	0.9	1.0	1.0	1.0
369 Other non-metallic	4.1	3.6	3.3	4.0	3.4	3.6
371 Iron and steel	5.6	7.0	6.1	6.0	5.3	5.9
372 Non-ferrous metals	0.9	1.2	1.2	1.1	1.2	1.1
381 Fabricated metal products	2.9	3.8	4.7	5.2	5.2	4.8
382 Non-electrical machinery	3.0	3.8	5.9	8.1	9.6	7.4
383 Electric machinery	7.9	9.7	14.3	14.5	18.1	14.7
384 Transport equipment	5.8	7.7	8.5	10.8	12.3	10.2
385 Professional equipment	0.8	0.9	1.2	0.9	1.0	1.0
390 Other manufactured	2.0	2.0	2.3	1.4	1.0	1.5

Notes: As in Table 5.6.

Source: Author's calculations.

Table 5.11   *Decomposition of output growth: average annual growth rates of output, input and TFP by industry in Korea, 1970–97*

Industry	Output growth	Input growth	TFP growth
311 Food products	12.1	9.4 (78%)	2.7 (22%)
321 Textiles	9.9	5.6 (57%)	4.3 (43%)
322 Wearing apparel	13.7	9.4 (69%)	4.3 (31%)
323 Leather products	17.4	13.3 (77%)	4.1 (23%)
324 Footwear	16.4	13.6 (83%)	2.8 (17%)
331 Wood products	8.3	3.5 (42%)	4.9 (58%)
332 Furniture	17.3	14.2 (82%)	3.0 (18%)
341 Paper and paper products	13.6	9.6 (70%)	4.0 (30%)
342 Printing and publishing	13.3	9.1 (69%)	4.2 (31%)
351 Industrial chemicals	13.6	10.3 (75%)	3.3 (25%)
352 Other chemicals	13.2	10.4 (79%)	2.7 (21%)
354 Miscellaneous petroleum	5.6	3.1 (56%)	2.4 (44%)
355 Rubber products	11.4	7.6 (66%)	3.9 (34%)
356 Plastic products	17.5	16.1 (92%)	1.4 (8%)
361 Pottery, china, earthenware	12.9	4.6 (36%)	8.3 (64%)
362 Glass and glass products	13.4	10.9 (81%)	2.5 (19%)
369 Other non-metallic minerals	12.4	6.7 (54%)	5.7 (46%)
371 Iron and steel	15.1	12.0 (79%)	3.1 (21%)
372 Non-ferrous metals	16.6	10.5 (63%)	6.1 (37%)
381 Fabricated metal products	16.5	12.8 (78%)	3.7 (22%)
382 Non-electrical machinery	20.3	16.1 (79%)	4.2 (21%)
383 Electric machinery	18.9	15.4 (81%)	3.5 (19%)
384 Transport equipment	17.5	14.6 (84%)	2.8 (16%)
385 Professional equipment	17.7	12.1 (68%)	5.6 (32%)
390 Other manufactured	9.3	6.7 (71%)	2.7 (29%)
300 Manufacturing	14.5	10.9 (75%)	3.6 (25%)

Notes:
1. Due to rounding, figures may not add up precisely.
2. Figures in parentheses denote contributions to output growth. The relative contributions are calculated based on the entire period, not annual input and TFP growth estimates.
3. The final weighted growth rate for manufacturing sector does not include the tobacco, beverages and petroleum industries.

Source: Author's calculations.

machinery industries was 20.3 and 18.9 per cent respectively. Moreover, double-digit output growth for Korean manufacturing industries occurred frequently. In spite of experiencing the lowest output growth in Korea, output of the miscellaneous petroleum industry still grew by 5.6 per cent per annum. To some extent, the spectacular output growth in Korean manufacturing industries was attributed to the extensive use of labour and capital inputs. For instance, the plastic, non-electrical machinery and electric machinery industries had input growth of more than 14 per cent a year. Overall, 14 of the 25 industries experienced input growth of more than 10 per cent per annum.

Input growth could not completely explain the impressive output growth as TFP growth also played a crucial role. For example, the TFP growth of the pottery industry increased by 8.3 per cent a year, followed by non-ferrous metals with 6.1 per cent and other non-metallic minerals with 5.7 per cent. With respect to the contribution of components to output growth, TFP growth accounted for 64 per cent of output growth in the pottery industry, 58 per cent in wood and 46 per cent in other non-metallic minerals. Nonetheless, the contribution of TFP growth turned out to be insignificant for the plastics (8 per cent), transport equipment (16 per cent) and footwear (17 per cent) industries.

Overall, the output growth of the Korean manufacturing sector between 1970 and 1997 increased substantially at an average annual rate of 14.5 per cent. In addition, input growth and TFP growth increased by 10.9 and 3.6 per cent per annum respectively. In terms of the contribution of components to output growth, input growth and TFP growth contributed 75 and 25 per cent respectively. Thus it is obvious that the physical inputs, namely labour and capital, remain the most important factor for explaining output growth in the Korean manufacturing sector. Needless to say, the impressive TFP growth, at an average annual rate of 3.6 per cent, also played a crucial part in shaping its success.

5.2.4 Singapore

Table 5.12 shows the average shares of individual industries in Singapore's manufacturing sector over the period 1970–97.[2] Three dominant industries with the highest share over the sample period were electric machinery with 24.4 per cent, non-electrical machinery with 18.5 per cent and transport equipment with 8.7 per cent. They accounted for roughly 52 per cent of total manufacturing output over the period 1970–97 and over 60 per cent during 1995–97. Given the high share contributed by the three leading industries, it is reasonable to hypothesise that the extent of the TFP growth estimate of the overall manufacturing sector will be heavily influenced by them. Table 5.13

shows the decomposition of output growth for Singapore's manufacturing industries over the 1970–97 period. The highest average annual output growth occurred in the non-electrical machinery industry with 18.2 per cent, followed by professional equipment with 15.9 per cent and plastic products with 11.8 per cent. Conversely, sizeable negative output growth occurred in several traditional industries, such as wood with –2.7 per cent, footwear with –2.0 per cent and rubber with –1.5 per cent. Except for the footwear (–2.7 per cent), wood (–2.5 per cent) and textiles (–1.4 per cent) industries, most industries experienced positive and substantial input growth.

Although the average annual output growth of 9.4 per cent for the Singaporean manufacturing sector between 1970 and 1997 was remarkable, it was completely explained by the extraordinary average annual input growth of 10.2 per cent. In contrast to the other East Asian manufacturing sectors, the decomposition analysis shows that the level of TFP in Singapore surprisingly fell by 0.8 per cent per annum. More specifically, 12 of 23 industries experienced TFP decline, ranging from –0.3 per cent in the wood industry to –3.2 per cent in electric machinery. Nonetheless, the remaining 11 industries gained positive TFP growth; in particular, the professional equipment industry achieved the highest annual TFP growth of 3.5 per cent, followed by textiles with 1.9 per cent and other manufactured products with 1.6 per cent.

Thus far, Singapore's manufacturing sector is the only sector to experience TFP decline. The theoretical interpretation of the result is that in order to maintain the same amount of output, manufacturing industries in Singapore had to utilise more resources over time. Or, given the same amount of inputs, the Singaporean manufacturers produced less output over time. Under the TFP framework, this does not imply that excess use of inputs is the cause for the technological decline, nor should this be linked with loss of knowledge or other production information (Kwong *et al.*, 2000). So why was there TFP decline in Singapore? Wasting inputs, changes in government policy, poor management and/or other uncontrollable factors, all could have contributed to undermining TFP growth.

The average annual 0.8 per cent TFP decline for Singapore's manufacturing sector established by the current study is in line with some previous literature. Tsao (1985) also found little evidence of TFP growth (0.08 per cent) for Singapore's manufacturing industries between 1970 and 1979. The result for Singapore in this study is also consistent with Young (1995), who suggested that Singapore's manufacturing sector experienced an average annual TFP growth rate of –1 per cent during the 1970–90 period. He explained that manufacturing industries in Singapore always adopted the most advanced technology, which might have led to productivity loss at the outset before they managed the new technology efficiently.[3] Young also stated that if the process of adopting new technology had continued in Singapore over the past three decades, the full benefits of applying new technology might not be entirely realised due to the lack of a learning-by-doing effect.[4]

Table 5.12 *The average shares of individual industries in overall manufacturing in Singapore, 1970–97*

Industry	1970–79	1980–84	1985–89	1990–94	1995–97	1970–97
311 Food products	4.6	3.4	3.1	2.6	2.6	3.1
313 Beverages	1.7	1.4	1.4	1.1	0.8	1.2
314 Tobacco	1.1	0.8	0.6	0.6	0.2	0.6
321 Textiles	2.7	1.2	0.6	0.5	0.2	0.9
322 Wearing apparel	3.2	3.3	3.0	1.8	0.7	2.2
323 Leather products	0.2	0.1	0.1	0.1	0.1	0.1
324 Footwear	0.3	0.2	0.1	0.1	0.0	0.1
331 Wood products	3.7	1.5	0.6	0.3	0.2	1.0
332 Furniture	0.7	1.1	1.0	0.7	0.6	0.8
341 Paper and paper products	1.1	1.3	1.6	1.5	1.3	1.4
342 Printing and publishing	3.8	4.0	4.2	4.7	4.4	4.3
351 Industrial chemicals	1.4	1.6	5.6	3.8	1.8	3.0
352 Other chemicals	3.6	4.4	5.5	5.6	7.7	5.6
353+354 Petroleum	15.9	14.9	6.5	7.1	5.1	8.9
355 Rubber products	2.2	0.8	0.4	0.3	0.3	0.7
356 Plastic products	1.5	2.0	2.2	2.8	2.5	2.3
361+362 Pottery, glass	0.4	0.3	0.1	0.3	0.5	0.3
369 Other non-metallic	2.6	2.9	1.6	1.6	1.5	1.9
371 Iron and steel	1.7	1.3	1.0	0.7	0.4	0.9
372 Non-ferrous metals	0.3	0.3	0.3	0.3	0.1	0.3
381 Fabricated metal products	4.9	6.3	6.0	6.4	6.0	6.0
382 Non-electrical machinery	7.2	9.4	9.9	24.2	30.6	18.5
383 Electric machinery	18.6	23.9	33.8	23.0	22.7	24.4
384 Transport equipment	12.9	10.7	7.8	7.5	7.1	8.7
385 Professional equipment	1.9	1.4	1.8	1.8	2.1	1.8
390 Other manufactured	1.4	1.3	1.3	0.7	0.5	1.0

Notes: As in Table 5.6.

Source: Author's calculations based on the UNIDO database.

Table 5.13   Decomposition of output growth: average annual growth rates of output, input and TFP by industry in Singapore, 1970–97

Industry	Output growth	Input growth		TFP growth	
311 Food products	5.5	5.4	(98%)	0.1	(2%)
313 Beverages	3.7	4.7	(129%)	−1.1	(−29%)
321 Textiles	0.5	−1.4	(−368%)	1.9	(372%)
322 Wearing apparel	3.9	4.3	(110%)	−0.4	(−10%)
323 Leather products	5.3	3.8	(72%)	1.5	(28%)
324 Footwear	−2.0	−2.7	†	0.8	†
331 Wood products	−2.7	−2.5	†	−0.3	†
332 Furniture	7.2	8.8	(123%)	−1.7	(−23%)
341 Paper and paper products	9.2	8.3	(90%)	0.9	(10%)
342 Printing and publishing	8.7	7.8	(90%)	0.9	(10%)
351 Industrial chemicals	9.5	9.9	(104%)	−0.4	(−4%)
355 Rubber products	−1.5	0.3	†	−1.8	†
356 Plastic products	11.8	12.4	(105%)	−0.6	(−5%)
361+362 Pottery and glass	7.0	5.9	(85%)	1.0	(15%)
369 Other non-metallic	7.7	6.7	(87%)	1.0	(13%)
371 Iron and steel	3.6	6.0	(166%)	−2.4	(−66%)
372 Non-ferrous metals	2.3	4.2	(180%)	−1.9	(−80%)
381 Fabricated metal products	8.4	10.3	(122%)	−1.9	(−22%)
382 Non-electrical machinery	18.2	18.1	(99%)	0.1	(1%)
383 Electric machinery	11.1	14.3	(129%)	−3.2	(−29%)
384 Transport equipment	6.8	7.6	(111%)	−0.8	(−11%)
385 Professional equipment	15.9	12.4	(78%)	3.5	(22%)
390 Other manufactured	2.7	1.2	(43%)	1.6	(57%)
300 Manufacturing	9.4	10.2	(109%)	−0.8	(−9%)

Notes:
1. Due to rounding, figures may not add up precisely.
2. Figures in parentheses denote contributions to output growth. The relative contributions are calculated based on the entire period, not annual input and TFP growth estimates.
3. The calculation of percentage contributions to negative output growth is not meaningful so it is denoted by '†'.
4. The final weighted growth rate for the manufacturing sector does not include the tobacco, other chemicals and petroleum refineries and miscellaneous petroleum industries.

Source: Author's calculations.

From the comprehensive data set contained in Table 5.4, it is possible to identify four major factors driving down TFP growth in Singapore's manufacturing sector through the above empirical analysis.[5] These can be described as follows: (1) choice of sample period, (2) negative influence by the leading industries, (3) implementation of quality adjustment in factor inputs and (4) active government policy. First, TFP growth for Singapore's manufacturing sector over the 1970–75 period was severely affected by external shocks, for example the oil crisis, leading to a significant TFP decline of –5.8 per cent. If this five-year period is excluded, the average annual TFP growth rate between 1975 and 1997 becomes a positive 0.4 per cent, as shown in Table 5.14. Thus TFP growth could be significantly raised by 1.2 per cent per annum if the first five years were eliminated from the sample. Hence it is believed that the choice of sample period has a significant impact on TFP growth estimates in Singapore's manufacturing sector. This also explicitly confirms that the large variation in TFP growth estimates for Singapore in the existing literature is to a large extent caused by the choice of sample period.

Second, industries that experienced TFP decline and had higher shares in the manufacturing sector, such as electric machinery, fabricated metal products and transport equipment, were more responsible for the negative TFP growth. For example, if the average annual TFP growth (–3.2 per cent) of the electric machinery industry with about a 25 per cent share could be raised to zero or positive, it would increase the TFP growth estimate by 0.8 percentage points per annum for the entire manufacturing sector. Consequently, the TFP growth for Singapore during 1970–97 would increase from –0.8 per cent to zero or positive.

Third, it is argued that the true depreciation rate of capital stock in Singapore's manufacturing sector may be higher than the figure of 0.1768 suggested by Jorgenson (1990). If the depreciation rate turned out to be higher, say 0.20 or 0.25, the new TFP growth estimate for Singapore would be higher. In addition to incorporating Jorgenson's depreciation rate of capital stock, this study adopts the labour quality adjustment index from Young (1995), where he suggested that there was an additional annual 1.6 per cent quality enhancement in labour input due to a growing number of better educated workers in Singapore. If the labour quality adjustment index turned out to be lower, say, 1 or 0.5 per cent, the new TFP growth estimate would rise again. In order to reinforce the findings of this study, a sensitivity analysis to further explore the assumptions of Jorgenson and Young is undertaken for Singapore's manufacturing sector in Chapter 6, section 6.4. The results of the sensitivity tests show that the TFP growth estimates for Singapore found in this study are fairly robust unless extreme depreciation rates of capital stock and labour quality adjustments are chosen.

Table 5.14   Decomposition of output growth: average annual growth rates of output, input and TFP by industry in Singapore, 1975–97

Industry	Output growth	Input growth		TFP growth	
311 Food products	6.0	5.5	(91%)	0.5	(9%)
313 Beverages	4.6	4.4	(95%)	0.2	(5%)
321 Textiles	–2.5	–6.3	†	3.8	†
322 Wearing apparel	1.0	–0.1	(–6%)	1.1	(107%)
323 Leather products	6.5	4.1	(63%)	2.4	(37%)
324 Footwear	–3.2	–4.2	†	1.0	†
331 Wood products	–2.4	–5.6	†	3.3	†
332 Furniture	8.2	7.5	(92%)	0.7	(8%)
341 Paper and paper products	9.1	7.4	(81%)	1.8	(19%)
342 Printing and publishing	8.9	7.8	(87%)	1.1	(13%)
351 Industrial chemicals	9.4	8.6	(92%)	0.7	(8%)
355 Rubber products	0.6	0.3	(42%)	0.4	(58%)
356 Plastic products	11.2	9.9	(88%)	1.3	(12%)
361 +362 Pottery and glass	9.6	9.2	(96%)	0.4	(4%)
369 Other non-metallic	4.6	4.8	(105%)	–0.2	(–5%)
371 Iron and steel	1.7	2.4	(142%)	–0.7	(–42%)
372 Non-ferrous metals	1.6	1.6	(103%)	0.0	(–3%)
381 Fabricated metal products	8.6	9.8	(113%)	–1.2	(–13%)
382 Non-electrical machinery	13.5	12.9	(96%)	0.6	(4%)
383 Electric machinery	9.3	10.5	(114%)	–1.3	(–14%)
384 Transport equipment	5.5	4.2	(76%)	1.3	(24%)
385 Professional equipment	7.3	2.9	(39%)	4.4	(61%)
390 Other manufactured	4.5	3.2	(72%)	1.2	(28%)
300 Manufacturing	8.5	8.1	(95%)	0.4	(5%)

Notes: As in Table 5.13.

Source: Author's calculations.

Fourth, in contrast to Hong Kong's *laissez faire* policy, the Singaporean government has been actively participating in economic activities and providing many schemes, grants and tax concessions to promote investment, as documented by Huff (1999) and Ermisch and Huff (1999). However, the excess investment may have resulted in lower capacity utilisation, indicating overestimation of capital input and understatement of TFP growth.[6] Even if the problem of low capacity utilisation did exist in Singapore, TFP growth for

Singapore's manufacturing sector remained insignificant according to the results of the sensitivity test.[7]

Among the four possible causes of low TFP growth, the choice of sample period and the fact that several leading industries experienced large negative TFP growth are most likely to be responsible for the negative TFP growth in Singapore. It may have recorded a slight positive TFP growth if these adverse factors had not operated. However, such an outcome would have been far below the other East Asian manufacturing sectors, and implies that the spectacular output growth in Singapore's manufacturing industries was mainly driven by factor accumulation.

5.2.5 Taiwan

Table 5.15 presents the average shares of individual industries in overall manufacturing in Taiwan between 1981 and 1999. The shares of the labour-intensive industries, including textiles, leather, wearing apparel and wood industries, fell over time. Notably, the share of the wearing apparel industry in overall manufacturing dropped drastically from 7.3 per cent in the 1981–85 period to 1.5 per cent in the 1996–99 period. As opposed to labour-intensive industries, the shares of capital–intensive industries in the manufacturing sector rose gradually, for instance the electrical and electronic machinery, machinery and equipment, and chemical products industries. During 1996–99, a fast-growing electrical and electronic machinery industry shared nearly 30 per cent of total manufacturing output. The petroleum and coal products industry comprised merely 5.5 per cent during the 1981–99 period, implying that the remaining 20 industries accounted for 94.5 per cent of total manufacturing output.

Table 5.16 presents the decomposition of output growth in Taiwanese manufacturing over the period 1981–99. Out of 20 industries, only three experienced negative output growth. These were wearing apparel with –3.2 per cent, wood products with –1.7 per cent and leather with –0.9 per cent. In terms of fast-growing industries, the electrical and electronic machinery, chemical products and chemical materials industries had average annual output growth of 13.2, 11.0 and 8.4 per cent respectively. The only industry with negative input growth was the wood products industry with –3.2 per cent per annum. Eleven out of 20 industries experienced negative TFP growth. It appears that labour-intensive industries were more likely to be associated with a TFP decline, such as leather with –5.5 per cent per annum, pulp and paper with –4.3 per cent, printing with –4.0 per cent and wearing apparel with –3.9 per cent; however, the furniture (2.7 per cent) and wood (1.5 per cent) industries exhibited significant gains in TFP. The highest average annual TFP growth of 3.9 per cent occurred in the chemical materials industry, followed by chemical products with 3.6 per cent and furniture with 2.7 per cent. The electrical and electronic machinery industry, with the highest share in the overall manufacturing sector, gained a moderate TFP progress of 1.7 per cent.

Table 5.15   The average shares of individual industries in overall manufacturing in Taiwan, 1981–99

Industry	1981–85	1986–90	1991–95	1996–99	1981–99
Food, beverages and tobacco	12.0	10.4	9.4	7.4	9.4
Textile mill products	8.9	7.5	5.7	4.2	6.2
Wearing apparel, accessories*	7.3	5.0	2.7	1.5	3.6
Leather, fur and products	1.7	1.6	0.8	0.5	1.0
Wood and bamboo products	1.7	1.8	1.0	0.5	1.2
Furniture and fixtures	1.2	1.5	1.5	1.3	1.4
Pulp, paper and paper products	3.4	2.9	2.0	1.7	2.3
Printing processings	1.4	1.3	1.3	1.1	1.2
Chemical materials	5.7	6.1	7.1	7.4	6.7
Chemical products	1.5	1.9	2.5	2.9	2.3
Petroleum and coal products	6.5	4.7	5.1	6.0	5.5
Rubber products	1.7	1.4	1.2	1.0	1.3
Plastic products	5.6	7.1	5.7	4.7	5.7
Non-metallic mineral products	4.5	4.0	4.8	4.1	4.4
Basic metal industries	6.3	6.6	7.5	7.6	7.1
Fabricated metal products	4.2	5.2	6.4	5.6	5.5
Machinery and equipment	3.2	4.0	5.0	5.0	4.5
Electrical and electronic mach.	10.6	14.5	19.3	29.4	19.9
Transport equipment	6.9	6.7	7.2	5.6	6.5
Precision instruments	1.1	1.1	0.9	0.7	0.9
Other industrial products	4.8	4.6	2.9	2.0	3.3

Notes:
1. As in Table 5.6.
2. * denotes wearing apparel, accessories and other textile products industry.

Source: Author's calculations based on dX for Windows 3.0, EconData: CEIC Database, Taiwan.

Table 5.16   *Decomposition of output growth: average annual growth rates of output, input and TFP by industry in Taiwan, 1981–99*

Industry	Output growth	Input growth		TFP growth	
Food, beverages and tobacco	3.3	3.7	(112%)	−0.4	(−12%)
Textile mill products	1.5	3.0	(204%)	−1.5	(−104%)
Wearing apparel, accessories	−3.2	0.8	†	−3.9	†
Leather, fur and products	−0.9	4.6	†	−5.5	†
Wood and bamboo products	−1.7	−3.2	†	1.5	†
Furniture and fixtures	6.1	3.4	(56%)	2.7	(44%)
Pulp, paper and paper products	1.7	6.0	(353%)	−4.3	(−253%)
Printing processings	4.2	8.2	(194%)	−4.0	(−94%)
Chemical materials	8.4	4.5	(53%)	3.9	(47%)
Chemical products	11.0	7.4	(67%)	3.6	(33%)
Rubber products	3.0	5.3	(175%)	−2.3	(−75%)
Plastic products	5.8	4.1	(71%)	1.7	(29%)
Non-metallic minerals	4.8	2.8	(59%)	2.0	(41%)
Basic metal industries	8.1	6.2	(77%)	1.9	(23%)
Fabricated metal products	7.6	9.0	(118%)	−1.3	(−18%)
Machinery and equipment	8.1	7.7	(95%)	0.4	(5%)
Electrical and electronic machinery	13.2	11.5	(87%)	1.7	(13%)
Transport equipment	4.0	6.2	(156%)	−2.2	(−56%)
Precision instruments	3.5	5.2	(147%)	−1.7	(−47%)
Other industrial products	0.9	2.5	(271%)	−1.6	(−171%)
Manufacturing	6.5	6.3	(96%)	0.2	(4%)

Notes:
1. Due to rounding, figures may not add up precisely.
2. Figures in parentheses denote contributions to output growth. The relative contributions are calculated based on the entire period, not annual input and TFP growth estimates.
3. The calculation of percentage contributions to negative output growth is not meaningful so it is denoted by '†'.
4. The final weighted growth rate of manufacturing does not include the petroleum and coal products industry.

Source: Author's calculations.

Comparing Table 5.15 with Table 5.16 shows that industries with increasing shares in Taiwan's manufacturing sector were always linked with significant positive TFP growth, for example the electrical and electronic machinery, basic metals, chemical materials and chemical products industries. Moreover, out of 20 industries, eight with decreasing shares in manufacturing were found to have negative TFP growth. This may suggest that less productive industries in Taiwan tended to lose shares in the manufacturing sector; that is, resources (labour and capital inputs) were likely to be allocated to industries with higher productivity over time, such as the electrical and electronic machinery industry.

The striking picture of declining TFP growth for Taiwanese manufacturing industries in the 1990s warrants further discussion. According to Figure 5.6 (see p. 124), deceleration of TFP growth took place after 1991.[8] After the Taiwanese government officially lifted the ban on indirect investment in mainland China in 1991, massive Taiwanese investment and funds flowed to the other side of the Taiwan Straits, particularly in labour-intensive industries due to rising labour costs and increasingly restrictive environmental regulations in Taiwan. Hence there is good reason to speculate that the slowdown of TFP growth in Taiwan's manufacturing sector was probably initiated by this large-scale outward investment. Given the fact that access to low-cost resources in mainland China was no longer prohibited, Taiwanese manufacturers had little incentive to upgrade production technology, which would require heavy investment in R&D and involve uncertainty. A sharp decline in TFP in the 1990s is therefore comprehensible (Kwong *et al.*, 2000). Due to limited data, this study is not able to analyse the causes of TFP slowdown but it would be worthwhile presenting the decomposition of output growth between 1981 and 1991, which is reported in Table 5.17.

Manufacturing output and factor inputs over the 1981–91 period increased by 7.5 and 4.7 per cent per annum respectively, suggesting 2.8 per cent TFP growth. Except for the wearing apparel and wood industries with small negative input growth, output growth and input growth were positive for all other industries. There were only five industries exhibiting negative TFP growth during the 1981–91 period in Table 5.17 in contrast to 11 industries by 1999 in Table 5.16. This is explained by the fact that a number of industries experienced remarkable TFP progress, such as chemical materials with 6.6 per cent per annum, plastics with 6 per cent and basic metal with 5.3 per cent. Moreover, the findings of this study for Taiwan's manufacturing sector during the period 1981–91 are consistent with Young (1995), where he found an average annual TFP growth rate of 2.7 per cent over the period 1980–90.

Table 5.17   *Decomposition of output growth: average annual growth rates of output, input and TFP by industry in Taiwan, 1981–91*

Industry	Output growth	Input growth		TFP growth	
Food, beverages and tobacco	5.2	3.7	(72%)	1.5	(28%)
Textile mill products	3.5	1.5	(41%)	2.1	(59%)
Wearing apparel, accessories	1.1	–0.5	(–45%)	1.6	(145%)
Leather, fur and products	5.5	6.9	(127%)	–1.5	(–27%)
Wood and bamboo products	3.9	–0.9	(–23%)	4.8	(123%)
Furniture and fixtures	8.1	4.9	(61%)	3.1	(39%)
Pulp, paper and paper products	2.1	5.2	(248%)	–3.1	(–148%)
Printing processings	5.4	10.2	(187%)	–4.7	(–87%)
Chemical materials	9.6	3.0	(31%)	6.6	(69%)
Chemical products	12.4	7.9	(64%)	4.5	(36%)
Rubber products	5.3	4.1	(78%)	1.2	(22%)
Plastic products	9.8	3.8	(39%)	6.0	(61%)
Non-metallic minerals	6.3	1.8	(28%)	4.5	(72%)
Basic metal industries	9.3	4.0	(43%)	5.3	(57%)
Fabricated metal products	11.5	9.9	(86%)	1.7	(14%)
Machinery and equipment	10.1	6.7	(66%)	3.4	(34%)
Electrical and electronic machinery	12.6	8.5	(68%)	4.1	(32%)
Transport equipment	7.1	4.7	(66%)	2.4	(34%)
Precision instruments	7.1	7.3	(102%)	–0.1	(–2%)
Other industrial products	4.2	4.6	(109%)	–0.4	(–9%)
Manufacturing	7.5	4.7	(62%)	2.8	(38%)

Notes:
1. Due to rounding, figures may not add up precisely.
2. Figures in parentheses denote contributions to output growth. The relative contributions are calculated based on the entire period, not annual input and TFP growth estimates.
3. The final weighted growth rate of manufacturing does not include the petroleum and coal products industry.

Source: Author's calculations.

5.3   ESTIMATES AND TRENDS IN TFP GROWTH IN THE EAST ASIAN MANUFACTURING SECTORS

This section discusses the estimates and trends in annual TFP growth for the five East Asian manufacturing sectors, which are depicted in Figures 5.1 to 5.6. The annual TFP growth estimates for individual industries will not be discussed here but the details are available in Tables 5.18 to 5.22.[9] The annual TFP growth estimates for the entire manufacturing sector in this study are computed by taking the average share of each industry in overall manufacturing in two consecutive years as a weight multiplied by the TFP growth rate of that industry.

Table A5.1 shows annual TFP growth estimates for manufacturing industries in Hong Kong from 1976 to 1997. Hong Kong's manufacturing sector was in general successful in terms of achieving progress in TFP. Sizeable TFP growth occurred in 1977–78 (14.3 per cent), 1982–83 (13.3 per cent) and 1985–86 (14.4 per cent) while the worst TFP performance of –15.7 per cent was in 1983–84. Despite the rapid relocation of manufacturing production to mainland China from the mid-1980s, Hong Kong's manufacturing sector continued to achieve TFP progress in the 1990s. Despite the slight downward trend in TFP growth, as indicated by Figure 5.1, moderate TFP growth for the manufacturing sector of Hong Kong was maintained throughout the period 1976–97.

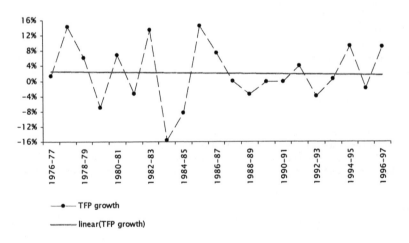

Source: The annual TFP growth estimates are available in Table A5.1.

Figure 5.1   Trend of annual TFP growth estimates in Hong Kong's manufacturing sector, 1976–97

Figure 5.2 shows the trend of annual TFP growth estimates in the manufacturing sector of Japan over the period 1965–98. The linear trend of TFP growth for the manufacturing sector was in significant decline. Table A5.2 presents annual TFP growth estimates for manufacturing industries in Japan over the 1965–98 period. The Japanese manufacturing sector had outstanding TFP growth in the late 1960s, 1970s and 1980s. The highest TFP growth of 13.7 per cent occurred in 1978–79 but the worst result of –10.9 per cent was in 1974–75 due to the oil crisis of the early 1970s. After that, TFP growth was managed at a reasonable level until 1990. Due to the slump of the Japanese economy in the last decade, TFP growth for the manufacturing sector was on average negative in the 1990s. To some extent, this outcome reflects the end of the technology borrowing phase in post-war Japan, that is, a catching up process which has recently been highlighted by Hayami and Ogasawara (1999).

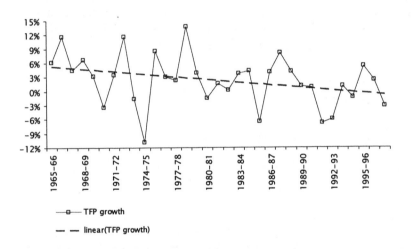

Source: The annual TFP growth estimates are available in Table A5.2.

Figure 5.2   Trend of annual TFP growth estimates in Japan's manufacturing sector, 1965–98

Likewise, the TFP growth of Korean manufacturing industries was seriously affected by the two major oil crises. Table A5.3 presents annual TFP growth estimates for manufacturing industries in Korea from 1970 to 1997. The 2-digit negative TFP growth rates took place in 1973–74 (–16.3 per cent) and 1978–80 (–13.6 per cent) and the highest TFP growth of 15.3 per cent occurred in 1972–73 and 1989–90. In spite of the external impacts,

Korean manufacturing industries during the 1970–97 period achieved on average the highest TFP growth among the five East Asian manufacturing sectors. Figure 5.3 shows the trend of annual TFP growth estimates in the manufacturing sector of Korea over the period 1970–97. In contrast to Hong Kong and Japan, this reveals that Korea's manufacturing sector has been achieving TFP growth since 1970 and shows no sign of slowing down.

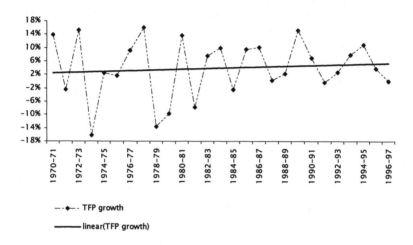

Source: The annual TFP growth estimates are available in Table A5.3.

Figure 5.3   Trend of annual TFP growth estimates in Korea's manufacturing sector, 1970–97

Table A5.4 presents annual TFP growth estimates for manufacturing industries in Singapore over the 1970–97 period. Similar to Japan and Korea, Singapore's manufacturing sector experienced significant negative TFP growth in the first half of the 1970s, such as in 1973–74 (–13.8 per cent) and 1974–75 (–11.5 per cent). After that, considerable negative TFP growth still took place over the 1979–83 and 1988–91 periods. In contrast, the best TFP growth of 13.5 per cent occurred in 1986–87 when the manufacturing sector rebounded from the economic recession in 1985. On average, TFP growth remained negative throughout the entire period 1970–97. To reconcile the findings for Singapore's manufacturing sector, several possible explanations have been described in section 5.2.

Figure 5.4 shows the trend of annual TFP growth estimates in the manufacturing sector of Singapore over the period 1970–97. As mentioned earlier, average annual TFP growth in Singapore during this period was –0.8 per cent. Regardless of the negative TFP growth, Singapore's manufacturing sector gradually reversed the extent of TFP decline, as seen in the upward-sloping trend of TFP growth in Figure 5.4. Likewise, Toh and Ng (2002) suggested that although TFP growth for the overall economy was negligible between 1971 and 1986, according to more recent data it had improved significantly over the period 1987–96, averaging 2.6 per cent per annum. Nevertheless, this interpretation must be applied only to Singapore's manufacturing sector. As stressed in section 5.2, the trend in TFP growth has much to do with the choice of the sample period. If the first half of the 1970s is excluded from the sample, the trend of TFP growth becomes downward-sloping. In other words, the level of TFP deteriorated over time; see Figure 5.5.

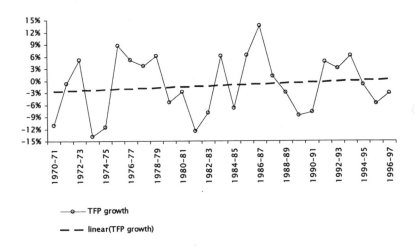

Source: The annual TFP growth estimates are available in Table A5.4.

Figure 5.4   Trend of annual TFP growth estimates in Singapore's manufacturing sector, 1970–97

Table A5.5 presents annual TFP growth estimates for manufacturing industries in Taiwan over the 1981–99 period. TFP in Taiwanese manufacturing industries progressed significantly in the 1980s, particularly over the 1982–84 and 1985–87 periods, but deteriorated sharply in the 1990s. The highest TFP growth of 12.1 per cent occurred in 1985–86 and the lowest growth of –5.7 per cent in 1997–98, which coincided with the Asian financial crisis. On average, Taiwan's manufacturing industries achieved a slight progress in TFP over the 1981–99 period.

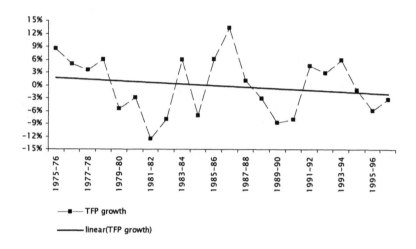

The annual TFP growth estimates are available in Table A5.4.

Figure 5.5   Trend of annual TFP growth estimates in Singapore's manufacturing sector, 1975–97

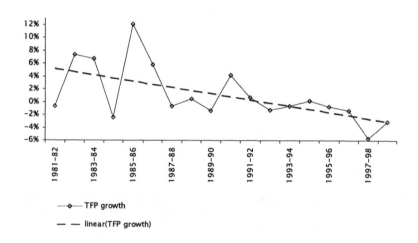

Source: The estimated annual TFP growth is available in Table A5.5.

Figure 5.6   Trend of annual TFP growth estimates in Taiwan's manufacturing sector, 1981–99

Figure 5.6 shows the trend of annual TFP growth estimates in the manufacturing sector of Taiwan over the period 1981–99. As in the Japanese manufacturing sector, the trend of TFP growth for Taiwan's manufacturing sector declined drastically, especially in the 1990s. This implies that the role of factor accumulation (or input growth) in determining output growth turned out to be more important than TFP growth.

In the literature on growth accounting, the idea of TFP growth has often been used synonymously with technological progress. In other words, the traditional concept of treating TFP growth as technological progress or technology advance ignores the importance of technical efficiency pertaining to industry organisation and effective use of available resources. As such, Chapter 6 examines the claim by the current study that technology progress and technical efficiency both contributed to TFP growth and were responsible for the structural transformation of the East Asian manufacturing sector.

NOTES

1. As the weighted TFP growth includes additional TFP growth due to shifts of labour and capital inputs from lower productivity industries to higher productivity industries, it differs from the TFP growth based on aggregate manufacturing data for two reasons. First, the latter TFP growth estimates do not take account of industry-specific characteristics and interactions between industries. Second, the potential production frontier is generated for the manufacturing industries at the 3-digit level not the manufacturing level. Hence this study derives the weighted TFP growth, and applies this process to input growth, technical efficiency change and technological progress for the manufacturing sectors.
2. It should be noted that the final weighted growth rate for the manufacturing sector does not include the beverages (1995–97) and footwear (1993–97) industries due to their exclusion from the sample; see Appendix A.3 for details.
3. As mentioned earlier, three industries – tobacco, other chemicals, and petroleum refineries and miscellaneous petroleum – are not included in the sample. However, the impact of the removal has been diminishing because the total share of the three industries in manufacturing has decreased from about 20% in the 1970s to less than 13% in the 1990s.
4. This proposition has been examined recently by Huggett and Ospina (2001). They found evidence that a large investment in equipment would simultaneously reduce TFP growth by 3–9 per cent from annual plant-level data in the Colombian manufacturing sector.
5. Young (1992, pp. 38–43) provided his bounded learning-by-doing model to reconcile the results for Singapore.
6. A number of studies, including Tsao (1985), Toh and Low (1996) and Swee and Low (1996), have provided other interpretations for the low estimated TFP growth for Singapore.
7. A recent study by Toh and Ng (2002) disagreed with this suggestion. They found that Singapore's returns from capital investment were similar to those of Hong Kong and

Taiwan, suggesting that Singapore did not over-invest. Note that their investigation focused on the entire economy, not the manufacturing sector.

8. The issue of decreasing capacity utilisation leading to overestimation of capital input growth is similar to that of employing a low depreciation rate. Thus it can be easily examined by changing the depreciation rates, as shown in Chapter 6, section 6.4.

9. Similarly, Kwong *et al.* (2000) argued that technology (or TFP) decline in Hong Kong's manufacturing industries was most likely caused by the relocation of manufacturing production to mainland China. The liberalisation in China since 1978 eliminated the need to upgrade local production technology because the rate of return from technology upgrade requiring heavy investment in R&D was uncertain.

10. Compared with the output growth graphs presented in Chapter 4, it is found that TFP growth and output growth in fact moved closely together. The rationale behind this outcome is not difficult to work out. As capital and labour inputs cannot be expanded or reduced considerably in a short period of time, if output growth follows the business cycle fluctuations, TFP growth will be affected by the business cycle as well.

6. Sources of TFP growth

According to the model outlined in Chapter 3, the potential production frontier for each of the five East Asian manufacturing sectors is constructed using the estimates of frontier coefficients shown in Tables 4.3 to 4.7. The potential output can be obtained by transposing actual labour and capital inputs into the potential production frontier. The actual output of each manufacturing sector can then be compared with its potential frontier output. Given a constant level of inputs, the closer the actual output is to the potential frontier output, the higher the technical efficiency (TE); likewise, the larger the shift in production frontier, the higher the technological progress. Applying these definitions, the focus of this chapter is to identify sources of TFP growth and to distinguish TFP growth from technological progress.

Following Nishimizu and Page (1982), TFP growth is decomposed into that of technological progress and technical efficiency change. Section 6.1 discusses the decomposition of TFP growth for the five East Asian manufacturing industries. Section 6.2 analyses the long-term trends in technical efficiency change and technological progress and provides empirical evidence with regard to structural transformation across the East Asian manufacturing sectors. For instance, it can be seen that since the early 1990s, technical efficiency improvement has gradually replaced the role of technological progress in Japan. Section 6.3 examines two hypotheses relating to high-tech and low-tech industries: first, that high-tech industries have a higher TFP growth than low-tech industries; and second, that technological progress and technical efficiency improvement are the main sources of TFP growth in high-tech and low-tech industries respectively. Section 6.4 conducts a series of sensitivity tests to confirm the decline in TFP in Singapore's manufacturing industries found by the current study, using various capital depreciation rates and labour quality adjustment indices. A comparison of earlier studies of the performance of TFP growth in the five East Asian manufacturing industries is then carried out in section 6.5.

6.1   SOURCES OF TFP GROWTH: TECHNOLOGICAL PROGRESS VERSUS TECHNICAL EFFICIENCY

In the literature on growth accounting, TFP growth has often been treated synonymously with technological progress.   This tendency obscures the nature of technology advance, and ignores the learning-by-doing effect and the importance of technical efficiency in the use of available resources.   TFP growth comprises a combination of technological progress and technical efficiency.   Following Nishimizu and Page (1982), who incorporated the concept of technical inefficiency into the production process, this study decomposes TFP growth into technological progress and technical efficiency change for the five East Asian manufacturing sectors.

6.1.1   Hong Kong

Table 6.1 presents the decomposition of TFP growth for Hong Kong's manufacturing industries over the period 1976–97. With the exception of the footwear industry (–1.0 per cent), all industries experienced positive TFP growth, ranging from 0.9 per cent a year in the beverages industry to 4.6 per cent in electric machinery.   Apart from the non-metal mineral products industry (–0.3 per cent), all industries achieved technological progress, from 0.1 per cent in the chemical products industry to 3.8 per cent in wearing apparel on an average annual basis.   Surprisingly, the highest rates of technological progress occurred in the wearing apparel industry, which is considered to be traditional and labour-intensive.   Other labour-intensive industries, such as wood, furniture and textiles, also experienced substantial technological progress.   One possible interpretation for the higher rates of technological progress in these labour-intensive industries relates to the gradual relocation of the production of low-end products to mainland China. As a result, the only way to sustain the higher labour costs was to upgrade production technology, which would allow the production of high-end products and thus enable the industries to survive competitively in international markets.

Among 21 industries, six experienced technical efficiency deterioration, especially wearing apparel with –2.0 per cent a year and footwear with –3.2 per cent.   Yet the non-metal mineral products industry enjoyed the highest average annual technical efficiency improvement of 4.3 per cent, followed by chemical and leather products with about 2.6 per cent.   On examining contributions to TFP growth, technological progress was wholly responsible for TFP growth in a number of industries, such as furniture and wearing apparel.   Interestingly, technological progress also appears to be the major contributor to TFP growth in several labour-intensive industries, including textiles, furniture, wood and wearing apparel. However, technical efficiency improvement also played a significant role; for example, it was totally responsible for TFP growth in the non-metal mineral industry.

Table 6.1 Sources of TFP growth: technological progress and technical efficiency change in Hong Kong's manufacturing industries, 1976–97

Industry	TFP growth	Tech. progress		TE change	
311 Food products	2.9	1.6	(54%)	1.3	(46%)
313 Beverages	0.9	0.9	(102%)	0.0	(–2%)
321 Textiles	2.3	2.4	(102%)	–0.1	(–2%)
322 Wearing apparel	1.9	3.8	(207%)	–2.0	(–107%)
323 Leather products	4.1	1.5	(37%)	2.6	(63%)
324 Footwear	–1.0	2.2	—	–3.2	—
331 Wood products	2.2	2.3	(106%)	–0.1	(–6%)
332 Furniture	1.7	2.2	(128%)	–0.5	(–28%)
341 Paper and paper products	2.4	1.7	(72%)	0.7	(28%)
342 Printing and publishing	2.7	1.7	(65%)	0.9	(35%)
351+352 Chemical products	2.7	0.1	(4%)	2.6	(96%)
355 Rubber products	3.3	1.7	(50%)	1.6	(50%)
356 Plastic products	3.0	2.5	(84%)	0.5	(16%)
36 Non-metal mineral products	4.0	–0.3	(–7%)	4.3	(107%)
371+372 Basic metals	1.6	0.9	(59%)	0.7	(41%)
381 Fabricated metal products	3.2	2.8	(87%)	0.4	(13%)
382 Non-electrical machinery	4.0	1.9	(48%)	2.1	(52%)
383 Electric machinery	4.6	2.7	(58%)	1.9	(42%)
384 Transport equipment	2.5	2.1	(84%)	0.4	(16%)
385 Professional equipment	2.8	1.7	(60%)	1.1	(40%)
390 Other manufactured	2.5	2.5	(101%)	0.0	(–1%)
300 Manufacturing	2.7	2.5	(90%)	0.2	(10%)

Notes:
1. TFP growth estimates may not add up precisely due to rounding. Percentages in parentheses are the contribution to TFP growth. The relative contributions are calculated based on the entire sample period, not annual estimates.
2. Non-metal mineral products industry (36) includes pottery, china, earthenware (361), glass and glass products (362) and other non-metallic minerals (369).
3. The final outcomes for the manufacturing sector exclude the tobacco industry and subsequently, beverages (1995–97) and footwear (1993–97).

On average, the manufacturing sector achieved 2.7 per cent annual TFP growth, stemming from 2.5 per cent technological progress and only 0.2 per cent technical efficiency improvement. Thus technological progress was the dominant contributor to TFP growth.

6.1.2 Japan

Table 6.2 presents the decomposition of TFP growth for Japan's manufacturing industries over the period 1965–98. Apart from the petroleum refineries industry, manufacturing industries in Japan experienced substantial TFP growth. The highest average annual TFP growth occurred in the beverages industry with 4.1 per cent, followed by professional equipment with 3.2 per cent and other non-metallic minerals with 3.0 per cent. All industries achieved considerable technological progress, ranging on an average annual basis from 2.5 per cent in the petroleum refineries industry to 3.7 per cent in textiles, wearing apparel and wood products. On the other hand, except for the beverages industry with 0.9 per cent annual technical efficiency improvement, technical efficiency deteriorated across industries, ranging from –0.2 per cent in the professional equipment industry to –1.9 per cent in petroleum refineries. With the exception of the beverages industry, TFP growth for all industries can be fully accounted for by technological progress.

The sweeping negative technical efficiency change and positive technological progress across Japan's 27 manufacturing industries are explicable. In practice, it always takes some time for new technology to be fully absorbed. This implies that firms will not benefit substantially until they become proficient in applying the latest technology. Referring to plant-level data from the Colombian manufacturing sector as an example, Huggett and Ospina (2001) suggested that TFP initially declines after new technology is adopted due to a fall in the level of technical efficiency, but may recover or exceed the previous technical efficiency level some time later when the technology upgrade is completed. However, they contended that technical efficiency would not improve if there was continuous technology upgrade due to the lack of the learning-by-doing effect.

6.1.3 Korea

Table 6.3 presents the decomposition of TFP growth for Korea's manufacturing industries over the period 1970–97. All industries increased TFP growth significantly by at least 1.4 per cent a year. Technological progress was widespread across Korean manufacturing industries, ranging from an average annual 1.1 per cent in the other manufactured products industry to 4.6 per cent in non-ferrous metals. Of 25 industries, 21 exhibited technical efficiency improvement. More specifically, apart from the plastics industry (−1.2 per cent), technical efficiency deterioration in the remaining three industries was negligible.

The decomposition results for the Korean manufacturing sector as a whole indicate that average annual technological progress of 2.5 per cent was the major contributor to TFP growth, accounting for about 70 per cent. Nonetheless, for some industries such as wearing apparel and other manufactured products, technical efficiency improvement played a more important role than technological progress in achieving TFP growth.

In practice, how can technical efficiency improvement and technological progress coexist? One possible explanation is that Korean manufacturing industries not only continuously upgraded production technology, possibly through imported technology, innovation (R&D) or technological diffusion, but also managed to master the new technology in a short period of time. This implies that regardless of a small fall in technical efficiency at the outset, Korean industries soon caught up or even exceeded earlier levels of technical efficiency. Another possibility is that inefficient firms were not able to survive after the structural and industrial reforms implemented by the Korean government; hence the aggregation of existing efficient firms to some extent raised the level of technical efficiency in the manufacturing sector as a whole. Furthermore, the considerable technical efficiency improvement in Korean manufacturing industries may have been a result of substantial investment in education and job-training programmes, gains from learning-by-doing by workers and firms, and technology spillovers. Other factors, including effective management and government policy, may have also contributed.

To some extent, this decomposition analysis reveals that Korean manufacturing industries have outperformed other nations in terms of applying both tangible technology, which induces technological progress, and intangible or efficiency-based technology gained through learning-by-doing, which results in technical efficiency improvements.

Table 6.2   Sources of TFP growth: technological progress and technical efficiency change in Japan's manufacturing industries, 1965– 98

Industry	TFP growth	Tech. progress		TE change	
311 Food products	2.1	3.6	(170%)	−1.5	(−70%)
313 Beverages	4.1	3.2	(78%)	0.9	(22%)
321 Textiles	2.9	3.7	(128%)	−0.8	(−28%)
322 Wearing apparel	2.2	3.7	(172%)	−1.6	(−72%)
323 Leather products	2.5	3.4	(135%)	−0.9	(−35%)
324 Footwear	2.9	3.3	(114%)	−0.4	(−14%)
331 Wood products	2.7	3.7	(136%)	−1.0	(−36%)
332 Furniture	2.8	3.6	(128%)	−0.8	(−28%)
341 Paper and paper products	2.1	3.4	(162%)	−1.3	(−62%)
342 Printing and publishing	2.7	3.5	(133%)	−0.9	(−33%)
351 Industrial chemicals	2.8	3.1	(110%)	−0.3	(−10%)
352 Other chemicals	2.9	3.3	(113%)	−0.4	(−13%)
353 Petroleum refineries	0.6	2.5	(420%)	−1.9	(−320%)
354 Miscellaneous petroleum	2.4	2.9	(123%)	−0.5	(−23%)
355 Rubber products	2.4	3.4	(143%)	−1.0	(−43%)
356 Plastic products	2.8	3.3	(120%)	−0.6	(−20%)
361 Pottery, china, earthenware	2.1	3.5	(170%)	−1.5	(−70%)
362 Glass and glass products	1.9	3.2	(164%)	−1.2	(−64%)
369 Other non-metallic	3.0	3.3	(110%)	−0.3	(−10%)
371 Iron and steel	2.8	3.2	(118%)	−0.5	(−18%)
372 Non-ferrous metals	1.8	3.2	(171%)	−1.3	(−71%)
381 Fabricated metal products	2.6	3.6	(139%)	−1.0	(−39%)
382 Non-electrical machinery	2.9	3.6	(125%)	−0.7	(−25%)
383 Electric machinery	1.9	3.6	(194%)	−1.8	(−94%)
384 Transport equipment	2.0	3.5	(174%)	−1.5	(−74%)
385 Professional equipment	3.2	3.4	(106%)	−0.2	(−6%)
390 Other manufactured	2.5	3.6	(141%)	−1.0	(−41%)
300 Manufacturing	2.5	3.5	(139%)	−1.0	(−39%)

Notes:
1. TFP growth estimates may not add up precisely due to rounding. Percentages in parentheses are the contribution to TFP growth. The relative contributions are calculated based on the entire sample period, not annual estimates.
2. The final outcomes for the manufacturing sector exclude the tobacco industry.

Table 6.3   *Sources of TFP growth: technological progress and technical efficiency change in Korea's manufacturing industries, 1970– 97*

Industry	TFP growth	Tech. progress		TE change	
311 Food products	2.7	2.0	(76%)	0.6	(24%)
321 Textiles	4.3	2.3	(53%)	2.0	(47%)
322 Wearing apparel	4.3	1.3	(31%)	2.9	(69%)
323 Leather products	4.1	2.5	(62%)	1.5	(38%)
324 Footwear	2.8	2.4	(88%)	0.3	(13%)
331 Wood products	4.9	2.9	(59%)	2.0	(41%)
332 Furniture	3.0	1.9	(62%)	1.1	(38%)
341 Paper and paper products	4.0	3.4	(83%)	0.7	(17%)
342 Printing, publishing	4.2	2.2	(53%)	1.9	(47%)
351 Industrial chemicals	3.3	3.6	(108%)	−0.2	(−8%)
352 Other chemicals	2.7	2.5	(93%)	0.2	(7%)
354 Miscellaneous petroleum	2.4	2.6	(106%)	−0.2	(−6%)
355 Rubber products	3.9	2.3	(60%)	1.6	(40%)
356 Plastic products	1.4	2.7	(185%)	−1.2	(−85%)
361 Pottery, china, earth.	8.3	3.9	(47%)	4.4	(53%)
362 Glass and glass products	2.5	2.6	(103%)	−0.1	(−3%)
369 Other non-metallic	5.7	4.2	(73%)	1.6	(27%)
371 Iron and steel	3.1	2.8	(91%)	0.3	(9%)
372 Non-ferrous metals	6.1	4.6	(76%)	1.5	(24%)
381 Fabricated metals	3.7	1.9	(51%)	1.8	(49%)
382 Non-electrical machinery	4.2	2.1	(50%)	2.1	(50%)
383 Electric machinery	3.5	2.4	(68%)	1.1	(32%)
384 Transport equipment	2.8	2.7	(95%)	0.1	(5%)
385 Professional equipment	5.6	3.2	(57%)	2.4	(43%)
390 Other manufactured	2.7	1.1	(41%)	1.6	(59%)
300 Manufacturing	3.6	2.5	(70%)	1.1	(30%)

Notes:
1. TFP growth estimates may not add up precisely due to rounding. Percentages in parentheses are the contribution to TFP growth. The relative contributions are calculated based on the entire sample period, not annual estimates.
2. The final results for the manufacturing sector do not include the tobacco, beverages and petroleum industries.

6.1.4 Singapore

Table 6.4 presents the decomposition of TFP growth for Singapore's manufacturing industries over the period 1970–97. Note that, due to prevalent negative TFP growth and technological progress, it is not meaningful to discuss the percentage contribution of the different components to TFP growth. Singapore's manufacturing sector is often regarded as a pioneer in adopting advanced technology and machinery; thus, capital stock is likely to depreciate more than the other manufacturing sectors in East Asia. This means that the growth rate of capital stock could be overestimated in Singapore, resulting in understatement of TFP growth. However, the problem of overestimating capital input growth has been overcome in this study by using a higher capital depreciation rate of 0.1768 (instead of 0.0925) for Singapore's manufacturing industries to calculate its TFP growth.

Even so, Singapore's manufacturing sector is the exception in East Asia, recording negative TFP growth due entirely to technological decline. Although 11 industries had positive TFP growth, the entire manufacturing sector experienced a 0.8 per cent TFP decline on an average annual basis. As for technological progress, all 23 industries experienced negative technological progress, varying from –0.9 per cent per annum in the wearing apparel and footwear industries to –1.4 per cent in industrial chemicals. In terms of technical efficiency change, only six industries declined in technical efficiency, with the electric machinery industry recording the greatest decline of –2.2 per cent a year. By contrast, the professional equipment industry enjoyed the highest technical efficiency improvement of 4.7 per cent per annum, followed by textiles with 3.0 per cent and other manufactured products with 2.7 per cent.

As mentioned earlier, in spite of negative technological progress, TFP growth can be achieved by an improvement in technical efficiency, as evidenced in the Singapore manufacturing sector. Among individual industries, the professional equipment industry achieved the largest average annual TFP growth rate of 3.5 per cent owing to substantial technical efficiency improvement, followed by textiles with 1.9 per cent and other manufactured products with 1.6 per cent. Analysis of the contributions made by the different components of TFP growth for the overall manufacturing sector shows that although technical efficiency improved by only 0.3 per cent a year, the level of technology declined by 1.1 per cent and was mainly responsible for the negative TFP growth, particularly during the 1970–75 period.[1]

Sources of TFP growth

133

Table 6.4   *Sources of TFP growth: technological progress and technical efficiency change in Singapore's manufacturing industries, 1970–97*

Industry	TFP growth	Tech. progress	TE change
311 Food products	0.1	−1.2	1.3
313 Beverages	−1.1	−1.1	0.0
321 Textiles	1.9	−1.1	3.0
322 Wearing apparel	−0.4	−0.9	0.5
323 Leather products	1.5	−1.0	2.5
324 Footwear	0.8	−0.9	1.7
331 Wood products	−0.3	−1.1	0.8
332 Furniture	−1.7	−1.0	−0.7
341 Paper and paper products	0.9	−1.1	2.0
342 Printing and publishing	0.9	−1.1	2.0
351 Industrial chemicals	−0.4	−1.4	1.0
355 Rubber products	−1.8	−1.0	−0.7
356 Plastic products	−0.6	−1.1	0.5
361 +362 Pottery and glass products	1.0	−1.1	2.2
369 Other non-metallic minerals	1.0	−1.1	2.1
371 Iron and steel	−2.4	−1.2	−1.2
372 Non-ferrous metals	−1.9	−1.2	−0.7
381 Fabricated metal products	−1.9	−1.1	−0.8
382 Non-electrical machinery	0.1	−1.0	1.1
383 Electric machinery	−3.2	−1.0	−2.2
384 Transport equipment	−0.8	−1.1	0.3
385 Professional equipment	3.5	−1.2	4.7
390 Other manufactured products	1.6	−1.1	2.7
300 Manufacturing	−0.8	−1.1	0.3

Notes:
1. TFP growth estimates may not add up precisely due to rounding.
2. The final results for the manufacturing sector do not include tobacco, other chemicals and petroleum refineries and miscellaneous petroleum industries.

6.1.5 Taiwan

Table 6.5 presents the decomposition of TFP growth for Taiwan's manufacturing industries over the period 1981–99, with nine industries achieving TFP growth and 11 experiencing negative TFP growth. The highest average annual TFP growth was in the chemical industry with 3.9 per cent, and the worst TFP performance by the leather industry with –5.5 per cent.

Apart from the precision instruments industry, Table 6.5 reveals that industries with negative TFP growth were always accompanied by technical efficiency deterioration, such as the food, textiles, wearing apparel and leather industries. However, several industries achieved both technical efficiency improvement and technological progress, such as the non-metallic minerals, and electrical and electronic machinery industries. For the furniture, wood and machinery equipment industries, TFP growth was entirely attributed to technical efficiency improvement. With respect to the overall manufacturing sector, TFP only increased by 0.2 per cent a year, stemming from 0.4 per cent technological progress and –0.2 per cent technical efficiency change.

To facilitate comparison with the analysis for Taiwan in Chapter 5, the decomposition of TFP growth for Taiwan's manufacturing industries over the shorter period 1981–91 is also presented in Table 6.6. The average annual TFP growth rate of 2.8 per cent for the manufacturing sector came from 1.0 per cent technological progress and 1.8 per cent technical efficiency change. In terms of relative contribution to TFP growth, the former accounted for 38 per cent of TFP growth and the latter 62 per cent. Unlike Japan and Korea, technological progress in Taiwan during the 1981–91 period played a relatively minor role in the process of TFP growth; that is, apart from the food, textiles, and electrical and electronic machinery industries, technical efficiency improvement was the major factor boosting TFP growth in Taiwan. Thus the comparison between Tables 6.5 and 6.6 indicates that the significant technical efficiency deterioration over the 1991–99 period was responsible for the slowdown of TFP growth in Taiwan's manufacturing sector. The decline in technical efficiency was due to the rapid changes in economic environment, such as appreciation of the New Taiwanese Dollar, rising wages and environmental issues in the 1990s, which prompted a number of labour-intensive industries to relocate overseas. The closure of firms in labour-intensive industries, indicated by diminishing shares in manufacturing, implies that learning-by-doing effects could not bear fruit and resulted in a substantial fall in technical efficiency, particularly in labour-intensive industries.

Table 6.5 Sources of TFP growth: technological progress and technical efficiency change in Taiwan's manufacturing industries, 1981–99

Industry	TFP growth	Tech. progress		TE change	
Food, beverages and tobacco	−0.4	0.8	—	−1.2	—
Textile mill products	−1.5	1.4	—	−2.9	—
Wearing apparel*	−3.9	−1.1	—	−2.9	—
Leather, fur and products	−5.5	−2.8	—	−2.7	—
Wood and bamboo products	1.5	−0.7	(−48%)	2.2	(−148%)
Furniture and fixtures	2.7	−2.0	(−75%)	4.7	(−175%)
Pulp, paper and paper products	−4.3	0.0	—	−4.3	—
Printing processings	−4.0	−1.8	—	−2.2	—
Chemical materials	3.9	1.8	(−47%)	2.1	(−53%)
Chemical products	3.6	−0.8	(−21%)	4.4	(−121%)
Rubber products	−2.3	−1.5	—	−0.8	—
Plastic products	1.7	0.8	(−46%)	0.9	(−54%)
Non-metallic mineral products	2.0	0.6	(−29%)	1.4	(−71%)
Basic metal industries	1.9	1.4	(−76%)	0.4	(−24%)
Fabricated metal products	−1.3	−0.2	—	−1.1	—
Machinery and equipment	0.4	−0.5	(−130%)	0.9	(−230%)
Electrical, electronic machinery	1.7	0.9	(−50%)	0.8	(−50%)
Transport equipment	−2.2	0.4	—	−2.6	—
Precision instruments	−1.7	−1.9	—	0.2	—
Other industrial products	−1.6	−0.9	—	−0.7	—
Manufacturing	0.2	0.4	(−195%)	−0.2	(−95%)

Notes:
1. TFP growth estimates may not add up precisely due to rounding. Percentages in parentheses are the contribution to TFP growth. The relative contributions are calculated based on the entire sample period, not annual estimates.
2. The final results for the manufacturing sector do not include the petroleum and coal products industry.
3. * denotes wearing apparel, accessories and other textile products.

Table 6.6   Sources of TFP growth: technological progress and technical efficiency change in Taiwan's manufacturing industries, 1981– 91

Industry (1981–91)	TFP growth	Tech. progress		TE change	
Food, beverages, tobacco	1.5	1.4	(98%)	0.0	(2%)
Textile mill products	2.1	2.4	(112%)	−0.3	(−12%)
Wearing apparel*	1.6	0.5	(30%)	1.1	(70%)
Leather, fur and products	−1.5	−2.1	—	0.6	—
Wood and bamboo products	4.8	−0.2	(−4%)	5.0	(104%)
Furniture and fixtures	3.1	−1.4	(−43%)	4.5	(143%)
Pulp, paper and paper products	−3.1	0.0	—	−3.1	—
Printing processings	−4.7	−1.8	—	−2.9	—
Chemical materials	6.6	1.4	(21%)	5.2	(79%)
Chemical products	4.5	−0.7	(−16%)	5.2	(116%)
Rubber products	1.2	−1.1	(−97%)	2.3	(197%)
Plastic products	6.0	1.9	(31%)	4.1	(69%)
Non-metallic minerals	4.5	1.1	(24%)	3.4	(76%)
Basic metal industries	5.3	1.4	(26%)	3.9	(74%)
Fabricated metal products	1.7	0.6	(38%)	1.0	(62%)
Machinery and equipment	3.4	0.3	(7%)	3.2	(93%)
Electrical and electronic	4.1	2.3	(57%)	1.8	(43%)
Transport equipment	2.4	1.0	(41%)	1.4	(59%)
Precision instruments	−0.1	−2.0	—	1.9	—
Other industrial products	−0.4	0.0	—	−0.4	—
Manufacturing	2.8	1.0	(38%)	1.8	(62%)

Notes:
1. TFP growth estimates may not add up precisely due to rounding. Percentages in parentheses are the contribution to TFP growth. The relative contributions are calculated based on the entire sample period, not annual estimates.
2. The final results for the manufacturing sector do not include the petroleum and coal products industry.
3. * denotes wearing apparel, accessories and other textile products.

6.2   LONG-TERM TRENDS IN TECHNOLOGICAL
        PROGRESS AND TECHNICAL EFFICIENCY CHANGE

Large-scale fluctuations in technical efficiency and technological progress
have prevented the long-term trend analysis being undertaken for Hong
Kong's manufacturing sector. The underlying cause of these fluctuations is
implicit in the estimates of frontier coefficients contained in Table 4.3, which
shows sizeable changes in the estimated constant terms, labour and capital
coefficients over time. Thus, in this section the analysis focuses on the
manufacturing sectors of Japan, Korea, Singapore and Taiwan only.[2] Note
that the comparison of the long-term trends in technological progress and
technical efficiency change can also be extended to individual industries.

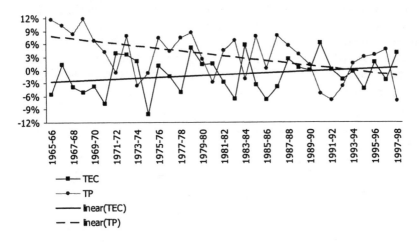

Notes: TEC and TP denote technical efficiency change and technological progress respectively.
          The linear trends in technical efficiency change and technological progress are obtained
          using *Microsoft Windows Excel* 2000.

Figure 6.1   *The trends in technical efficiency change and technological*
              progress in Japan's manufacturing sector, 1965–98

Figure 6.1 presents the trends in technical efficiency change and
technological progress in Japan's manufacturing sector over the period 1965–
98. It clearly shows that there has been a systematic transformation in the
components of TFP growth over time, as indicated by the trend for technical
efficiency change and technological progress to move in opposite directions.
The impressive technological progress in Japan's manufacturing sector
slowed down over time and even became negative after 1993. Although

technical efficiency change was negative at the beginning, it became positive after 1993. This trend persisted even when the sample period was reduced to the 1980–98 period, as shown in Figure 6.2.

A salient fact emerging from Figure 6.1 is that technical efficiency improvement has been playing an increasing role in maintaining TFP growth in Japan's manufacturing industries. Two possible explanations are offered for the change in the relative importance of the components of TFP growth. First, since production technology has reached a mature stage in Japan, extensive investments in R&D are required in order to upgrade production technology, so Japan may have chosen the less costly option of raising TFP growth by pursuing technical efficiency through learning-by-doing, on-the-job training and investment in human capital. Second, ongoing structural change and market reform in Japan, such as the withdrawal of the government subsidy on R&D, may have led to the exit of inefficient firms, which in turn raised the overall technical efficiency level for the entire manufacturing sector. Such an increase in technical efficiency improvement may be viewed as *efficiency-based* or intangible technology, in contrast to physical technology, which induces technological progress and deserves more empirical study.

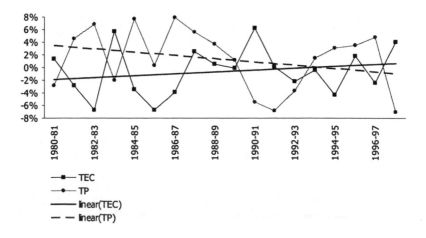

Notes: TEC and TP denote technical efficiency change and technological progress respectively. The linear trends in technical efficiency change and technological progress are obtained using *Microsoft Windows Excel* 2000.

Figure 6.2   *The trends in technical efficiency change and technological progress in Japan's manufacturing sector, 1980–98*

Figure 6.3 presents the trends in technical efficiency change and technological progress in Korea's manufacturing sector over the period 1974–97 to avoid the large-scale fluctuations experienced during the early 1970s due to the oil crisis. Note that, even if the sample period commences from 1970, the slopes of both trends remain almost unchanged. The current study found that both trends in technical efficiency improvement and technological progress were upward-sloping over the period 1974–97. On the one hand, the combination of these two rising trends indicates the sustainability of TFP growth in Korea's manufacturing sector; on the other hand, this outcome contradicts the general perception regarding the interaction between technological progress and technical efficiency change. Although Huggett and Ospina (2001) suggested that technological progress often accompanied deterioration in technical efficiency, the findings of this study reject such a proposition for Korea and demonstrate that Korean manufacturing industries can upgrade their technology (technological progress) and master the new technology concurrently (technical efficiency improvement).

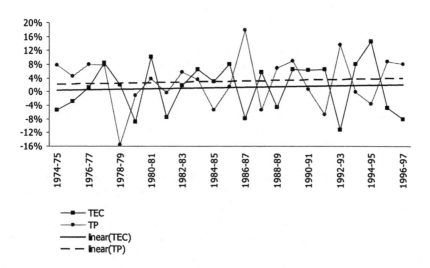

Notes: TEC and TP denote technical efficiency change and technological progress respectively. The linear trends in technical efficiency change and technological progress are obtained using *Microsoft Windows Excel* 2000.

Figure 6.3 *The trends in technical efficiency change and technological progress in the Korean manufacturing sector, 1974–97*

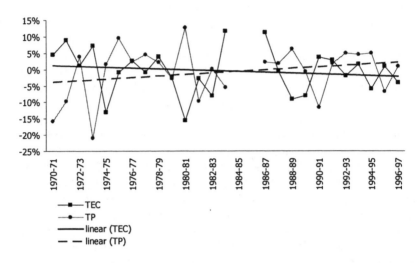

Notes: TEC and TP denote technical efficiency change and technological progress respectively.
          The linear trends in technical efficiency change and technological progress are obtained
          using *Microsoft Windows Excel* 2000.

Figure 6.4   **The trends in technical efficiency change and technological
               progress in Singapore's manufacturing sector, 1970–84 and
               1986–97**

Figure 6.4 presents the trends in technical efficiency change and
technological progress in Singapore's manufacturing sector over the periods
1970–84 and 1986–97. Substantial technological decline combined with
moderate technical efficiency improvement resulted in negative TFP growth
in the 1970s. With the decline in technical efficiency in the early 1980s, TFP
growth on average remained negative over the 1980s. Finally, the moderate
technological progress in the 1990s was unable to reverse (offset or
compensate) a large decline in the level of technical efficiency and resulted in
negative TFP growth. Similar to Japan, there has been a systematic
transformation in the components of TFP growth for Singapore over time, as
indicated by the trends for technical efficiency change and technological
progress to move in opposite directions. Nonetheless, the upward-sloping
trend in technological progress and the downward-sloping trend in technical
efficiency are the reverse of the Japanese scenario.

Given that technical efficiency improvement is often deemed to be the
result of the learning-by-doing effect, on-the-job training and other
investments in human capital, Singapore's manufacturing industries have
failed to enhance TFP through technical efficiency improvement. By

extension, the pursuit of modern and advanced technology unaccompanied by technical efficiency enhancement may explain the poor TFP performance in the Singapore manufacturing industries after the mid-1980s. The result of the current study is consistent with Young (1992, 1995) and Mahadevan and Kalirajan (2000). Young (1992) pointed out that the continual adoption of the latest technology represented by technological progress and failure to master existing production technology denoted by technical efficiency deterioration should be responsible for negative TFP growth, because the benefit of advanced technology cannot be entirely realised within a short period of time. Mahadevan and Kalirajan (2000) found evidence that technical efficiency deterioration was the main factor driving down TFP growth in Singapore. The ongoing structural transformation from technical efficiency improvement in the 1970s towards technological progress in the 1990s deserves more empirical research to uncover the process of such transformation.

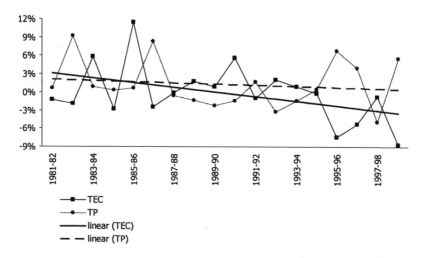

Notes: TEC and TP denote technical efficiency change and technological progress respectively. The linear trends in technical efficiency change and technological progress are obtained using *Microsoft Windows Excel* 2000.

Figure 6.5   *The trends in technical efficiency change and technological progress in Taiwan's manufacturing sector, 1981–99*

Figure 6.5 presents the trends in technical efficiency change and technological progress in Taiwan's manufacturing sector over the period 1981–99. Taiwan's manufacturing sector experienced a downward trend in both technical efficiency change and technological progress. On average, the improvement in technical efficiency fell drastically and became negative after 1990. Despite technological progress remaining positive, the declining trend implied that technological progress would soon become negative. Hence this study questions the sustainability of Taiwan's manufacturing industries due to the sharp slowdown of TFP growth that is attributed to a deterioration in technical efficiency, which significantly exceeded that of technological decline.

6.3   SOURCES OF TFP GROWTH: HIGH-TECH VERSUS LOW-TECH INDUSTRIES

Intuitively, high-tech industries are often associated with high TFP growth, yet such empirical comparison has rarely been carried out in the literature. Therefore, this section compares high-tech with low-tech industries based on two hypotheses. The first is that high-tech industries have higher TFP growth than low-tech ones. The second is that the sources of TFP growth for high-tech industries stem from technological progress, whereas low-tech industries derive TFP growth from technical efficiency improvement.[3] In the literature, there is no precise definition regarding the classification of high-tech and low-tech industries. Therefore, on the basis of capital–labour ratio comparisons, low-tech industries, also known as labour-intensive or traditional industries, are defined in this study as textiles, wearing apparel, leather products, footwear, wood products and furniture.[4]

Although the capital–labour ratio for the chemicals, petroleum and iron and steel industries are generally among the highest, these industries are usually characterised as heavy rather than high-tech industries. Based on the nature of technology rather than capital–labour ratio, this study classifies the following industries as high-tech: non-electrical machinery, electric machinery, and professional equipment (or precision instruments).

High-tech industries in Hong Kong were more productive than low-tech industries according to Table 6.1. For instance, the average annual TFP growth rates for the high-tech non-electrical machinery and electric machinery industries were over 4 per cent. However, the low-tech leather products industry also experienced over 4 per cent TFP growth, while the other low-tech industries experienced average annual TFP growth at around 2 per cent; and the footwear industry underwent TFP decline of –1.0 per cent. While the first hypothesis proved inconclusive, the second hypothesis failed. Not only did five of the six low-tech industries in Hong Kong suffer technical efficiency deterioration, but both technical efficiency improvement and technological progress contributed equally to TFP growth in Hong Kong's high-tech industries.

The hypotheses also proved to be incorrect for Japan's manufacturing industries, as both high-tech and low-tech industries enjoyed comparable TFP growth, at roughly 2.7 per cent per annum. As can be seen in Table 6.2, the sources of TFP growth appeared to be similar in that all industries benefited from technological progress but declined in technical efficiency. The first hypothesis is also rejected for Korean manufacturing industries for similar reasons to Japan and the second hypothesis is rejected because technological progress and technical efficiency both contributed to TFP growth in both high-tech as well as low-tech industries.

The results revealed in Table 6.4 are used to test the two hypotheses for Singapore's manufacturing industries. One of the high-tech industries, electric machinery, experienced the worst TFP growth of −3.2 per cent, but the professional equipment industry achieved the highest TFP growth of 3.5 per cent and the non-electric industry gained only 0.1 per cent TFP growth. Three low-tech industries recorded negative TFP growth while two others, the textiles and leather products industries, had slight TFP growth. Therefore, the proposition that high-tech industries have higher TFP growth in Singapore is incorrect.

In terms of sources of TFP growth, both high-tech and low-tech industries in Singapore experienced negative technological progress. Nevertheless, with the exception of the furniture industry, low-tech industries achieved considerable technical efficiency improvement, especially textiles and leather products. Hence the proposition of low-tech industries gaining TFP growth through technical efficiency improvement was valid only for the textiles and leather products industries.

As with Singapore, mixed results emerged from the comparison between Taiwan's high-tech and low-tech industries, as evidenced in Table 6.5. As far as high-tech industries are concerned, the electrical and electronic machinery industry gained average annual TFP growth of 1.7 per cent, but TFP growth for the precision instruments industry fell by 1.7 per cent annually. As for the low-tech industries, the wood and furniture industries recorded TFP growth of 1.5 per cent and 2.7 per cent, while the textiles, wearing apparel and leather industries experienced average annual TFP growth of −1.5 per cent, −3.9 per cent and −5.5 per cent respectively. Consequently, the first hypothesis is rejected because the high-tech industries in Taiwan did not enjoy higher TFP growth than low-tech ones.

Regarding the second hypothesis, it can be seen that TFP growth in Taiwan's high-tech electrical and electronic machinery industry was enhanced equally by technical efficiency improvement and technological progress. Instead of achieving TFP growth from technological progress, the precision instruments industry suffered a technological decline of –1.9 per cent, leading to negative TFP growth. Two low-tech industries, wood and furniture, considerably improved their level of technical efficiency, by 2.2 per cent and 4.7 per cent respectively, whereas the textile mills products gained in technological progress. Therefore, the statement that sources of TFP growth for low-tech industries stemmed from technical efficiency improvement turns out to be valid only for the wood and furniture industries, so the second hypothesis is also proved incorrect.

6.4 SENSITIVITY ANALYSIS

It has been established that a larger labour quality adjustment index generates higher input growth, resulting in lower TFP growth, and a larger capital depreciation rate creates higher TFP growth because less capital is used. Hence concerns over the negative TFP growth for Singapore's manufacturing industries have raised a number of questions regarding the choice of labour quality adjustment index and capital depreciation rate; Chen (1997) has argued that the quality improvement embodied in labour and capital inputs could be over-adjusted in Young (1992, 1995). As the current study used a labour quality adjustment index of 1.6 per cent per annum and a capital depreciation rate of 17.68 per cent to calculate the TFP growth estimates for Singapore, it conducted two sensitivity tests to examine the impact of varying these rates on the TFP growth estimates.

The first sensitivity test examines how changes in the labour quality adjustment indices and capital depreciation rates influence TFP growth estimates. Table 6.7 shows the sensitivity analyses for Singapore's TFP growth estimates over the period 1970–97 using three capital depreciation rates (0.20, 0.25 and 0.30) and labour quality improvement indices (1 per cent, 0.5 per cent and 0 per cent, per annum).[5] It is evident that an increase in capital depreciation rate and decrease in labour quality index generated an impact on the TFP growth estimates for Singapore.[6] Yet, these impacts appear to be insignificant unless the extreme capital depreciation rate (0.3) and labour quality adjustment index (0 per cent) are selected. Even so, it could only raise average annual TFP growth from a negative estimate of –0.8 per cent to a slight positive 0.4 per cent, which is insignificant in comparison to that of the Hong Kong, Japanese and Korean manufacturing sectors.

The current study used frontier coefficients; the second sensitivity test compares its findings with results gained from the use of mean coefficients with no random effect, based on the conventional econometric approach. On the basis of the mean coefficients in Table 4.6, along with the three capital depreciation rates and labour quality adjustment indices, the result of a

Table 6.7   Sensitivity analyses for Singapore's TFP growth estimates, 1970–97

Labour quality indices (%)	Depreciation rate (%)	Output growth (%)	Input growth (%)	TFP growth (%)	TE change (%)	Tech. progress (%)	Annual TFP growth (%)
1.6	**17.68**	**252.6**	**274.8**	**–22.1**	**6.8**	**–29.0**	**–0.8**
	20	252.6	272.5	–19.9	8.9	–28.8	–0.7
	25	252.6	268.4	–15.8	12.7	–28.4	–0.6
	30	252.6	265.2	–12.5	15.6	–28.1	–0.5
1.0	17.68	252.6	266.2	–13.6	15.4	–29.0	–0.5
	20	252.6	264.0	–11.3	17.5	–28.8	–0.4
	25	252.6	259.9	–7.2	21.2	–28.4	–0.3
	30	252.6	256.6	–4.0	24.1	–28.1	–0.1
0.5	17.68	252.6	259.1	–6.5	22.5	–29.0	–0.2
	20	252.6	256.8	–4.2	24.6	–28.8	–0.2
	25	252.6	252.7	–0.1	28.3	–28.4	0.0
	30	252.6	249.5	3.2	31.3	–28.1	0.1
0	17.68	252.6	251.9	0.7	29.7	–29.0	0.0
	20	252.6	249.6	3.0	31.8	–28.8	0.1
	25	252.6	2.455	7.1	35.5	–28.4	0.3
	30	252.6	2.423	10.3	38.5	–28.1	0.4

Notes:
1. Figures may not add up precisely due to rounding.
2. The results above are derived from the estimated frontier coefficients in Table 4.6. If the new labour and capital inputs are used to generate new frontier coefficients, it is believed that the new frontier coefficients and the results of using them will be very similar to Tables 4.6 and 6.7 respectively.
3. The result from this study is shown in bold.
4. If a lower depreciation rate of 9.25 per cent is used for Singapore, TFP growth over the 1970–97 period becomes –33.4 per cent, that is, –1.2 per cent per annum.

sensitivity test for TFP growth estimates as demonstrated in Table 6.8 turns out to be parallel to Table 6.7. The three average annual TFP growth estimates in Table 6.8 increase uniformly by approximately 0.2 per cent and the TFP growth rates of the manufacturing sector over the period 1970–97 rise by 6–7 per cent. Moreover, it is shown that the mean production frontier technology over the period 1970–97 changed very little, represented by the insignificant technological decline of 0.1 per cent, if the labour quality adjustment index and depreciation rate remain as usual (1.6 per cent and

0.1768).   But there was considerable deterioration in technical efficiency, which indicates that actual output in 1997 was further away from the average production frontier.

Table 6.8   *Sensitivity analyses for Singapore's TFP growth estimates using frontier coefficients versus conventional mean coefficients in Singapore, 1970–97*

Labour quality indices (%)	Depreciation rate (%)	Output growth (%)	Input growth (%)	TFP growth (%)	TE change (%)	Tech. progress (%)	Annual TFP growth (%)
1.6	**17.68**	**252.6**	**274.8**	**–22.1**	**6.8**	**–29.0**	**–0.8**
1.6	17.68	252.6	268.3	–15.7	–15.6	–0.1	–0.6
	20	252.6	266.1	–13.5	–13.7	0.2	–0.5
	25	252.6	262.2	–9.6	–10.3	0.8	–0.4
	30	252.6	259.1	–6.4	–7.7	1.3	–0.2
1.0	17.68	252.6	259.8	–7.2	–7.1	–0.1	–0.3
	20	252.6	257.6	–5.0	–5.2	0.2	–0.2
	25	252.6	253.7	–1.0	–1.8	0.8	0.0
	30	252.6	250.5	2.1	0.8	1.3	0.1
0.5	17.68	252.6	252.6	0.0	0.0	–0.1	0.0
	20	252.6	250.4	2.2	2.0	0.2	0.1
	25	252.6	246.5	6.1	5.4	0.8	0.2
	30	252.6	243.4	9.3	8.0	1.3	0.3
0	17.68	252.6	245.4	7.2	7.2	–0.1	0.3
	20	252.6	243.2	9.4	9.2	0.2	0.3
	25	252.6	239.3	13.3	12.5	0.8	0.5
	30	252.6	236.2	16.4	15.2	1.3	0.6

Notes: As in Table 6.7.

Note that the composition of TFP growth in Table 6.7, namely technical efficiency change and technological progress, differs significantly from that in Table 6.8. Intuitively, the former implies that the best practice production frontier in Singapore moved downwards, bringing the actual output closer to the production frontier and, as a result, technical efficiency improved by 6.8 per cent while technological progress fell by 29 per cent. Nonetheless, the latter shows that there was little change (–0.1 per cent) in mean frontier production technology.

More importantly, it should be stressed that the modelling of industry-specific characteristics in the frontier production function is theoretically favourable. Because the conventional stochastic frontier approach does not take industry-specific characteristics into account and simply assumes that the application of production technology is identical across industries, it is fundamentally flawed. Finally, the sensitivity analyses show that there is no significant change in the TFP growth estimates using three different labour adjustment indices and capital depreciation rates, which explicitly confirms that the empirical results of this study are robust.

6.5   COMPARISONS WITH EARLIER TFP STUDIES

This section compares the findings of this study with earlier TFP studies of the manufacturing industries in East Asia. In general, the comparison will be carried out at the manufacturing sector level rather than the industry level, although the detailed TFP growth estimates are available in Tables 6.11 to 6.15. Although there is a wide range of TFP studies on East Asia in the literature, many of them focus on the economy level or manufacturing level.[7] Except for Young (1995) and Timmer and Szirmai (2000), comparative TFP studies among East Asian manufacturing sectors are few. The following comparison with earlier TFP studies for manufacturing industries begins with East Asia as a whole, followed by the industries of Hong Kong, Japan, Korea, Singapore and Taiwan.

6.5.1   Comparison for East Asia

Table 6.9 summarises the components of output growth for the five East Asian manufacturing sectors. Korea enjoyed the highest annual output and input growth rates of 14.5 per cent and 10.9 per cent respectively, followed by Singapore with 9.4 per cent and 10.2 per cent respectively. Hong Kong's manufacturing sector experienced negative output and input growth due to the partial relocation of its manufacturing production to mainland China from the mid-1980s. The largest gain in TFP growth occurred in Korea with 3.6 per cent a year, followed by Hong Kong with 2.7 per cent and Japan with 2.5 per cent. Taiwan achieved little TFP growth, at 0.2 per cent and Singapore's manufacturing sector was the only sector that experienced negative TFP growth, of –0.8 per cent, in East Asia.

Table 6.9   Decomposition   of   output   growth   for   five   East   Asian
             manufacturing sectors

Country	Period	Output growth (%)	Input growth (%)	TFP growth (%)	TE change (%)	Tech. progress (%)
Hong Kong	1976–97	−0.3	−3.1	2.7	0.3	2.5
Japan	1965–98	4.8	2.3	2.5	−1.0	3.5
Korea	1970–97	14.5	10.9	3.6	1.1	2.5
Singapore	1970–97	9.4	10.2	−0.8	0.3	−1.1
Taiwan	1981–99	6.5	6.3	0.2	−0.2	0.4

Sources: From earlier tables presented in Chapters 5 and 6.

Technical efficiency improvement played an important role in TFP growth
in Korea and Taiwan (over the 1981–91 period, see Table 6.6). On the other
hand, deterioration in the level of technical efficiency was responsible for the
drastic slowdown of TFP growth in Taiwan in the 1990s. In other words, a
significant improvement in technical efficiency could raise TFP growth but
failure to maintain the technical efficiency level could also lower TFP growth,
as evidenced in the Japanese case. On examining the contribution to TFP
growth, technological progress has been crucial in the manufacturing sectors
of Hong Kong, Japan, Korea and Taiwan. In the case of Japan and Taiwan,
TFP growth was entirely due to technological progress while the decline in
technological progress was the main cause of negative TFP growth in
Singapore.

Despite the use of different methodologies, the findings of this study have
coincided with some recent empirical studies of East Asian manufacturing
sectors. Table 6.10 presents a brief comparison between this study, Young
(1995) and Timmer and Szirmai (2000). Regrettably, Hong Kong and Japan
are not covered in these two studies. However, this study revealed that the
Hong Kong and Japanese manufacturing sectors enjoyed 2.7 per cent and 2.5
per cent annual TFP growth respectively, over the 1976–97 and 1965–98
periods. For Korea, this study found average annual TFP growth of 3.6 per
cent over the period 1970–97, which is between the 4.5 per cent of Timmer
and Szirmai (2000) and the 3.0 per cent found by Young (1995). As for
Singapore's manufacturing sector, the current study found an average annual
TFP growth rate of −0.8 per cent during the 1970–97 period, which is in line
with the −1.0 per cent of Young (1995).

Table 6.10   Estimates of TFP growth for manufacturing sectors in East Asia

Country	Period	This study	Timmer and Szirmai (2000)	Young (1995)
Hong Kong	1976–97	2.7	—	—
Japan	1965–98	2.5	—	—
Korea	1970–97	3.6	4.5 (1963–93)	3.0 (1966–90)
Singapore	1970–97	−0.8	—	−1.0 (1970–90)
	1975–97	0.4	—	−1.1 (1980–90)
Taiwan	1981–99	0.2	2.0 (1963–93)	1.4 (1966–90)
	1981–91	2.8	—	2.7 (1980–90)

Notes:
1. The figures in parentheses denote the sample period.
2. The TFP growth of the manufacturing sector in Timmer and Szirmai (2000) is at the aggregate level and is not output–weighted TFP growth and the result for the Korean manufacturing sector excludes firms with less than five people. For Taiwan, their study includes all firms.

Sources: Timmer and Szirmai (2000, p. 380, Table 2); Young (1995, p. 660, Table VII and p. 661, Table III).

For Taiwan, the sample period of this study differs from those of Young (1995) and Timmer and Szirmai (2000).[8] As shown in Table 6.10, this study suggests that Taiwan's manufacturing sector achieved 2.8 per cent and 0.2 per cent annual TFP growth over the periods 1981–91 and 1981–99 respectively. Because the slowdown of TFP growth in Taiwan's manufacturing sector occurred after 1991, as indicated in Figure 5.6, the estimated annual TFP growth rates of 2.0 per cent and 1.4 per cent over the periods 1963–93 and 1966–90 by Timmer and Szirmai (2000) and Young (1995) respectively, appear to be higher than this study's finding of 0.2 per cent over the period 1981–99. However, if the period of TFP slowdown, 1992–99, is excluded, the finding of 2.8 per cent annual TFP growth in this study for the period 1981–91 is consistent with the 2.7 per cent over the 1980–90 period reported by Young (1995). Finally, it should be noted that this study derives the (weighted) TFP growth estimates for each manufacturing sector in East Asia while Young (1995) estimates TFP growth by employing aggregate data at the manufacturing level. Quite often, differences may arise because of aggregation problems. A detailed comparison for each economy is presented next.

6.5.2 Comparison for Hong Kong

Despite having done relatively less empirical work on TFP, Kwong *et al.* (2000) offer a comprehensive study for Hong Kong's manufacturing industries. Table 6.11 provides a detailed comparison between Kwong *et al.* (2000) and this study. In spite of 15 out of 29 industries recording TFP growth, they found evidence that the overall manufacturing sector experienced a surprising decline of 13.8 per cent in TFP during 1984–93, due to the rapid relocation of manufacturing production to mainland China. In contrast, this study, which examines the performance of 21 industries, suggests a somewhat optimistic result of 23.3 per cent TFP growth over the same period. In some industries, such as the beverages, wearing apparel and rubber industries, the TFP growth estimates are comparable to some extent between the two studies with respect to signs and magnitudes. However, there are large differences in other industries, such as non-metallic minerals, basic metals, non-electrical machinery and transport equipment.

Except for 1989–90, the annual TFP growth rate for the entire manufacturing sector suggested by Kwong *et al.* (2000, p. 186, Table 2) appeared to be stable at roughly between –3 per cent and 1 per cent, whereas, as indicated earlier in Figure 5.1, this study shows that annual TFP growth fluctuated significantly. Overall, there are substantial differences between the two studies during the 1984–87 period due to the different methodologies and measurements of manufacturing output. Kwong *et al.* (2000) use 'gross output' instead of value added and implicitly claim that the use of value added would overstate the true contribution of factor inputs in Hong Kong.[9] Other TFP studies on Hong Kong's manufacturing industries, such as Imai (2001) and Tuan and Ng (1995), are incomplete and have already been described in Chapter 2. Their results are not reiterated here.

6.5.3 Comparison for Japan

Table 6.12 reports a comparison of the current study with some of the earlier TFP studies for Japan's manufacturing industries. With respect to individual industries, this study finds that the average annual TFP growth rates for the industrial chemicals and other chemicals industries over the period 1965–98 were 2.8 per cent and 2.9 per cent respectively, which are higher than that of an earlier study by Kumbhakar *et al.* (2000), indicating a TFP growth rate of 1.553 per cent to 1.716 per cent for the chemical industry during the period 1968–87.

Table 6.11   TFP growth estimates for manufacturing industries in Hong Kong

Industry	Kwong *et al.* (2000) 1984–93	This study 1984–93	This study 1976–97
Food manufacturing	50.641	20.3	61.1
Beverages	57.093	43.6	19.2
Tobacco manufacturing	−38.376	—	—
Wearing apparel	10.653	12.2	48.8
Textiles	42.498	9.0	38.9
Leather products	9.220	37.0	86.1
Footwear (non-rubber)	−11.068	−72.4	−21.8
Wood and cork products	−5.626	10.3	46.6
Furniture (non-metal)	−1.700	11.8	36.3
Paper and paper products	16.938	38.9	50.2
Printing and publishing	69.813	30.6	56.0
Chemicals	−64.548	28.3	56.4
Petroleum and coal[#]	−80.850	—	—
Rubber	35.674	35.5	69.0
Plastics	−25.692	18.3	63.2
Non-metallic minerals	−37.367	68.4	84.8
Basic metals	−18.314	57.0	33.8
Fabricated metals	18.189	39.0	66.8
Non-electrical machinery*	−40.745	22.7	83.0
Office machinery[$]	−1.882	—	—
Consumer electronics*	17.079	36.3	97.4
Radio, TV, comm. equipment[$]	1.475	—	—
Electrical and electronic parts*	18.604	—	—
Electronic parts and components[$]	26.626	—	—
Electrical apparatus, electronic toys[$]	−4.677	—	—
Scientific equipment	10.117	31.3	51.5
Transport equipment	−52.739	41.9	59.0
Other machinery[$]	30.221	13.0	51.5
Others (products not classified)	−54.587	—	—
Manufacturing	−13.827	23.3	57.4

Notes: 1. (#) The sample period is from 1988–93, (*) from 1984–89 and ($) from 1990–93.
2. The electrical and electronic parts industry includes parts, machinery and parts and the electronic parts and components industry include circuit boards.
Source: Kwong *et al.* (2000, p. 188, Table 3).

Table 6.12   TFP growth estimates for manufacturing industries in Japan

Industry	This study	Jorgenson *et al.* (1987b)	Griliches and Mairesse (1990)	Denny *et al.* (1992)	Nakajima *et al.* (1998)
	1965–98	1960–79	1973–80	1954–88	1964–88
311 Food products	2.1	−1.23	0.7	0.23	2.167
313 Beverages	4.1	as food	as food	as food	as food
314 Tobacco	—	—	—	—	—
321 Textiles	2.9	0.29	—	2.40	2.281
322 Wearing apparel	2.2	1.01	—	—	5.027
323 Leather products	2.5	0.67	—	—	3.996
324 Footwear	2.9	—	—	—	—
331 Wood products	2.7	1.88	—	—	2.313
332 Furniture	2.8	1.01	—	—	4.135
341 Paper and paper product	2.1	0.88	—	1.26	2.961
342 Printing, publishing	2.7	−0.08	—	—	—
351 Industrial chemicals	2.8	2.45	0.6	1.99	2.956
352 Other chemicals	2.9	—	—	—	—
353 Petroleum refineries	0.6	−3.16	—	1.42	5.489
354 Miscellaneous petrol.	2.4	—	—	—	—
355 Rubber products	2.4	0.59	as chemical	—	4.627
356 Plastic products	2.8	—	—	—	as rubber
361 Pottery, china, earth.	2.1	1.20	—	1.35	3.196
362 Glass and glass products	1.9	as pottery	—	as pottery	as pottery
369 Other non-metallic	3.0	as pottery	—	as pottery	as pottery
371 Iron and steel	2.8	0.90	1.6	1.14	4.480
372 Non-ferrous metals	1.8	0.12	as iron	as iron	3.759
381 Fabricated metal prod.	2.6	1.91	—	2.05	3.218
382 Non-electrical mach.	2.9	1.29	4.6	1.85	2.707
383 Electric machinery	1.9	3.28	8.4	3.23	5.186
384 Transport equipment	2.0	3.07	4.4	2.05	4.332
385 Professional equip.	3.2	2.63	8.1	3.28	4.324
390 Other manufactured	2.5	2.89	1.7	1.87	—
300 Manufacturing	2.5	0.83	3.6	1.86	3.731

Notes:
1. Thirteen industries covered in Denny *et al.* (1992) are not parallel to other studies due to industry aggregation; in particular, miscellaneous manufacturing industry contains eight industries. The detail of aggregation is available in Denny *et al.* (1992, p. 589).
2. The average annual TFP growth rates for the manufacturing sector in Nakajima *et al.* (1998), Denny *et al.* (1992) and Jorgenson *et al.* (1987b) reported here are simple averages of individual industries. Since these results are not weighted by industry share in manufacturing GDP, they must be interpreted with caution.

Source: The estimates in Nakajima *et al.* (1998) are from p. 325, Table 2; in Denny *et al.* (1992) from p. 590, Table 1; in Jorgenson *et al.* (1987b) from pp. 12–15, Table II; and in Griliches and Mairesse (1990) from p. 325, Table 11.5.

According to the studies reported in Table 6.12, all industries enjoyed varying rates of positive TFP growth, with the exception of three industries with negative TFP growth in Jorgenson *et al.* (1987b). Significant TFP growth was seen in the electric machinery (8.4 per cent) and professional equipment (8.1 per cent) industries in Griliches and Mairesse (1990). The professional equipment industry was reported to have had relatively higher TFP growth and, except for Nakajima *et al.* (1998), most studies described the petroleum refineries industry as experiencing relatively lower TFP growth.

As for the entire manufacturing sector, TFP growth ranges from 0.83 per cent in Jorgenson *et al.* (1987b) to 3.73 per cent in Nakajima *et al.* (1998). Unlike other studies, the current study extends the sample period to the 1990s, which was characterised as a period of economic recession and slowdown in TFP growth. Hence the average annual TFP growth estimates reported in this study are lower than those of Griliches and Mairesse (1990) and Nakajima *et al.* (1998). On the other hand, the TFP growth estimate of this study for the overall manufacturing sector is substantially higher than that of Norsworthy and Malmquist (1983), Jorgenson *et al.* (1987b) and Morrison (1990a), but is similar to Prasad (1997) and Sato (2002), who also extend the sample period to the 1990s.

6.5.4 Comparison for Korea

Table 6.13 presents a comparison of recent TFP studies on Korea's manufacturing industries. Apart from the study by Kim (2000) and the glass industry in Dollar and Sokoloff (1990), all studies indicate that TFP growth was positive across industries over the different periods of time. It should be mentioned that the classification of industries differs in several studies. For instance, paper and printing are considered as one industry in Pilat (1995), Okuda (1997) and Kim and Han (2001) but are considered separately in this study. Moreover, compared with the industrial classification of the UNIDO database, which has 28 industries at the 3-digit level, Kim (2000) covers 36 manufacturing industries. As a result, some of his TFP growth estimates are simply averages and need to be interpreted with caution. More specific details are available in the notes to Table 6.13.

With the use of different time periods and methodologies, the annual TFP growth rates for individual industries vary a great deal across the studies, from –1.7 per cent in Kim (2000) to over 7 per cent in Dollar and Sokoloff (1990) for the food industry. Another example is the leather industry, ranging from 1.1 per cent in Kim (2000) to 12.7 per cent in Dollar and Sokoloff (1990). Except for Kim (2000), there is some consensus regarding the extent of TFP growth for a number of industries. For instance, the average annual TFP growth rate for wearing apparel was over 3 per cent and for the non-electrical machinery industry over 4 per cent.

With respect to the entire manufacturing sector, Kim (2000) claimed that the Korean manufacturing sector experienced a small annual TFP growth rate of 0.5 per cent between 1966 and 1988, whereas the average annual TFP growth estimates ranged from 3.2 per cent in Okuda (1997) to 7.3 per cent in Kim and Han (2001). This comparison for the Korean manufacturing sector is not exhaustive. The TFP growth estimates at the manufacturing level are also available in Kwon (1986), Kang and Kwon (1993), Park and Kwon (1995), Young (1995), Hwang (1998), Kwack (2000), Timmer and Szirmai (2000), Yuhn and Kwon (2000) and so on; see Chapter 2 for details.[10]

6.5.5 Comparison for Singapore

Table 6.14 shows a comparison of TFP studies for Singapore's manufacturing industries. The estimated annual TFP growth rates for the manufacturing sector range from –0.8 per cent in this study to 2.8 per cent in Leung (1997). Given the double-digit output growth, Tsao (1985) found that TFP grew at only 0.08 per cent annually. Wong and Gan (1994) and Leung (1997) both claimed that Singapore's manufacturing sector made slight TFP progress in the 1980s despite the economic recession in 1985. Nonetheless, by using a longer data set, this study suggests that Singapore's manufacturing sector experienced an average annual TFP growth rate of –0.8 per cent between 1970 and 1997, which is consistent with Young (1995), who estimates –1 per cent TFP growth over the 1970–90 period.

As in the Korean manufacturing industries, the TFP growth estimates at the industry level vary widely. On the basis of Tsao (1985), Wong and Gan (1994) and this study, the electrical machinery industry, regarded as high-tech, experienced negative TFP growth. By contrast, it gained substantial TFP progress according to Leung (1997), Bloch and Tang (1999) and Koh *et al.* (2002). Such inconsistent TFP growth estimates also appear in other industries, for example leather and industrial chemicals.

Table 6.13   TFP growth estimates for manufacturing industries in Korea

Industry	This study	Nishimizu and Robinson (1984)	Dollar and Sokoloff (1990)	Pilat (1995)	Okuda (1997)	Kim (2000)	Kim and Han (2001)
	1970–97	1960–77	1963–79	1967–87	1970–93	1966–88	1980–94
311 Food products	2.7	5.26	7.2	0.7	3.3	-1.7	7.1
313 Beverages	—	—	6.5	—	—	2.0	—
314 Tobacco	—	—	8.0	—	—	6.4	—
321 Textiles	4.3	4.51	4.5	5.4	3.0	0.7[a]	7.7
322 Wearing apparel	4.3	1.62	9.3	1.5	—	0.7	—
323 Leather products	4.1	2.80	12.7	3.1	—	1.1	—
324 Footwear	2.8	—	—	—	—	as leather	—
331 Wood products	4.9	5.62	3.0	7.0	—	0.4	—
332 Furniture	3.0	4.88	9.2	—	—	as wood	—
341 Paper and paper products	4.0	4.52	0.9	6.8	4.4	-0.7	5.4
342 Printing, publishing	4.2	—	6.0	—	—	-2.3	—
351 Industrial chemicals	3.3	4.49	1.2	2.1	1.5	2.6	6.1
352 Other chemicals	2.7	—	12.6	—	—	-1.0	—
353 Petroleum refinery	—	0.68	10.8	—	0.0	-0.4	—
354 Miscellaneous petroleum	2.4	—	—	—	—	0.2	—
355 Rubber products	3.9	5.88	8.3	7.5	—	0.5	—
356 Plastic products	1.4	—	10.2	as rubber	—	1.5	—
361 Pottery, china, earthenware	8.3	4.33	3.6	2.6	1.6	1.2	5.1
362 Glass and glass products	2.5	—	-4.1	—	—	-0.4	—

369 Other non-metallic	5.7	—	0.1	—	—	0.0	—
371 Iron and steel	3.1	1.87	2.5	2.3	8.4	0.3	5.8
372 Non-ferrous metals	6.1	—	8.1	—	—	-0.6	—
381 Fabricated metal products	3.7	6.01	10.4	—	—	1.0	9.4
382 Non-electrical	4.2	5.73	6.2	9.7	7.6	2.1[b]	—
383 Electric machinery	3.5	7.25	10.4	10.4	3.8	-1.1[c]	—
384 Transport equipment	2.8	5.10	8.7	—	6.0	-0.4[d]	—
385 Professional equipment	5.6	—	8.0	—	—	4.6	—
390 Other manufactured	2.7	—	—	8.2	0.7	1.5	—
300 Manufacturing	3.6	3.71	6.1	4.3	3.2	0.5	7.3

Notes:

1. The following figures in parentheses denote average annual TFP growth estimates. (a) This result is derived from a simple average of three industries: fibre yarn and textile fabrics (0.01), fabric products (–0.02) and other fabricated textiles (0.03). (b) The estimate consists of three industries: power generating machinery (0.030), metalworking and industrial machinery (0.019) and office and other general machinery (0.015). (c) This estimate includes four industries: electrical industrial apparatus (–0.008), electronic and commercial equipment (0.026), household electrical appliances (–0.045) and other electrical equipment (–0.015). (d) The estimate constitutes shipbuilding and repairing (–0.012), railroad vehicles (0.007), motor vehicles (0.002), and aircraft and transport equipment (–0.013).

2. The empirical result of Kim and Han (2001) is based on the manufacturing firms listed on the Korean Stock Exchange and subsequently grouped into seven industries at the 2-digit level. The seven industries are wood, textiles, paper, chemical, non-metal, basic metal and fabrication.

3. Okuda (1997) regrouped the 28 Korean manufacturing industries into 11 industries in his paper. For more details, see Okuda (1997, p. 380).

4. The industry entitled 'manufactures, n.e.c.' in Dollar and Sokoloff (1990) cannot be matched with this study; hence it is assumed to be the professional equipment industry.

5. Nishimizu and Robinson (1984) examined 16 Korean manufacturing industries.

Sources: The result in Kim (2000) is from p. 77, Table 7; in Nishimizu and Robinson (1984) from p. 201, Table A.1; in Pilat (1995) from p. 141, Table 8; in Kim and Han (2001) from p. 277, Table 4; in Okuda (1997) from p. 364, Table I; and in Dollar and Sokoloff (1990) from p. 319, Table 4.

The studies by Rao and Lee (1995) and Mahadevan and Kalirajan (2000) coincidently excluded the 1984–87 period of economic recession. After estimating TFP growth for two separate periods, their results contradict each other. Rao and Lee (1995) indicated that Singapore's manufacturing sector experienced –0.4 per cent TFP growth over the 1976–84 period but Mahadevan and Kalirajan (2000) arrived at an average annual TFP growth of 0.92 per cent for the same period. The results remain inconsistent over the later period 1987–94, that is, 3.2 per cent in Rao and Lee (1995) versus –0.52 per cent in Mahadevan and Kalirajan (2000). In line with Tsao (1985) and Young (1995), the conclusion emerging from the current study indicates that TFP growth in Singapore over the past two and a half decades was negligible but the extent of TFP decline abated gradually in later years. While Tsao (1985), Young (1995), Huff (1999) and Ermisch and Huff (1999) have offered a number of explanations for the causes of negative TFP growth, case studies on individual industries, for example the electric machinery (electronics) industry, will contribute more insight to this controversial debate. Likewise, Koh *et al.* (2002) estimate that TFP growth for the overall manufacturing sector was 2.7 per cent on an annual basis over the period 1975–98.

6.5.6 Comparison for Taiwan

Table 6.15 reports a comparison of the current study with some of the earlier TFP studies for Taiwan's manufacturing industries.[11] Despite the similarities and differences revealed in this table, these results must be interpreted with care because the estimated TFP growth rates are derived from different sample periods, methodologies and industrial classifications. For example, Okuda (1994) aggregated 18 industries into 11, and using firm-level data, Aw *et al.* (2001) grouped Taiwan's firms into 11 industries at the 2-digit level.

The current study finds an average annual TFP growth rate of 2.8 per cent for Taiwan's manufacturing sector between 1981 and 1991, which is parallel to many earlier studies, such as Okuda (1994), Young (1995), Liang and Jorgenson (1999), and Färe *et al.* (2001). For the period 1981–99, this study shows that the average annual TFP growth rate fell to only 0.2 per cent, implying a dramatic slowdown of TFP growth over the last decade. In contrast, Hu and Chan (1999) and the report by DGBAS (Republic of China, 2000) optimistically recorded average annual 3.1 per cent and 1.9 per cent TFP growth rates for the manufacturing sector over the periods 1979–96 and 1978–98 respectively. With regard to the extent of TFP growth for individual industries, there appears to be a consensus. For instance, the precision instruments industry experienced negative TFP growth, and apart from Liang (1995), all studies reported that the electronics industry achieved reasonable TFP progress, ranging from 1.7 per cent in this study to 5 per cent in Okuda (1994).

Table 6.14   TFP   growth   estimates   for   manufacturing   industries   in   Singapore

Industry	This study	Tsao (1985)	Wong and Gan (1994)	Leung (1997)	Bloch and Tang (1999)	Koh *et al.* (2002)
	1970–97	1970–79	1981–90	1983–93	1975–94	1975–98
311 Food products	0.1	0.62	1.51	3.0	—	−0.4
313 Beverages	−1.1	1.73	−2.14	−1.0	—	as food
314 Tobacco	—	3.22	11.22	−1.3	4.85	as food
321 Textiles	1.9	−3.23	−5.21	4.8	—	2.6
322 Wearing apparel	−0.4	−2.11	2.05	1.6	−0.94	0.6
323 Leather products	1.5	−3.06	−4.67	3.0	0.27	−0.4
324 Footwear	0.8	−9.91	0.49	5.8	5.61	as leather
331 Wood products	−0.3	−6.57	−4.59	5.3	0.29	1.8
332 Furniture	−1.7	−2.44	−2.01	3.3	—	—
341 Paper and paper products	0.9	2.18	−3.97	3.4	−4.78	1.9
342 Printing and publish.	0.9	−1.36	0.35	−1.2	0.07	1.4
351 Industrial chemicals	−0.4	−0.24	−2.99	2.4	4.03	0.8
352 Other chemicals	—	4.80	2.48	7.3[d]	−5.61	as chemical
353 Petroleum refineries	—	—	—	2.6	0.73	0.3
354 Miscellaneous petrol.	—	1.49	2.64	—	as petrol.	as petrol.
355 Rubber products	−1.8	−1.57	−4.65	3.0	−0.82	2.5
356 Plastic products	−0.6	−3.16	−6.07	4.5	−7.46	as rubber
361 Pottery, china, earth.	1.0	−3.03	−19.67[b]	−3.0	—	1.2
362 Glass and glass products	as pottery	as pottery	as pottery	as pottery	—	as pottery
369 Other non-metallic	1.0	−1.17[a]	−4.71[c]	4.1[e]	—	as pottery
371 Iron and steel	−2.4	3.41	−0.77	0.6	1.17	0.9
372 Non-ferrous metals	−1.9	−13.87	2.81	0.8	—	as iron
381 Fabricated metals	−1.9	−3.59	−3.35	3.8	−3.46	1.0
382 Non-electrical mach.	0.1	−3.28	−2.32	4.3	0.22	4.0
383 Electric machinery	−3.2	−0.04	−0.54	3.8[f]	6.54	3.7[f]
384 Transport equipment	−0.8	1.27	5.56	3.7	0.00	4.8
385 Professional equip.	3.5	—	0.39	2.3	−2.46	6.6

Table 6.14   (continued)

390 Other manufactured	1.6	—	—	0.8	−8.14	—
300 Manufacturing	−0.8	0.80	1.60	2.8	—	2.7

Notes:
1. (a) This is a simple average of the annual TFP growth rates for concrete, structural clay and cement products, which were −0.0536, −0.0563 and −0.0378 respectively. (b) This figure is from Wong (1993) because it is not reported in Wong and Gan (1994). However, these TFP growth estimates are derived from the same author. (c) The average annual TFP growth rates for concrete, structural clay and cement products were 0.1072, −0.0554 and 0.0468 respectively. (d) This estimate is for the pharmaceutical industry. (e) The average annual TFP growth rates for the bricks/tiles, cement and concrete product industries were 0.049, 0.099 and 0.022 respectively. (f) This includes the electronics industry, which had an average annual TFP growth rate of 0.008.
2. In addition, Bloch and Tang (1999) used conventional growth accounting to estimate TFP growth for the 19 industries, which is available in Table 1, p. 700.

Sources: The result from Leung (1997) is from p. 526, Table 1; Bloch and Tang (1999) from p. 700, Table 1; Tsao (1985) from p. 29, Table 1; Wong and Gan (1994) from p. 182, Table 2; Bloch and Tang (1999) from p. 700, Table 1; and Koh *et al.* (2002) from p. 263, Table 4.

In terms of sources of TFP growth, Färe *et al.* (2001) pointed out that technological progress (2.56 per cent) accounted for most of the TFP growth (2.89 per cent) in Taiwan's manufacturing sector during the 1978–92 period. Yet this study demonstrates that the contribution of technical efficiency improvement to TFP growth outweighed that of technological progress over the period 1981–91, as shown in Table 6.6.

In summary, there are a number of reasons for the differences in the results of this study and earlier studies. First, in contrast to the growth accounting assumption of firms with full efficiency, the model used in this study makes allowance for inefficient behaviour by firms. Second, different approaches used to construct the production frontier may explain the discrepancies. The varying coefficients frontier approach used in this study considers the possibility of heterogeneous applications of production technology, and develops the concept of the best practice production frontier for individual industries. Conversely, the conventional stochastic frontier approach does not allow for industry-specific characteristics and applies constant capital and labour shares across industries, ignoring firms' heterogeneous behaviour in applying the best available technology. Finally, the adjustment of quality improvement embodied in capital and labour inputs has been cautiously employed by the current study using the estimates of Young (1995), whereas the earlier studies do not make this adjustment and therefore underestimate input growth and thus overstate TFP growth.

Table 6.15   TFP growth estimates for manufacturing industries in Taiwan

Industry	This study	This study	Chen and Tang (1990)	Liang (1995)	Liang and Jorgenson (1999)
	1981–99	1981–91	1968–82	1973–82	1982–93
Food processing	—	—	−0.15	4.32	3.09
Beverages and tobacco	—	—	0.88	0.05	4.76
Food, bev. and tobacco	−0.4	1.5	—	—	—
Textile mill products	−1.5	2.1	3.46	4.56	3.0
Wearing apparel, acces.*	−3.9	1.6	2.02	−2.88	−0.41
Leather, fur and products	−5.5	−1.5	4.13	4.91	−0.22
Wood and bamboo	1.5	4.8	−0.76	−17.44	0.57
Furniture and fixtures	2.7	3.1	—	as wood	as wood
Pulp, paper products	−4.3	−3.1	−0.01	−12.02	0.85
Printing processings	−4.0	−4.7	—	as paper	as paper
Chemical materials	3.9	6.6	−0.67	0.15	10.75
Chemical products	3.6	4.4	—	as chemical	3.32
Petroleum and coal	—	—	−0.63	−14.47	0.68
Rubber products	−2.3	1.2	2.07	−2.39	2.01
Plastic products	1.7	6.0	—	as chemical	−1.7
Non-metallic minerals	2.0	4.5	0.99	−1.37	4.51
Basic metal industries	1.9	5.3	0.04	0.02	8.58
Fabricated metals	−1.3	1.7	1.42	−3.96	1.45
Machinery and equipment	0.4	3.4	3.63	−0.01	4.75
Electrical and electronic	1.7	4.1	2.12	−1.68	4.44
Transport equipment	−2.2	2.4	2.26	−1.76	2.71
Precision instruments	−1.7	−0.1	—	—	—
Other industrial products	−1.6	−0.4	—	2.75	1.33
Manufacturing	0.2	2.8	—	0.12	2.72

Industry	Okuda (1994)	Hu and Chan (1999)	Republic of China (2000)	Färe et al. (2001)	Aw et al. (2001)
	1978–91	1979–96	1978–98	1978–92	1981–91
Food processing	—	—	0.9	4.84	—
Tobacco	—	—	1.7	—	—
Food, beverages	2.3	0.9	—	—	—

Table 6.15   (continued)

Textile mill products	3.9	2.2	2.0	5.74	3.17
Wearing apparel	2.1	1.9	-0.9	1.13	0.78
Leather, fur and products	2.8	1.5	-0.4	0.07	—
Wood and bamboo	2.1	1.7	1.7	0.12	—
Furniture and fixtures	—	as wood	as wood	as wood	—
Pulp, paper and products	0.5	-1.2	-1.5	1.72	—
Printing processings	—	as paper	as paper	as paper	—
Chemical materials	1.0	4.0	4.0	8.49	3.66
Chemical products	—	as chemical	as chemical	as chemical	—
Petroleum and coal	—	2.9	-2.3	—	—
Rubber products	—	as chemical	as chemical	3.13	—
Plastic products	—	as chemical	1.4	as chemical	2.38
Non-metallic minerals	1.0	2.0	2.0	3.80	—
Basic metal industries	1.2	1.3	1.9	5.28	2.85
Fabricated metals	—	2.2	0.9	1.41	1.04
Machinery and equipment	3.0	3.3	3.2	3.74	0.84
Electrical and electronic	5.0	2.9	3.6	4.68	3.46
Transport equipment	—	2.4	1.3	3.00	-0.39
Precision instruments	—	-2.5	-0.2	-0.66	—
Other industrial products	—	as precision	-2.1	0.27	—
Manufacturing	2.6	3.1	1.9	2.89	3.24

Notes:
1. The TFP growth rates for the periods 1961–73 and 1973–82 are available in Liang (1995) and for the period 1961–82 in Liang and Jorgenson (1999).
2. Asterisk (*) denotes the 1969–82 period in Chen and Tang (1990).
3. Liang and Jorgenson (1999) also calculated TFP growth using gross output, which is available in their paper (p. 277, Table 12.2).
4. The TFP growth estimates of Hu and Chan (1999) in this Table are calculated using employees as labour input; 'hours worked' as labour input is also available in their paper (p. 15, Table 1.1).
5. The estimates of DGBAS (Republic of China, 2000) are derived using value added with capital and labour inputs. Other results of DGBAS using gross output are available in Table 20 of the report.

Sources: The TFP growth estimates of Liang (1995) are from pp. 22–3, Table 3; of Chen and Tang (1990) from p. 580, Table 1; of Liang and Jorgenson (1999) from p. 277, Table 12.2; of Okuda (1994) from p. 438, Table I; of Hu and Chan (1999) from p. 32, Table 3; of DGBAS (Republic of China, 2000) from pp. 104–9, Table 19; of Färe *et al.* (2001) from p. 1919, Table 5; of Aw *et al.* (2001) from p. 76, Table 8.

NOTES

1. If the 1970–75 period is excluded, this study suggests that technical efficiency deterioration was the main cause of low TFP growth in Singapore over the 1975–97 period. This outcome is consistent with the findings of Mahadevan and Kalirajan (2000).
2. If the frontier production function was estimated with a small upward bias due to data or other unknown problems, thus obtaining a larger constant term and labour and capital frontier coefficients, the upward bias of the frontier production function would give rise to a smaller technical efficiency improvement but higher technological progress. As a result, there is little change in TFP growth estimates, implying that a large fluctuation in the estimated frontier coefficients has little impact on the calculation of TFP growth estimates.
3. This comparison was motivated by a conversation with Professor Nirvikar Singh.
4. The R&D expenditure ratio is also a good indicator in defining high-tech and low-tech industries, yet such data are unavailable. The ranking of the capital–labour ratio for manufacturing industries is based on Japan's data in 1990 and 1995. Although the capital–labour ratio for the other manufactured products industry is ranked at the 6th from the bottom, this study considers the textile industry (7th from the bottom) instead.
5. It should be noted that a 'zero' labour quality improvement index might not necessarily imply that there was no quality improvement in labour input at all. Provided that actual labour input 'hours worked' dropped sharply, the use of number of employees might overstate the actual labour input. The overstatement, say of 0.5 per cent, can be interpreted as labour quality improvement (0.5 per cent) if the labour quality adjustment index is set to be zero. Nevertheless, in this case the labour quality improvement index will be very small, but is unlikely to be zero. Yet, if the true labour input 'hours worked' has not changed over time, the zero labour quality adjustment index will indeed imply no quality improvement in labour input.
6. In addition, it is observed that when the capital depreciation rate is fixed, say at 0.20, an increase in the labour quality adjustment index only alters technical efficiency improvement and not technological progress because the calculation of technological progress is based on the initial capital and labour input.
7. Many existing TFP studies concentrate on the overall economy. For instance, in terms of cross-country TFP studies, see the World Bank (1993), Young (1994), Collins and Bosworth (1996) and Klenow and Rodriguez-Clare (1997); for TFP studies on East Asia and the Asia Pacific, refer to, among others, Kim and Lau (1994), Young (1995), Sarel (1995), Drysdale and Huang (1997), Gapinski (1997), Singh and Trieu (1999), Chang and Luh (1999) and Hsieh (1999, 2002).
8. The average annual TFP growth estimates of 4.5 per cent for Korea and 2 per cent for Taiwan's manufacturing sector are calculated at the aggregate level in Timmer and Szirmai (2000). The output–weighted sectoral TFP growth rates are estimated to be higher for Korea at 4.9 per cent per annum and lower for Taiwan at 1.7 per cent.
9. Kwong et al. (2000, p. 173) explain the reason for using gross output instead of value added in footnote 4.

10. It is worth pointing out that Park and Kwon (1995) and Hwang (1998) employ two different methods to obtain two different results.

11. It should be noted that some TFP studies for Taiwan's manufacturing sector are not included in Table 6.15. Chuang (1996) and Timmer and Szirmai (2000) provided TFP growth estimates only for the manufacturing sector. For details, see Chapter 2, TFP studies review for Taiwan.

7. Summary and conclusions

The findings of a number of studies that TFP growth had little to do with the economic miracle achieved by four East Asian countries have drawn considerable attention to this controversial debate. Although there is a consensus on the importance of TFP growth in the process of economic growth, the major concern of the debate is that different methods or assumptions used to calculate it have often led to different results. Despite the prevailing deficiencies and limitations, such as the assumptions of constant returns to scale, perfect competition and Hicks-neutral technology, growth accounting appears to have been the most popular approach used in the literature. Regardless of its wide popularity, it has recently been questioned as to whether is appropriate for shedding light on the role of technological progress in the East Asian economic miracle achieved by Hong Kong, Korea, Singapore and Taiwan (see Chen, 1997; Felipe, 1999; Nelson and Pack, 1999; Rodrigo, 2000). Furthermore, the use of TFP growth as synonymous with technological progress in the earlier growth accounting based studies concluded that the East Asian economies achieved insufficient technological progress.

   Using the data from the UNIDO Industrial Statistics Database at the 3-digit level and the varying coefficients frontier model outlined in Chapter 3, this study has examined whether TFP growth played a role in the manufacturing industries of Hong Kong, Japan, Korea, Singapore and Taiwan. Following Nishimizu and Page (1982), the decomposition of TFP growth into technological progress and change in technical efficiency is carried out. This book explicitly distinguishes TFP growth from technological progress as well as recognising the importance of technical efficiency in raising TFP growth in East Asian manufacturing.

7.1 SUMMARY OF THE MAIN RESEARCH FINDINGS

As seen in the literature review in Chapter 2, existing empirical results suggest no consensus on the issue of the role of TFP growth in the success of the East Asian manufacturing sectors. For Korea's manufacturing sector, the average annual TFP growth estimates vary extensively, ranging from –1.6 per cent in Park and Kwon (1995) to as high as 7.3 per cent in Kim and Han (2001). The empirical TFP studies on Singapore's manufacturing sector seem even more divided. Positive TFP growth was found for Singapore's manufacturing sector in Leung (1997) and Wong and Gan (1994), whereas Tsao (1985) and Young (1995) claimed that TFP growth was almost zero or negative. Unlike Singapore, there are relatively more studies confirming that Japan and Taiwan experienced various degrees of positive TFP growth.

The current study offers the following explanations for the discrepancies in the results reported on TFP growth by other studies. First, different methodologies have been used to calculate TFP growth, including the growth accounting, DEA (Malmquist productivity index) and stochastic frontier approaches. Although growth accounting has been applied frequently in many TFP studies, different specifications of the production function could have resulted in different outcomes. Second, different types and sources of data sets, for example firm-level and industry-level (aggregate) data, may have influenced the results. Third, industrial classifications and aggregations are not always the same, even for the same country, and could distort findings. Lastly, with regard to the construction and adjustment of variables, quality improvement embodied in labour and capital inputs has frequently been ignored, leading to overestimation of the extent of TFP growth in some studies; for example, the use of 'working hours' or 'number of employees' as the measure of labour input can give rise to a variety of conclusions.

Next, by using the varying coefficients frontier model instead of the conventional stochastic frontier approach (Aigner *et al.*, 1977) to calculate TFP growth, this study avoids the assumption of homogeneous behaviour in applying the best practice production technology across industries. Empirically, given the same levels of inputs, data often show that different levels of actual output are obtained, because different firms utilise their resources differently. In order to account for such differences, it is vital to take account of the heterogeneity of firms' behaviour and estimate the variations in both intercepts and slope coefficients across firms and over time for the same firm, namely reflecting a non-neutral shift in production frontier.

The specification of the varying coefficients frontier model is bolstered by the results of the Breusch–Pagan LM test, because the hypothesis of homogeneous industries is statistically rejected for the Korean and Singaporean manufacturing industries in most years. Although the results of the Breusch–Pagan LM test do not statistically favour the manufacturing industries of Hong Kong, Japan and Taiwan (see Table 4.2), in most cases there are certain variations in the estimated coefficients of labour input, indicating different applications of their human resources.

Third, the analysis of the sources of output growth reveals mixed results. This study finds evidence to support strongly the role of TFP growth in the manufacturing sectors of Hong Kong, Japan, Korea and Taiwan (only for the 1981–91 period). However, despite the fact that these countries enjoyed average annual TFP growth of 2.7 per cent, 2.5 per cent, 3.6 per cent and 2.8 per cent (1981–91) respectively, the study found that factor accumulation remains the most important factor in shedding light on output growth in the five East Asian manufacturing sectors.

More specifically, TFP growth contributed as much as 52 per cent to output growth in Japan, roughly 25 per cent in Korea and 38 per cent in Taiwan. Despite a drastic fall in input growth, Hong Kong suffered only a slight decline in output growth due to considerable TFP. On the other hand, the study finds that TFP growth played no role in the Singaporean manufacturing sector, having found an annual 0.8 per cent decline in Singapore's TFP over the 1970–97 period, although TFP growth improved slightly in the 1980s and 1990s in comparison to the early 1970s. Even when the 1970–74 period is removed, overall TFP growth in Singapore over the period 1975–97 remained around 0.4 per cent per annum, which is insignificant in comparison with the other four East Asian manufacturing sectors. In spite of vigorous sensitivity testing, the result for Singapore remains pessimistic.

Fourth, having decomposed TFP growth, this study was able to give due recognition to each component, namely technical progress and technical efficiency. It found that technological progress was completely responsible for raising TFP growth in Japan and was the main factor contributing to TFP growth for both Hong Kong and Korea's manufacturing sectors. Technical efficiency change accounted for only 10 and 30 per cent of TFP growth in Hong Kong and Korea respectively. Thus the decomposition analysis in this study reveals that Korean manufacturing industries have outperformed other nations in terms of applying both tangible (technology progress) and intangible (technical efficiency improvement) technologies. Singapore's negative TFP growth over the 1970–97 period was due mainly to a substantial technological decline, but if the 1970–74 period is excluded, technical efficiency deterioration was responsible. This was also the case for the slowdown of TFP growth in Taiwan, particularly in the 1990s.

Fifth, using the long-term trend analysis of the evolution of technological progress and technical efficiency change, the study has implicitly revealed the nexus between structural transformation and technological progress in the Japanese, Korean and Taiwanese manufacturing industries. In particular, these outcomes have significant implications for policy makers.

For Japan, the importance of technical efficiency improvement has gradually replaced the role of technological progress in the content of TFP growth. As production technology is at a mature stage in Japan, it is conjectured that technology upgrade has become costly, and one of the alternatives for maintaining future growth and competitiveness is to engage in improving technical efficiency. The long-term trend analysis indicates that over the 1970–97 period the Korean manufacturing sector not only upgraded technology (technological progress) but simultaneously mastered the new technology quickly (technical efficiency improvement). This explains why Korean industries could maintain both technological progress and technical efficiency improvement and enjoy remarkable TFP growth.

In contrast to Japan, this study suggests that Singapore's manufacturing industries failed to enhance TFP through technical efficiency improvement due to the continual adoption of the latest technology with no time lag to master it. In the case of Taiwan, it was found to experience downward-sloping trends in both technological progress and technical efficiency change; this implies a diminishing role played by TFP growth and questions future output growth in Taiwan's manufacturing sector.

7.2 LIMITATIONS OF THE ANALYSES

The findings of this study are subject to some limitations that could have a slight effect on the outcomes. First, capital utilisation is implicitly assumed to be constant in this study. If utilisation of capital input decreases over time, the growth of capital input will be overstated, leading to understatement of TFP growth, and vice versa. Furthermore, due to lack of data, this study adopts employee numbers as labour input instead of working hours. If working hours fell sharply over time, actual labour input could be overestimated, resulting in TFP growth being understated slightly.

Second, due to the lack of detailed data on the components of factor inputs, labour and capital quality adjustment indices are taken from the estimates of Young (1995). However, it is believed that the impact of quality adjustment indices on the TFP growth estimates is minimal, as demonstrated by the sensitivity tests.

Third, investment in physical and human capital generally depends on the extent of TFP growth. Higher TFP growth always encourages firms to invest more. As a result, the contribution of TFP growth to output growth should be higher if TFP-induced increases in inputs are regarded as part of TFP growth. However, this study does not consider the endogeneity effect on factor inputs. Finally, it was outside the scope of this research to allow for the implications of ongoing structural transformations or trade and industrial policies when assessing TFP growth for the five East Asian manufacturing sectors, although their impact on TFP growth would be evident in the 1990s. For instance, TFP growth in Hong Kong's manufacturing sector was heavily affected by the relocation of manufacturing production to mainland China and the diminishing manufacturing share in GDP. The estimated TFP growth for Korean manufacturing industries does not take account of the recent financial crisis and hence requires some modification before predicting the sustainability of future output growth.

The economic recession in Japan, which has been occurring for over a decade, has undoubtedly influenced the progress of technological upgrading in the manufacturing industries. For Taiwan, the official ban on cross-straits investment was lifted in 1991, triggering a massive outflow of capital, particularly to mainland China. Many of the firms in traditional labour-intensive industries transferred their production to mainland China to avoid rising wages and the appreciation of the New Taiwan Dollar and so on.

7.3   POLICY IMPLICATIONS AND FUTURE AGENDA

The role of TFP growth in East Asia is not only crucial for the future of the region but of particular importance for less developed countries because a successful experience can serve as a model for them to follow. After analysing the sources of output growth and TFP growth in Chapters 5 and 6, several policy implications can be drawn from the empirical findings of this study. First, slowdown of TFP growth was prevalent in the East Asian manufacturing sectors apart from Korea. Since TFP growth is critical to the sustainability of East Asian economic growth, this study recommends the adoption of more productive technologies and effective modes of management and organisation. As demonstrated earlier, TFP growth stems from a combination of technological progress and technical efficiency improvement, so this study suggests that policy makers facilitate the allocation of limited resources so as to raise TFP growth through both components. In other words, pursuing the latest technologies alone may not be the most cost-effective approach for raising TFP growth. This has often been ignored.

Second, according to a decomposition analysis, technological progress has had a downward trend in Japan and Taiwan, as seen in Figures 6.2 and 6.5, and has consequently undermined TFP growth significantly in the last decade. If technological decline is due to lack of investment in R&D, it is suggested that the implementation of an innovation policy, which offers tax concessions and research grants, may encourage technological innovation and diffusion.

Third, the downward-sloping trend of technical efficiency change in Figures 6.4 and 6.5 reveals that there was a considerable slowdown in TFP growth in the manufacturing sectors of Singapore and Taiwan. If the decline in technical efficiency is due to a lack of learning-by-doing effects, then policy should be aimed at ensuring the effectiveness of organisational management and job training. In addition, competition policy and market reforms may be useful in promoting the efficiency of production and eliminating inefficient operators.

It is hoped that the findings of this study can offer more understanding of the sources of TFP growth, facilitate the efficient allocation of resources and enhance the effectiveness of policy implementation. To explore this issue of TFP growth fully, more research is required to assess the current status of East Asian manufacturing. Hence a future agenda may include the discussion of why Japan's manufacturing industries have shifted their attention to intangible technology (technical efficiency improvement) rather than physical technology. Despite the recognition of substantial TFP progress in the 1980s for Taiwan's manufacturing industries, there is little consensus on the role of TFP growth in the 1990s due to the conflicting results between this study and studies by Hu and Chan (1999) and the DGBAS (Republic of China, 2000). Hence it is critical to uncover the reasons for TFP slowdown in Taiwan's manufacturing industries.

Finally, on the basis of the UNIDO database and the varying coefficients frontier model, this study has measured the extent of TFP growth for manufacturing industries in the five East Asian economies and analysed the proposed questions in detail. Yet, due to the limited data set, some of the findings may not be conclusive. Therefore, the completion of this study should not be viewed as an end to the research. Rather, based on these findings, this study indicates that more fieldwork and case studies of individual industries across East Asian countries are required to shed light on the success of the East Asian growth experience.

Appendix

A.1 THE UNIDO INDUSTRIAL STATISTICS AND INDUSTRY COVERAGE

The database is based on the International Standard Industrial Classification (ISIC) of All Economic Activities code (3-digit level) at Revision 2, which has 29 divisions, as shown in Table A1.1.

Table A1.1   ISIC codes

Code	Industry	Code	Industry
300	Total manufacturing	354	Miscellaneous petroleum and coal products
311	Food products	355	Rubber products
313	Beverages	356	Plastic products
314	Tobacco	361	Pottery, china, earthenware
321	Textiles	362	Glass and glass products
322	Wearing apparel, except footwear	369	Other non-metallic mineral products
323	Leather products	371	Iron and steel
324	Footwear, except rubber or plastic	372	Non-ferrous metals
331	Wood products, except furniture	381	Fabricated metal products
332	Furniture, except metal	382	Machinery, except electrical
341	Paper and paper products	383	Machinery, electric
342	Printing and publishing	384	Transport equipment
351	Industrial chemicals	385	Professional and scientific equipment
352	Other chemicals	390	Other manufactured products
353	Petroleum refineries		

A.2   GROWTH ACCOUNTING APPROACH

Following Jorgenson *et al.* (1987a) and Young (1995), value added is specified as a translog function of capital and labour inputs:

$$\ln Y = \alpha_0 + \alpha_K \ln K + \alpha_L \ln L + \alpha_T \cdot T + 1/2\,\beta_{KK}(\ln K)^2 + \beta_{KL} \ln K \ln L +$$
$$\beta_{KT} \ln K \cdot T + 1/2\beta_{LL}(\ln L)^2 + \beta_{LT} \ln L \cdot T + 1/2\,\beta_{TT} \cdot T^2, \tag{A2.1}$$

where Y, K, L and T denote value added, capital input, labour input and time. Under the assumption of constant returns to scale, the parameters satisfy the following conditions:

$$\alpha_K + \alpha_L = 1, \; \beta_{KK} + \beta_{KL} = \beta_{KT} + \beta_{LT} = \beta_{KL} + \beta_{LL} = 0. \tag{A2.2}$$

Because the data sets are only available at discrete points of time, say T and $T-1$, the growth rate of output can be expressed as a first difference of $\ln Y(T)$ and $\ln Y(T-1)$:

$$\ln Y(T) - \ln Y(T-1) = \overline{S}_K[\ln K(T) - \ln K(T-1)] + \overline{S}_L[\ln L(T) - \ln L(T-1)]$$
$$+ \overline{TFP}_T, \tag{A2.3}$$

where S_K and S_L represent the elasticities of output with respect to capital and labour inputs and $\overline{S}_i = [S_i(T) + S_i(T-1)]/2$, $i = K, L$ and $\overline{TFP}_T = [TFP(T) + TFP(T-1)]/2$. The expression of the average rate of technical change, $\overline{TFP}_{T+1}$, is also called the translog index of the rate of total factor productivity growth, where $TFP(T)$ and $TFP(T-1)$ denote the level of total factor productivity at time T and *T-1* respectively. The translog index is often referred to as the discrete version of the Divisia index or the Törnqvist index. Under the assumption of perfect competition, the elasticity with respect to each input is equal to its share in total factor payments. Since the sum of capital and labour shares is one, the capital share can be obtained by one minus the labour share.[1]

Because aggregate capital and labour inputs consist of a number of components such as machinery, transport equipment and buildings, aggregate capital and labour inputs are assumed to be the translog function of their components:

$$\ln K = \alpha_1^K \ln K_1 + \alpha_2^K \ln K_2 + \cdots + \alpha_M^K \ln K_M + 1/2 \beta_{11}^K (\ln K_1)^2 +$$
$$\beta_{12}^K \ln K_1 \ln K_2 + \cdots + 1/2 \beta_{MM}^K \ln(K_M)^2, \tag{A2.4}$$

$$\ln L = \alpha_1^L \ln L_1 + \alpha_2^L \ln L_2 + \cdots + \alpha_N^L \ln L_N + 1/2 \beta_{11}^L (\ln L_1)^2 +$$
$$\beta_{12}^L \ln L_1 \ln L_2 + \cdots + 1/2 \beta_{NN}^L \ln(L_N)^2. \tag{A2.5}$$

Similarly, under the assumption of constant returns to scale, the parameters in equation (A2.4) again satisfy the following conditions:[2]

$$\sum_p \alpha_p^K = 1 \text{ and } \sum_p \beta_{pq}^K = \sum_q \beta_{pq}^K = 0 \quad p \neq q \text{ and } p, q = 1, 2, \dots M \tag{A2.6}$$

Thus, taking first difference of the equations (A2.4) and (A2.5) provides the growth rates of aggregate capital and labour inputs as weighted averages of the growth rates of their subinputs:

$$\ln K(T) - \ln K(T-1) = \sum \bar{s}_{Km} [\ln K_m(T) - \ln K_m(T-1)], \tag{A2.7}$$

$$\ln L(T) - \ln L(T-1) = \sum \bar{s}_{Ln} [\ln L_n(T) - \ln L_n(T-1)], \tag{A2.8}$$

where $\bar{s}_{ij} = [s_{ij}(T+1) + s_{ij}(T)]/2$, $i = K, L$, $j = m, n$, $m = 1, 2, \dots M$ and $n = 1, 2, \dots N$. The elasticity of each aggregate input with respect to each of its component subinputs is denoted by s_{ij}; that is, assuming perfect competition, the share of each subinput in total payments to its aggregate factor. The expressions for the capital and labour input in equations (A2.7) and (A2.8) are considered as translog indices of capital and labour inputs. In fact, the indices adjust for quality improvement of aggregate capital and labour inputs. Jorgenson *et al.* (1987a) illustrate the importance of disaggregating the inputs by quality levels; for example, labour input is classified by sex, age, education, employment status and occupation of employees. As can be seen from equation (A2.8), the growth rate of aggregate labour input is a weighted average of the growth rates of subinputs, weights being the associated income shares, s_{Ln}. Hence, if the average education level rises over time, the procedure will capture the quality

Appendix173

improvement of labour input by assigning a higher weight for category n because of the higher wage, w_n.

Finally, if the TFP growth is interpreted as a shift in an aggregate production, the associated variables have to be measured as flows. Therefore, the flow of labour services is assumed to be proportional to total hours of work and the flow of capital services is proportional to the estimated capital stock, that is, $L_n(T) = \gamma_{Ln} H_n(T)$ and $K_m(T) = \gamma_{km} C_m(T)$, with

$$\ln K(T) - \ln K(T-1) = \sum \overline{s}_{Km}[\ln C_m(T) - \ln C_m(T-1)], \qquad (A2.9)$$

$$\ln L(T) - \ln L(T-1) = \sum \overline{s}_{Ln}[\ln H_n(T) - \ln H_n(T-1)], \qquad (A2.10)$$

where H_n and C_m denote the total hours of work and estimated capital stock respectively.

A.3   NUMBER OF INDUSTRIES AND SAMPLE PERIODS

The sample periods and number of industries examined in this study depend on the availability of data and the number of industries in the sample. Ideally, there are 28 industries at the 3-digit level for each country in the UNIDO database. In reality, the availability of data for each manufacturing sector varies from country to country. To be consistent, this study made the following adjustments depending on the nature of individual manufacturing sectors.

A3.1   Use of Aggregate Data

Due to the lack of firm-level data for the five East Asian manufacturing sectors, this study has no choice but to use the aggregate data at the 3-digit level and further assumes that all manufacturing industries within each economy use more or less similar production technologies, although this approach could be challenged. Nonetheless, while analysing the sources of economic growth for the East Asian NICs, Kim and Lau (1994) also assumed that the four East Asian NICs and a group of the five developed countries had the same meta-production function at the economy level. Moreover, it is worth mentioning that both studies applied a micro concept approach to analyse a macroeconomic issue, and the use of the production function in

A3.2   Replacement of 3-digit Level Industry with 2-digit Level Industry

When the data for some 3-digit level industries are missing or unavailable, an alternative approach to maintain the maximum number of industries is to include industries at the 2-digit level. For instance, because the pottery, china and earthenware (ISIC 361), glass products (ISIC 362) and other non-metal mineral products (ISIC 369) industries in Hong Kong had a lot of missing data, the combination of these three industries, that is, ISIC 36, is instead included in the sample. A similar process was applied to Singapore.

A3.3   Use of Interpolation and Extrapolation

These were occasionally resorted in order to reconstruct missing data.

A3.4   Exclusion of the 'Problematic' Industries

A3.4.1   The tobacco industry

The inclusion of the tobacco industry influences dramatically the estimation of the production function and the convergence of estimation; due to divergence, this makes it difficult to obtain the frontier coefficients. Even if the estimated coefficients are obtained, preliminary results have found that the tobacco industry unduly extends the production frontier and simultaneously lowers the actual output of other industries. For example, if the tobacco industry is included in the estimation for Hong Kong, it achieves 100 per cent technical efficiency, but lowers that of other industries to about 10 per cent, in contrast to around 60 per cent without the tobacco industry. Other adverse effects resulting from the inclusion of the tobacco industry include technology regression across most industries and large swings in technical efficiency and technological progress over time. Furthermore, the volatility of GFCF data in the tobacco industry in Hong Kong creates difficulty in estimating capital stock.[3] In order to obtain accurate estimation results, the tobacco industry is excluded from the manufacturing samples examined in this study except for Taiwan, where the tobacco industry is combined with two other industries (food and beverages) and so the above problems do not appear.

With regard to actual data, it is found that the output–capital and/or output–labour ratios of the tobacco industry are much higher than those of other industries. This is commonly the case for state-owned industries such as tobacco and petroleum refineries, which generally operate as monopolies. As a result, the output prices (measured in value added) are usually overvalued because they are often regulated by government. This view is also shared by Färe *et al.* (2001) and they exclude the beverages, tobacco, petroleum and coal industries in their study on productivity growth in 16 Taiwanese manufacturing industries. Because these two industries operate as near monopolies in Taiwan, their output values are unavoidably inflated by monopoly profits and tax revenues, suggesting the exaggeration of relative productivity of monopolies. In addition, Färe *et al.* observe that the inclusion of these two industries results in peculiar outcomes, namely technology regression.

Finally, the speculation may not be completely ruled out that some of the manufacturing industries, for example tobacco, utilise different types of frontier production technology. This may explain the anomalies that occur when the tobacco industry is included, and account for the discrepancies in the output–capital and output–labour ratios. However, more empirical evidence and econometric hypothesis testing are required to examine this speculation.

The exclusion of industries in this study is based on the above reasons or criteria. However, the decision to exclude industries cannot be taken by comparing output–capital ratios with output–labour ratios alone; as indicated below, the results of the estimated frontier coefficients, returns to scale and convergence also need to be considered.

A3.4.2 Irregular output–capital/–labour ratios

The evidence of irregular (or extreme) output–capital, output–labour or capital–labour ratios is presented in Figures A3.1 to A3.5. Moreover, it should be noted that the output–labour ratio of Hong Kong in Figure A3.1 may not be comparable with those of other manufacturing sectors since manufacturing value added is measured in local currency and the periods covered are different.

The output–capital ratio against output–labour ratio in Hong Kong's manufacturing industries between 1976 and 1980 is shown in Figure A3.1. The distinctive industry marked in Figure A3.1 is the tobacco industry. The number of industries examined for Hong Kong between 1976 and 1992 fell to 21 due to the removal of the tobacco industry; after 1993 the number of industries declined still further because of the removal of the footwear and beverages industries. The footwear industry was temporarily deleted from the sample from 1993 because its output–capital ratio was far below the average.[4] The beverages industry was removed from 1995 to 1997 because of negative capital stock in the period 1995–96; this was caused by the large negative GFCF.[5] Overall, during the 1993–94 and 1995–97 periods, the number of industries covered in Hong Kong was reduced to 20 and 19 respectively.

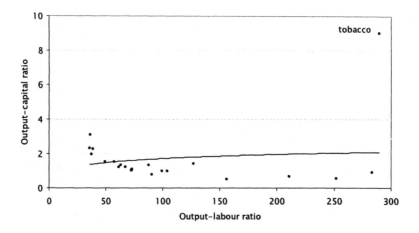

Note: The unit of output–labour ratio is HK$ thousands/person.

Source: UNIDO database deflated at constant 1990 prices and author's calculations.

Figure A3.1   Average output–capital ratio against average output–labour ratio in Hong Kong's manufacturing industries, 1976–80

The missing data for Hong Kong's manufacturing industries deserves some explanation. First, the data for petroleum refineries (ISIC 353) and miscellaneous petroleum and coal products (ISIC 354) in the UNIDO database show up as zero over the period 1976–87. Compared with other economies, Hong Kong is a service-oriented state; hence it is conceivable that Hong Kong may not have had those two heavy industries during that period, or that such data are unavailable in Hong Kong. Consequently, those two industries are excluded.

Second, the existing missing data and 'combined data' have led to the combination of some 3-digit level industries to maintain a larger sample size.[6] In terms of missing data, the use of interpolation has reconstructed the data of manufacturing GFCF and value added for the pottery industry (ISIC 361) in 1992, 1993 and 1995, the glass industry (ISIC 362) in 1994 and the data of manufacturing GFCF for the other non-metal mineral industry (ISIC 369) in 1992. As far as the combined data are concerned, the industrial chemicals and other chemicals industries are combined into a single chemical products industry (ISIC 351+352). Three industries, pottery, glass and other non-metal minerals, are joined as a 2-digit level industry, non-metal mineral products (ISIC 36). The iron (ISIC 371) and steel and non-ferrous metals (ISIC 372) industries are combined into a 2-digit level industry, basic metals

(ISIC 37). Most of the GFCF data for manufacturing industries are not available over the period 1974–75, so the construction of capital stock starts from 1976. Thus, the sample period for Hong Kong's manufacturing industries runs from 1976 to 1997.

For Japan, there are 27 industries during the 1963–84 period and 28 industries from 1985 onwards, because the data of value added and number of employees for the tobacco industry are available only after 1985. Accordingly, the tobacco industry is excluded and 27 manufacturing industries at the 3-digit level are included in this study.[7] The data for manufacturing value added and number of employees are available from 1963 to 1998 and data for GFCF from 1963 to 1997. Overall, Japan has retained the maximum number of industries and the sample period covers 1965 to 1998.

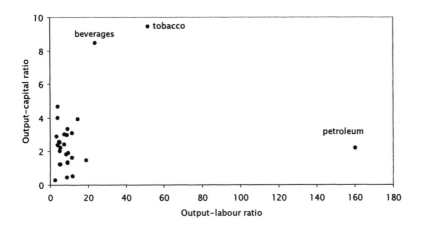

Note: The unit of output–labour ratio is Korean Won millions/person.

Source: UNIDO database deflated at constant 1990 prices and author's calculations.

Figure A3.2 Average output–capital ratio against average output–labour ratio in Korea's manufacturing industries, 1970–72

As with Japan, the data for Korea's manufacturing industries are well established, apart from the combined data for manufacturing GFCF in 1991 and the data for manufacturing value added, number of employees and GFCF in the period 1996–97 for the petroleum refineries (ISIC 353) and miscellaneous petroleum and coal products (ISIC 354) industries. Thus it is assumed that the value of GFCF for 1991 in the petroleum and coal products

178   *The growth process in East Asian manufacturing industries*

industry is a simple average of 1990 and 1992. Then the value of GFCF for the petroleum refineries industry can be obtained by subtracting the GFCF of the petroleum and coal products industry from the combined data.

Figure A3.2 shows the output–capital ratio against output–labour ratio for Korean manufacturing industries between 1970 and 1972. The three industries marked in Figure A3.2 are the tobacco, petroleum refineries and beverages industries. For similar reasons to Hong Kong, these three industries are excluded from the sample for Korea.[8] Despite their removal, the remaining 25 industries accounted for over 93 per cent of total manufacturing value added output in the 1990s. In spite of the availability of complete manufacturing GFCF data from 1967 to 1997 and manufacturing value added and number of employees from 1963 to 1997, the study for the Korean manufacturing sector only covers the period 1970 to 1997 due to the unavailability of the deflators between 1967 and 1969.

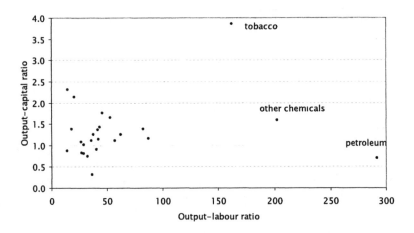

Note: The unit of output–labour ratio is S$ thousands/person.

Source: UNIDO database deflated at constant 1990 prices and author's calculations.

Figure A3.3 Average output–capital ratio against average output–labour ratio in Singapore's manufacturing industries, 1985–90

In Singapore, the petroleum refineries and petroleum and coal products industries have to be merged as a single industry (ISIC 353+354) because the data are combined. As the data for the glass industry are available only from 1970 to 1974 and the data after 1974 is merged with the pottery industry, these two industries are joined as a single industry (ISIC 361+362). Figure

A3.3 shows the output–capital ratio against output–labour ratio for Singapore's manufacturing industries during the period 1985–90. Similar to Hong Kong and Korea's manufacturing sectors, the three industries marked in Figure A3.3 and eliminated from the sample are tobacco, petroleum and other chemicals industries. One of the three industries is easily detected at the outset but the other two are found in the late 1980s because the estimation of frontier coefficients becomes difficult. Therefore, the number of industries examined for Singapore is 23 and the sample period is from 1970 to 1997.

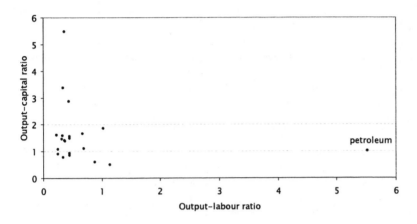

Note: The unit of output–labour ratio is NT$ millions/person.

Source: Author's calculations and data deflated at constant 1990 prices.

Figure A3.4   Average output–capital ratio against average output–labour ratio in Taiwan's manufacturing industries, 1981–85

The sample period for Taiwan's manufacturing industries is from 1981 to 1999 due to the change of industrial classification from 1981 and to lack of employment data (based on the new industrial classification) before 1979. Despite the existence of manufacturing value added and GFCF data from 1966 and employment data from 1974 in the *Statistical Yearbook of the Republic of China* published by the DGBAS, the industrial classifications of these two separate data series differed between 1974 and 1980. Even though the employment data are available from the *Monthly Bulletin of Manpower Statistics* published by the DGBAS from 1979, the beginning of the sample period cannot be brought forward to 1979 because of the significant reduction in the number of industries. Also, Taiwan's manufacturing sector was divided into 17 industries before 1981 but into 22 industries after 1981 in the *National Income in Taiwan Area of the Republic of China*, published by the DGBAS. To maintain the maximum number of industries, this study uses the sample period from 1981 to 1999.

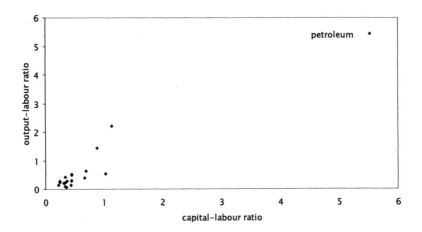

Note: The unit of output–labour ratio is NT$ millions/person.

Source: Author's calculations and data deflated at constant 1990 prices.

Figure A3.5   Average output–labour ratio against average capital–labour ratio in Taiwan's manufacturing industries, 1981–85

Figures A3.4 and A3.5 present the detailed evidence of the output–labour ratio against output–capital and capital–labour ratios for Taiwan's manufacturing industries during the period 1981–85.   The change of industrial classification in 1981 creates a difficulty for the beverages industry, which was classified with tobacco as a single industry before 1981 but was combined with the food industry after 1981. To overcome the problem, this study aggregates these three industries, food, beverages and tobacco, as a single industry. For similar reasons to those discussed earlier for Hong Kong and Korea, this study excludes the petroleum and coal products industry, as marked in Figures A3.4 and A3.5.[9] Thus, the number of industries studied for Taiwan is 20.   The numbers of manufacturing industries and sample periods examined for the five East Asian manufacturing sectors are summarised in Table A3.1.

Finally, the decision to commence the analysis of capital stock in 1980 in Taiwan warrants an explanation. To retain the industries of 1981 in the sample, the data for GFCF for 1980 were required. Therefore, an extrapolation was required to generate the GFCF data of 1980 for five industries, namely precision instruments, plastic products, chemical products, printing and furniture.

Table A3.1   The number of 3-digit manufacturing industries and time periods examined

Country	Period	No. of industries	Industries excluded
Hong Kong	1976–92	21	Tobacco
	1993–94	20	Tobacco, footwear
	1995–97	19	Tobacco, footwear, beverages
Japan	1965–98	27	Tobacco
Korea	1970–97	25	Tobacco, petroleum refineries, beverages
Singapore	1970–97	23	Tobacco, petroleum refineries and miscellaneous petroleum and coal products$, other chemicals
Taiwan	1981–99	20	Petroleum and coal products

Note: $ indicates the petroleum refineries, and miscellaneous petroleum and coal products are classified as a single industry ISIC 353+354.

A.4   ESTIMATES OF VARYING COEFFICIENTS ACROSS INDUSTRIES IN SELECTED YEARS

This appendix presents the actual varying coefficients (intercepts and coefficients of labour and capital) across manufacturing industries. To conserve space, results will only be presented for two selected years. For Japan, Korea, and Singapore, they are 1980 and 1995; for Taiwan they are 1981 and 1995. Due to the smaller sample size in 1995 in Hong Kong, they are 1980 and 1990.

An example of the empirical output generated by the computer program TERAN for Japan in 1980 is shown in Figure A4.1. The results here correspond to Table A4.2.

Table A4.1   Estimates of intercept and coefficients of labour and capital for individual industries in Hong Kong in 1980 and 1990

	Constant	Labour	Capital	Constant	Labour	Capital
		1980			1990	
311 Food products	7.631	0.504	0.409	7.830	0.682	0.335
313 Beverages	**7.662**	**0.541**	**0.409**	**7.909**	**0.730**	**0.335**
321 Textiles	7.623	0.491	0.409	7.791	0.654	0.335
322 Wearing apparel	7.646	0.525	0.409	7.783	0.652	0.335
323 Leather products	7.631	0.503	0.409	7.783	0.655	0.335
324 Footwear	7.654	0.532	0.409	7.704	0.609	0.335
331 Wood products	7.639	0.510	0.409	7.783	0.655	0.335
332 Furniture	7.639	0.513	0.409	7.791	0.660	0.335
341 Paper and paper products	7.639	0.508	0.409	7.791	0.660	0.335
342 Printing, publishing	7.639	0.510	0.409	7.822	0.682	0.335
351+352 (chemicals)	7.639	0.515	0.409	7.854	0.698	0.335
355 Rubber products	7.600	0.462	0.409	7.743	0.638	0.335
356 Plastic products	7.623	0.492	0.409	7.775	0.644	0.335
36 Non-metal minerals	7.631	0.501	0.409	7.854	0.698	0.335
371+372 (Basic metals)	7.646	0.519	0.409	7.854	0.694	0.335
381 Fabricated metal	7.639	0.511	0.409	7.783	0.653	0.335
382 Non-electrical machinery	7.639	0.509	0.409	7.830	0.688	0.335
383 Electric machinery	7.639	0.516	0.409	7.775	0.644	0.335
384 Transport equip.	7.639	0.507	0.409	7.854	0.698	0.335
385 Professional equip.	7.639	0.513	0.409	7.799	0.663	0.335
390 Other manufactured	7.639	0.515	0.409	7.799	0.663	0.335

Notes:
1. In 1995, the number of manufacturing industries falls to 19, as seen in Table 3.2. Instead of showing the results for 1995, those for 1990 are presented here.
2. Non-metal mineral products (36) industry includes pottery, china, earthenware (361), glass and glass products (362) and other non-metallic mineral (369) industries.
3. The figures in bold denote the frontier coefficients.

Source: Author's calculations using the computer program TERAN.

Table A4.2   Estimates of intercept and coefficients of labour and capital for individual industries in Japan in 1980 and 1995

	Constant	Labour	Capital	Constant	Labour	Capital
		1980			1995	
311 Food products	9.316	0.472	0.468	9.577	0.512	0.445
313 Beverages	9.316	0.473	0.468	9.764	0.539	0.445
321 Textiles	9.230	0.461	0.468	9.469	0.496	0.445
322 Wearing apparel	9.278	0.468	0.468	9.518	0.502	0.445
323 Leather products	9.373	0.479	0.468	9.636	0.520	0.445
324 Footwear	9.354	0.477	0.468	9.685	0.527	0.445
331 Wood products	9.306	0.471	0.468	9.597	0.515	0.445
332 Furniture	9.335	0.475	0.468	9.626	0.520	0.445
341 Paper and paper products	9.201	0.457	0.468	9.518	0.504	0.445
342 Printing and publishing	9.440	0.490	0.468	9.666	0.527	0.445
351 Industrial chemicals	9.249	0.464	0.468	9.656	0.523	0.445
352 Other chemicals	**9.536**	**0.502**	**0.468**	**9.833**	**0.551**	**0.445**
353 Petroleum refineries	9.565	0.500	0.468	9.715	0.529	0.445
354 Miscellaneous petroleum	9.134	0.454	0.468	9.459	0.499	0.445
355 Rubber products	9.239	0.464	0.468	9.518	0.504	0.445
356 Plastic products	9.306	0.472	0.468	9.548	0.507	0.445
361 Pottery, china, earthenware	9.259	0.466	0.468	9.479	0.499	0.445
362 Glass and glass products	9.297	0.471	0.468	9.518	0.505	0.445
369 Other non-metallic minerals	9.287	0.469	0.468	9.607	0.516	0.445
371 Iron and steel	9.278	0.468	0.468	9.508	0.502	0.445
372 Non-ferrous metals	9.287	0.469	0.468	9.449	0.494	0.445
381 Fabricated metal products	9.345	0.477	0.468	9.636	0.521	0.445
382 Non-electrical machinery	9.383	0.482	0.468	9.626	0.520	0.445
383 Electric machinery	9.354	0.479	0.468	9.557	0.508	0.445
384 Transport equipment	9.297	0.470	0.468	9.567	0.510	0.445
385 Professional equipment	9.287	0.469	0.468	9.577	0.512	0.445
390 Other manufactured prod.	9.326	0.474	0.468	9.626	0.519	0.445

Note: The figures in bold denote the frontier coefficients.

Source: Author's calculations using the computer program TERAN.

Table A4.3   Estimates of intercept and coefficients of labour and capital for individual industries in Korea in 1980 and 1995

	Constant	Labour	Capital	Constant	Labour	Capital
		1980			1995	
311 Food products	8.646	0.389	0.523	7.969	0.610	0.475
321 Textiles	8.585	0.358	0.523	7.716	0.610	0.467
322 Wearing apparel	8.637	0.385	0.523	8.091	0.610	0.478
323 Leather products	8.567	0.353	0.523	8.050	0.610	0.477
324 Footwear	8.567	0.351	0.523	7.879	0.610	0.473
331 Wood products	8.489	0.316	0.523	7.969	0.610	0.475
332 Furniture	8.567	0.354	0.523	7.757	0.610	0.469
341 Paper and paper products	8.593	0.364	0.523	7.985	0.610	0.476
342 Printing and publishing	8.646	0.388	0.523	**8.156**	**0.610**	**0.480**
351 Industrial chemicals	8.646	0.388	0.523	8.042	0.610	0.477
352 Other chemicals	**8.733**	**0.428**	**0.523**	8.140	0.610	0.480
354 Miscellaneous petrol.	8.707	0.411	0.523	8.018	0.610	0.477
355 Rubber products	8.602	0.365	0.523	7.895	0.610	0.473
356 Plastic products	8.611	0.372	0.523	8.075	0.610	0.478
361 Pottery, china, earth.	8.559	0.348	0.523	7.863	0.610	0.472
362 Glass and glass products	8.602	0.367	0.523	8.091	0.610	0.478
369 Other non-metallic minerals	8.611	0.369	0.523	7.977	0.610	0.476
371 Iron and steel	8.576	0.354	0.523	8.026	0.610	0.477
372 Non-ferrous metals	8.611	0.371	0.523	8.010	0.610	0.477
381 Fabricated metal	8.593	0.361	0.523	7.961	0.610	0.475
382 Non-electrical mach.	8.567	0.349	0.523	7.985	0.610	0.476
383 Electric machinery	8.611	0.370	0.523	8.099	0.610	0.479
384 Transport equipment	8.593	0.360	0.523	7.936	0.610	0.474
385 Professional equipment	8.602	0.369	0.523	8.067	0.610	0.478
390 Other manufactured	8.611	0.369	0.523	7.977	0.610	0.475

Note: The figures in bold denote the frontier coefficients.

Source: Author's calculations using the computer program *TERAN*.

Table A4.4   Estimates of intercept and coefficients of labour and capital for individual industries in Singapore in 1980 and 1995

	Constant	Labour	Capital	Constant	Labour	Capital
	1980			1995		
311 Food products	3.424	0.303	0.689	2.888	0.415	0.660
313 Beverages	3.739	0.341	0.689	2.992	0.415	0.675
321 Textiles	3.275	0.283	0.689	2.839	0.415	0.653
322 Wearing apparel	3.470	0.309	0.689	2.811	0.415	0.649
323 Leather products	3.566	0.320	0.689	3.026	0.415	0.677
324 Footwear	3.278	0.289	0.689	2.928	0.415	0.666
331 Wood products	3.305	0.287	0.689	2.919	0.415	0.664
332 Furniture	3.405	0.302	0.689	2.922	0.415	0.665
341 Paper and paper products	3.517	0.316	0.689	2.925	0.415	0.665
342 Printing and publishing	3.509	0.315	0.689	2.974	0.415	0.673
351 Industrial chemicals	3.447	0.307	0.689	2.888	0.415	0.660
355 Rubber products	3.536	0.318	0.689	2.928	0.415	0.666
356 Plastic products	3.351	0.294	0.689	2.863	0.415	0.656
361+362 Pottery, glass	3.302	0.293	0.689	2.946	0.415	0.668
369 Other non-metallic	3.659	0.333	0.689	**3.069**	**0.415**	**0.686**
371 Iron and steel	**3.839**	**0.352**	**0.689**	2.882	0.415	0.660
372 Non-ferrous metals	3.467	0.310	0.689	2.866	0.415	0.658
381 Fabricated metal	3.497	0.314	0.689	2.891	0.415	0.660
382 Non-electrical mach.	3.555	0.322	0.689	3.044	0.415	0.684
383 Electric machinery	3.566	0.325	0.689	2.900	0.415	0.662
384 Transport equipment	3.624	0.333	0.689	2.916	0.415	0.664
385 Professional equipment	3.263	0.281	0.689	2.983	0.415	0.674
390 Other manufactured	3.497	0.313	0.689	2.824	0.415	0.651

Note: The figures in bold denote the frontier coefficients.

Source: Author's calculations using the computer program *TERAN*.

Table A4.5   Estimates of intercept and coefficients of labour and capital for individual industries in Taiwan in 1981 and 1995

	Constant	Labour	Capital	Constant	Labour	Capital
	1981			1995		
Food, beverages, tobacco	**2.573**	**0.577**	**0.395**	0.377	0.643	0.592
Textile mill products	2.066	0.577	0.378	0.246	0.580	0.592
Wearing apparel	2.437	0.577	0.389	0.329	0.619	0.592
Leather, fur and products	2.249	0.577	0.383	0.289	0.602	0.592
Wood and bamboo products	1.737	0.577	0.368	0.298	0.607	0.592
Furniture and fixtures	1.974	0.577	0.376	0.383	0.643	0.592
Pulp, paper and paper products	2.316	0.577	0.386	0.240	0.579	0.592
Printing processings	2.375	0.577	0.387	0.280	0.597	0.592
Chemical material	2.120	0.577	0.380	**0.386**	**0.645**	**0.592**
Chemical products	1.755	0.577	0.369	0.325	0.617	0.592
Rubber products	2.017	0.577	0.377	0.309	0.610	0.592
Plastic products	1.770	0.577	0.368	0.269	0.591	0.592
Non-metallic minerals	2.058	0.577	0.378	0.349	0.628	0.592
Basic metal industries	2.141	0.577	0.380	0.317	0.614	0.592
Fabricated metal products	2.064	0.577	0.378	0.289	0.600	0.592
Machinery and equip.	2.061	0.577	0.378	0.344	0.627	0.592
Electrical and electronic	2.035	0.577	0.377	0.326	0.619	0.592
Transport equipment	2.411	0.577	0.389	0.346	0.628	0.592
Precision instruments	2.105	0.577	0.380	0.317	0.614	0.592
Other industrial products	2.365	0.577	0.387	0.353	0.630	0.592

Note: The figures in bold denote the frontier coefficients.

Source: Author's calculations using the computer program *TERAN*.

```
technical efficiency estimates for the individual period  1

the ols estimates are :

                    coefficient   standard-error        t-ratio

  intercept        .93495327E+01  .90673422E+00   .10311216E+02
  x 1              .47571898E+00  .49527078E-01   .96052302E+01
  x 2              .46577218E+00  .41939700E-01   .11105758E+02
  sigma-squared    .52297198E-01

  breusch-pagan chi-squared value    .79806940E+01
               with degree of   2

the variance coefficient estimates are :

                    coefficient   standard-error        t-ratio

  intercept        .25172371E-01  .23045379E-01   .10922958E+01
  x 1              .26709587E-03  .10306175E-03   .25916100E+01
  x 2              .00000000E+00  .38425552E-04   .00000000E+00
  sigma-squared    .59701253E-02

the final wls estimates are :

                    coefficient   standard-error        t-ratio

  intercept        .93177261E+01  .22537865E+00   .41342542E+02
  x 1              .47316646E+00  .12177618E-01   .38855419E+02
  x 2              .46804184E+00  .10327099E-01   .45321714E+02
  sigma-squared    .52304607E-01

the frontier coefficients are :

  intercept        .95646585E+01
  x 1              .50197013E+00
  x 2              .46804184E+00

number of firms =   27

number of periods =    1

total number of observations =   27

technical efficiency estimates :

input specific technique efficiencies for period 2
firm no.,   intercept,   x1,   x2,   ...
   1          .974       .941    1.000
   2          .974       .942    1.000
   3          .965       .918    1.000
   4          .970       .933    1.000
   5          .980       .955    1.000
   6          .978       .950    1.000
   7          .973       .938    1.000
   8          .976       .946    1.000
```

```
 9       .962      .911     1.000
10       .987      .977     1.000
11       .967      .924     1.000
12       .997     1.000     1.000
13      1.000      .997     1.000
14       .955      .904     1.000
15       .966      .924     1.000
16       .973      .940     1.000
17       .968      .929     1.000
18       .972      .938     1.000
19       .971      .935     1.000
20       .970      .932     1.000
21       .971      .935     1.000
22       .977      .951     1.000
23       .981      .961     1.000
24       .978      .954     1.000
25       .972      .936     1.000
26       .971      .935     1.000
27       .975      .945     1.000

firm-no. tech.-eff.%        allo.-eff%        econ.-eff.%

 1       .51502932E+02
 2       .55732729E+02
 3       .40914759E+02
 4       .48486901E+02
 5       .64930283E+02
 6       .62315566E+02
 7       .51363269E+02
 8       .57019292E+02
 9       .39467765E+02
10       .75587229E+02
11       .45586140E+02
12       .97409314E+02
13       .98295330E+02
14       .40461676E+02
15       .45981857E+02
16       .52665318E+02
17       .49358959E+02
18       .54026632E+02
19       .50032358E+02
20       .48021707E+02
21       .51201708E+02
22       .57433109E+02
23       .63044901E+02
24       .58647571E+02
25       .49199812E+02
26       .50433723E+02
27       .55921286E+02
mean technical   eff. =   .56112671E+02%
     negative values are excluded in calculating mean effs.
```

Figure A4.1   The output of the computer program TERAN

A.5 ESTIMATES OF VARYING COEFFICIENTS ACROSS INDUSTRIES IN SELECTED YEARS

Table A5.1   Annual TFP growth rates by industry in Hong Kong

Industry	1976 –77	1977 –78	1978 –79	1979 –80	1980 –81	1981 –82	1982 –83	1983 –84	1984 –85	1985 –86	1986 –87
311	9.1	13.2	–4.6	–7.1	8.8	15.1	6.9	–21.3	–6.3	6.0	12.9
313	15.8	–18.7	–0.2	–1.0	–6.0	7.6	12.2	–39.8	31.8	12.4	–18.6
321	–15.7	24.6	7.9	–12.7	0.5	0.5	29.6	–16.4	–1.8	24.5	3.3
322	–0.1	9.8	5.2	0.4	–1.4	–3.1	10.8	–12.7	–7.4	9.9	11.8
323	15.9	22.2	6.9	–14.1	–4.4	–3.1	26.2	–23.0	–23.9	27.8	12.6
324	–10.5	26.8	5.9	15.1	–15.3	–10.6	13.9	–15.5	5.5	–1.4	–7.2
331	6.8	19.2	–14.7	–23.4	40.8	–22.1	20.9	–36.0	–4.0	13.0	10.3
332	6.1	24.8	6.5	–19.4	18.6	–10.7	3.5	–27.1	4.1	3.4	17.8
341	–4.3	29.0	0.4	–7.2	2.0	0.4	18.8	–24.9	–5.6	23.8	–4.8
342	9.1	12.6	9.9	–9.8	21.6	–8.5	5.1	–12.0	2.9	–4.9	13.1
351+352	8.9	12.1	12.1	–7.8	2.8	–7.5	17.5	–13.7	–6.2	4.5	3.3
355	–7.4	–2.3	27.8	–25.8	3.2	5.8	0.2	–9.7	5.5	–13.0	16.1
356	5.4	12.3	8.4	–12.3	9.7	–3.8	11.2	–2.5	–7.0	14.0	–11.6
36	35.9	32.2	–4.7	–12.8	7.0	–29.6	18.7	–41.1	17.3	21.4	21.0
371+372	2.1	19.5	–9.0	–24.2	–10.9	–1.7	9.9	–26.2	–19.8	28.4	68.9
381	1.7	20.9	8.7	–12.1	0.7	–9.0	15.8	–16.8	–2.7	13.2	10.2
382	–1.4	29.3	1.5	–2.2	30.8	–6.3	25.4	–26.8	–24.3	12.7	0.2
383	16.5	10.0	8.2	–4.8	20.4	–3.8	6.5	–20.5	–30.0	22.9	14.2
384	–1.0	–14.5	14.8	–15.3	9.5	12.0	–14.5	–2.6	–0.7	11.7	7.5
385	11.4	15.8	12.1	–9.0	4.2	–9.4	18.9	–18.1	–10.1	15.2	1.8
390	0.9	16.6	–4.4	–3.8	12.1	–3.8	12.0	–5.6	–10.5	9.9	17.3
300	**1.3**	**14.3**	**6.2**	**–7.1**	**6.8**	**–3.4**	**13.3**	**–15.7**	**–8.4**	**14.4**	**7.3**

Industry	1987 –88	1988 –89	1989 –90	1990 –91	1991 –92	1992 –93	1993 –94	1994 –95	1995 –96	1996 –97
311	14.9	–10.1	5.7	–4.5	0.1	–2.4	–0.7	19.1	5.0	–1.1
313	33.5	–1.2	2.2	–12.3	6.5	1.2	0.2	#	#	#
321	–7.0	–2.2	–0.7	–0.7	5.1	–13.4	–2.7	12.3	–1.7	11.2
322	–6.2	–3.2	–2.0	–1.3	4.8	–5.7	–4.6	14.2	3.2	6.1
323	–16.1	7.2	–6.5	–12.3	21.2	–7.4	29.7	–13.6	–15.0	26.9

Table A5.1   (continued)

Industry	1987 –88	1988 –89	1989 –90	1990 –91	1991 –92	1992 –93	1993 –94	1994 –95	1995 –96	1996 –97
324	11.0	0.7	–46.8	–2.7	–4.4	–57.8	15.5	13.1	8.9	3.3
331	–10.5	–24.4	5.8	–12.6	8.8	–2.5	18.6	9.5	–21.7	25.1
332	–17.7	5.3	–1.0	–3.9	–3.3	–19.3	–19.3	18.5	39.9	–22.3
341	–9.7	–10.0	10.3	5.7	3.9	1.5	–13.6	4.5	–1.9	11.6
342	7.3	–3.8	7.8	–8.6	6.0	–0.7	–1.9	–13.6	9.9	4.7
351+352	13.3	6.6	4.0	18.4	–12.7	–2.0	–0.9	1.3	14.2	–0.3
355	2.1	4.6	4.5	–17.3	4.0	11.3	–12.8	24.6	–5.1	8.4
356	9.0	–1.6	–3.3	–1.9	–2.1	–1.5	–10.2	23.4	–5.1	9.2
36	8.6	19.0	0.9	–5.8	–13.3	20.9	3.2	33.6	–113.3	84.3
371+372	47.7	–54.7	–29.1	3.9	–0.2	–0.2	–14.7	38.8	–26.2	13.5
381	3.4	–7.1	–1.4	3.4	2.1	4.2	0.6	1.5	–7.7	16.9
382	13.1	–4.4	17.3	–2.8	3.1	–14.0	–0.5	17.0	3.8	1.0
383	–7.9	–6.4	–8.8	11.5	9.1	1.0	19.8	10.6	–6.7	12.0
384	9.9	18.6	0.7	–3.2	4.7	0.4	–7.1	10.2	–12.3	14.2
385	17.7	–6.4	–0.4	–2.1	3.0	–0.6	5.4	9.0	–10.5	16.8
390	–13.7	–4.0	–7.5	–1.0	5.2	0.5	1.6	2.2	–2.3	12.8
300	**–0.1**	**–3.6**	**–0.2**	**–0.3**	**3.9**	**–4.1**	**0.4**	**9.1**	**–1.9**	**8.8**

Notes:
1. # denotes the removal of the industry due to negative capital stock in 1995 and 1996.
2. Non-metal mineral products industry (36) includes pottery, china, earthenware (361), glass and glass products (362) and other non-metallic minerals (369).
3. The figures in bold denote annual TFP growth rates for manufacturing sector.

Source: Author's calculations.

Table A5.2   Annual TFP growth rates by industry in Japan

Industry	1965 –66	1966 –67	1967 –68	1968 –69	1969 –70	1970 –71	1971 –72	1972 –73	1973 –74	1974 –75	1975 –76
311	4.6	2.7	1.6	3.2	4.2	7.4	9.6	1.5	2.2	2.9	5.6
313	10.6	9.8	1.7	8.4	7.4	8.5	2.7	1.7	–7.4	9.6	–5.8
321	6.2	8.8	1.3	6.0	5.3	–0.1	6.6	18.5	–19.0	–5.6	13.2
322	10.3	5.4	4.6	7.1	3.1	1.7	10.1	11.0	–10.9	2.2	8.9
323	–1.1	3.4	4.0	13.2	–1.8	3.8	11.5	3.9	–4.6	3.2	7.8
324	1.6	8.6	–1.3	13.4	17.7	–6.9	15.5	7.1	7.3	–10.9	24.2
331	10.0	6.2	3.8	4.7	6.1	–6.4	15.1	25.0	–21.7	–10.7	8.1
332	8.0	6.7	3.1	5.9	5.2	2.4	9.2	10.4	–3.6	–4.7	4.0
341	3.7	0.3	5.4	3.9	7.3	–4.8	–0.5	14.8	16.9	–28.2	4.4
342	12.7	6.6	4.4	5.7	1.7	0.9	5.5	6.5	0.2	5.4	4.7
351	4.5	17.4	3.2	11.5	–0.9	–8.1	–4.7	11.4	–0.7	–20.6	5.3
352	5.9	8.5	4.7	11.2	3.1	5.9	–2.9	6.8	1.6	–0.9	4.7
353	–4.6	17.0	9.7	–3.3	1.9	4.9	–7.9	18.3	12.2	–26.2	18.3
354	–16.6	4.9	–6.6	20.5	2.8	8.6	–11.8	9.8	27.5	–10.3	–23.0
355	6.8	10.5	–4.2	–1.3	4.3	3.4	10.2	5.9	0.7	–11.3	8.5
356	13.7	10.0	11.3	10.6	1.9	2.2	8.3	15.1	3.1	–19.8	11.0
361	0.5	7.9	3.7	8.9	4.4	0.3	3.0	6.3	4.9	2.6	1.1
362	–4.0	19.7	5.4	8.5	–0.7	–2.3	2.2	8.2	–9.1	–14.8	27.8
369	10.0	7.3	10.6	5.2	2.9	0.1	6.9	15.5	1.0	–14.6	0.8
371	6.6	23.9	–12.1	14.4	2.2	–11.7	6.5	25.7	1.4	–30.7	10.9
372	13.5	8.6	–5.9	10.8	–4.8	–10.6	7.2	25.2	0.3	–38.3	14.9
381	7.8	9.4	9.3	12.4	2.6	–4.6	–3.1	10.7	1.3	–13.3	5.8
382	6.9	20.3	13.3	7.8	4.3	–6.6	–3.1	10.6	5.8	–11.2	4.3
383	6.3	16.0	5.8	6.5	3.8	–12.0	7.4	5.7	–5.5	–16.4	19.1
384	–0.5	9.3	7.0	–4.7	3.8	–2.5	3.5	7.9	–8.8	–1.3	11.9
385	14.0	11.3	5.4	8.3	–2.4	6.1	–1.0	8.3	7.4	–5.9	2.5
390	7.1	6.8	5.0	8.0	1.1	–2.8	4.7	10.9	–5.0	2.5	9.0
300	**6.2**	**11.6**	**4.4**	**6.7**	**3.2**	**–3.5**	**3.4**	**11.6**	**–1.6**	**–10.9**	**8.5**

Industry	1976 –77	1977 –78	1978 –79	1979 –80	1980 –81	1981 –82	1982 –83	1983 –84	1984 –85	1985 –86	1986 –87
311	4.4	–0.2	6.9	0.1	–1.3	4.3	1.6	2.0	4.7	–1.5	4.6
313	10.5	7.8	–2.4	8.4	5.7	4.9	6.3	0.5	1.6	1.1	2.9

Table A5.2   (continued)

Industry	1976 -77	1977 -78	1978 -79	1979 -80	1980 -81	1981 -82	1982 -83	1983 -84	1984 -85	1985 -86	1986 -87
321	-3.4	3.4	13.7	0.1	-2.7	2.8	0.7	3.0	5.0	-4.0	6.0
322	-3.6	1.8	8.0	-1.0	-0.3	0.1	1.3	-0.5	4.6	1.4	3.2
323	1.4	-1.0	9.3	-2.0	-0.7	-1.1	4.1	-0.3	11.6	-0.6	1.3
324	-5.1	0.2	12.1	-6.5	-4.9	1.1	-2.8	-3.8	6.0	3.2	4.2
331	4.9	4.4	16.6	-0.4	-13.9	4.4	2.2	-1.9	6.0	2.8	10.6
332	3.6	3.6	14.6	1.0	-7.7	4.4	1.9	-1.4	6.1	-0.1	6.5
341	1.6	-0.8	11.1	3.5	-2.4	2.6	4.4	5.4	0.7	2.9	7.0
342	1.5	4.6	10.7	5.1	0.6	2.1	0.0	-1.1	3.2	-1.0	2.1
351	3.1	6.2	20.2	-3.8	-5.6	5.0	10.3	14.0	2.1	3.8	8.1
352	5.5	5.5	10.6	1.6	1.1	2.1	4.8	-4.1	5.0	1.5	9.2
353	-6.2	-20.0	53.9	24.6	-16.8	8.6	-11.8	-4.2	-1.9	-21.1	29.9
354	14.0	4.1	17.7	5.5	22.6	-23.2	-12.3	-8.5	-1.4	12.0	1.5
355	1.7	3.8	10.0	5.2	-5.2	0.2	3.1	1.4	6.3	-4.6	8.7
356	0.2	6.2	12.9	-1.1	-3.6	1.1	4.5	5.0	3.1	-5.0	2.5
361	7.0	-6.2	7.2	9.5	-7.3	-1.9	2.8	3.2	-7.8	-8.5	4.0
362	3.3	-1.9	6.1	2.2	1.5	2.3	6.5	4.1	4.1	-14.4	7.3
369	4.8	11.4	13.8	2.8	-0.5	-2.3	0.9	1.6	4.8	2.4	8.7
371	-2.0	10.4	32.0	2.3	-8.5	1.1	-14.2	14.9	8.6	-16.8	10.2
372	3.0	-1.4	28.0	14.0	-15.7	-10.0	-5.3	12.1	-5.8	-8.4	4.9
381	6.0	6.5	9.5	3.3	-1.0	1.5	-1.1	2.5	10.2	-3.5	4.0
382	2.0	1.4	14.7	8.0	1.0	3.7	-4.7	5.5	5.9	-8.6	-2.1
383	4.4	2.6	11.7	5.5	0.8	1.8	1.4	6.1	-3.4	-13.4	-0.3
384	5.2	-7.0	8.2	4.8	5.1	-1.3	3.0	-0.3	10.4	-12.9	5.3
385	11.0	0.3	3.9	5.0	-0.9	-3.9	1.6	-0.7	9.6	-9.5	-8.5
390	4.5	-4.3	11.3	2.5	2.6	1.4	5.2	3.3	3.4	-3.8	3.6
300	**3.0**	**2.3**	**13.7**	**3.8**	**-1.5**	**1.7**	**0.2**	**3.7**	**4.3**	**-6.5**	**4.0**

Industry	1987 -88	1988 -89	1989 -90	1990 -91	1991 -92	1992 -93	1993 -94	1994 -95	1995 -96	1996 -97	1997 -98
311	2.3	0.5	-0.9	2.5	1.4	-2.3	-7.1	-1.5	1.4	0.2	-1.3
313	9.2	-2.7	-4.1	-1.0	-5.0	0.8	41.6	-4.6	6.5	1.5	-4.0
321	5.9	0.3	-1.1	1.2	-2.7	-9.0	0.7	-1.6	3.0	4.6	22.3
322	2.7	2.2	-1.1	5.3	-4.4	-8.2	-5.4	3.0	3.0	0.0	2.2
323	6.9	1.0	-1.9	2.6	-6.9	-15.5	7.7	0.1	-0.1	-8.8	26.0

Table A5.2 *(continued)*

Industry	1987 –88	1988 –89	1989 –90	1990 –91	1991 –92	1992 –93	1993 –94	1994 –95	1995 –96	1996 –97	1997 –98
324	0.3	5.3	3.1	−1.3	−5.0	−9.5	24.0	7.3	0.5	0.3	−8.4
331	3.9	2.9	1.2	2.5	−3.7	0.5	5.0	0.8	2.4	−2.2	−5.6
332	8.8	5.5	−2.3	0.5	−7.2	−8.7	14.2	−0.4	4.4	−0.8	−6.3
341	5.9	3.8	−3.9	−2.5	−5.0	1.5	5.9	−2.8	6.3	1.5	−4.8
342	3.7	2.3	−1.1	−0.9	−5.0	−4.0	−0.6	1.4	5.5	2.5	−4.8
351	13.2	6.4	−1.9	0.0	−1.7	−7.8	−1.0	−1.5	0.2	6.0	−5.5
352	3.5	4.0	−0.7	−2.4	−3.4	−1.1	2.5	−0.4	2.9	2.4	−6.8
353	−5.9	−15.0	−25.0	46.2	14.5	9.5	9.2	−38.2	−22.0	−30.2	−0.7
354	2.1	20.2	−1.1	0.2	3.1	3.6	2.1	−6.1	11.5	−3.0	0.8
355	5.5	−0.4	5.8	−0.3	−2.6	−8.8	0.9	−2.6	6.7	7.7	−6.4
356	3.4	3.0	−1.1	3.5	−5.8	−6.3	−0.6	−6.0	4.0	2.3	−2.4
361	7.4	0.3	−2.2	1.4	−2.3	−1.3	7.9	0.3	2.2	3.9	−3.7
362	10.9	5.2	−5.6	−9.2	−8.2	−5.6	10.4	−15.1	6.5	6.6	−2.9
369	8.8	2.4	1.8	3.1	−3.1	−2.8	2.9	−5.2	4.0	−0.3	−8.2
371	22.9	7.3	1.1	2.9	−9.3	−10.8	−5.9	−5.3	4.8	9.5	−6.5
372	19.1	7.1	0.0	−3.6	−7.0	−5.4	1.0	−4.0	9.0	4.4	−2.3
381	8.6	2.9	3.8	3.9	−6.0	−8.7	1.6	−1.0	5.3	−1.1	−5.0
382	13.0	7.5	4.9	0.6	−13.9	−12.7	4.6	0.2	8.5	2.1	−3.3
383	8.4	3.4	0.7	1.2	−13.3	−4.3	−3.5	2.0	5.4	3.4	−2.7
384	6.0	7.9	5.2	−4.8	−5.4	−5.3	−2.0	0.3	10.5	3.8	−2.7
385	8.2	4.9	1.2	0.5	−9.6	−5.0	24.6	4.5	10.5	5.6	−2.2
390	1.8	5.3	3.0	5.0	−1.8	−6.8	1.7	−4.2	2.5	1.2	−7.0
300	**8.1**	**4.2**	**1.1**	**0.8**	**−6.8**	**−5.9**	**1.1**	**−1.3**	**5.3**	**2.3**	**−3.1**

Note: The figures in bold denote annual TFP growth rates for manufacturing sector.

Source: Author's calculations.

Table A5.3   Annual TFP growth rates by industry in Korea

Industry	1970 -71	1971 -72	1972 -73	1973 -74	1974 -75	1975 -76	1976 -77	1977 -78	1978 -79
311	17.0	-18.1	-23.3	-28.1	37.2	13.5	19.1	10.0	-18.8
321	12.5	15.1	19.2	-31.1	11.8	6.3	-6.4	21.1	-10.1
322	14.0	-6.1	7.5	-19.1	-5.6	9.5	-3.8	18.1	-11.5
323	28.4	-4.3	81.6	-27.2	12.6	-55.1	-24.1	42.5	-28.0
324	-17.0	-26.3	33.1	1.2	-2.5	13.2	23.0	6.1	-21.7
331	44.4	-4.6	25.0	-29.6	-13.4	-1.8	11.2	29.3	-34.0
332	10.0	6.8	-15.7	10.3	-4.0	36.0	22.4	52.5	-33.7
341	14.5	-1.6	34.2	-24.3	-15.4	11.5	22.2	12.6	-19.4
342	24.8	-19.2	-18.1	19.5	3.4	-5.9	27.7	21.6	-4.5
351	2.8	-0.1	-7.8	4.5	7.5	-12.3	10.2	16.6	-13.1
352	20.1	-8.0	1.4	0.5	10.6	6.0	10.3	11.9	-15.6
354	53.6	-6.4	46.4	-67.8	5.2	-11.4	14.2	11.2	32.7
355	8.1	-9.2	3.3	-7.0	1.5	14.6	3.9	16.3	4.8
356	1.9	41.2	-1.3	-49.0	-50.0	17.2	27.0	31.0	13.8
361	11.4	21.4	39.2	-23.8	12.9	25.2	48.3	31.9	7.5
362	-18.4	-3.2	5.0	21.1	20.1	-5.8	22.3	14.1	-18.9
369	24.8	5.9	18.5	-4.6	24.8	-7.1	14.8	2.6	2.4
371	16.7	1.9	43.2	-13.6	-18.6	-12.4	-2.7	26.4	-0.5
372	39.0	-16.2	55.7	-10.2	-9.9	9.6	38.4	19.2	-24.0
381	-5.7	-4.4	30.2	11.0	-20.5	-2.0	23.6	35.2	-25.3
382	10.6	-2.2	42.6	-20.0	-2.5	10.1	-3.2	21.1	-18.1
383	6.9	-1.8	20.6	-3.1	-16.2	-13.7	8.6	15.5	-18.9
384	4.4	-23.4	30.3	-23.0	-10.3	20.4	39.6	-7.9	-34.0
385	-4.0	37.0	32.6	-29.5	30.0	8.3	-23.3	16.8	-6.1
390	-10.7	-26.9	23.9	-6.2	10.8	6.2	-0.4	15.8	-13.9
300	**14.0**	**-2.5**	**15.3**	**-16.3**	**2.4**	**1.7**	**9.2**	**16.1**	**-13.6**

Industry	1979 -80	1980 -81	1981 -82	1982 -83	1983 -84	1984 -85	1985 -86	1986 -87	1987 -88
311	0.8	7.6	-1.7	0.4	-1.6	-2.8	4.5	4.9	0.4
321	-4.2	15.7	-14.3	4.9	15.4	2.7	12.5	12.3	-3.5
322	1.5	22.2	-17.2	2.0	12.8	-7.6	11.3	12.4	1.9
323	-17.6	47.4	-29.0	1.2	11.2	6.1	19.8	17.0	-7.1

Table A5.3   (continued)

Industry	1979 -80	1980 -81	1981 -82	1982 -83	1983 -84	1984 -85	1985 -86	1986 -87	1987 -88
324	-13.4	13.8	1.7	15.0	3.5	-0.7	9.1	6.0	7.7
331	-37.8	5.0	30.5	-4.1	-1.3	-4.9	6.6	17.2	13.1
332	-41.8	8.1	-3.7	19.8	7.6	-5.3	-0.3	11.8	15.8
341	-5.3	13.2	-9.2	19.1	2.8	-2.9	10.2	10.7	-1.1
342	-10.1	5.1	5.3	15.6	2.8	-12.5	3.7	13.7	2.4
351	14.6	0.6	-22.6	12.0	11.1	0.7	4.9	7.9	0.1
352	-2.4	1.3	-0.3	7.8	1.4	-5.1	-2.5	19.9	-4.3
354	3.5	18.5	-14.8	0.3	0.2	9.8	3.2	-1.8	-3.5
355	-19.2	-2.8	-18.3	4.7	20.3	6.6	12.2	11.1	2.5
356	-27.3	7.4	-16.9	18.5	20.0	-8.4	0.9	9.7	8.3
361	-10.4	11.3	-19.4	17.2	1.2	-1.9	7.2	11.2	-2.8
362	-18.6	-5.8	-16.8	13.2	14.4	2.7	7.2	-8.1	3.7
369	-1.7	2.6	-23.2	24.3	4.3	-2.9	8.6	8.2	9.2
371	-29.3	29.0	-2.5	-11.3	13.7	1.5	8.6	15.1	-9.1
372	15.3	-21.2	-24.1	25.6	5.3	0.1	14.9	19.3	7.6
381	-33.6	26.6	-2.0	-1.1	1.5	2.0	15.4	14.0	7.3
382	-37.1	14.4	-8.9	21.0	14.4	1.2	18.0	10.0	8.5
383	-10.8	20.7	-2.1	17.0	18.5	-13.7	12.3	6.0	-0.5
384	-8.3	24.0	2.9	7.5	8.8	0.8	3.9	6.0	-6.1
385	-6.6	-4.3	-6.4	0.5	23.6	-5.3	18.1	10.4	11.4
390	-1.6	22.3	-7.8	5.0	-0.4	-2.4	23.7	14.1	-3.2
300	**-9.8**	**13.7**	**-7.8**	**7.5**	**10.0**	**-2.5**	**9.4**	**10.1**	**0.2**

Industry	1988 -89	1989 -90	1990 -91	1991 -92	1992 -93	1993 -94	1994 -95	1995 -96	1996 -97
311	9.2	17.4	10.8	7.2	3.5	0.3	3.8	7.8	2.3
321	-5.2	0.3	16.2	9.8	0.8	3.0	5.7	6.4	2.8
322	2.7	9.3	7.1	1.3	21.6	7.0	15.2	2.0	2.3
323	-2.3	22.9	-0.7	11.6	-2.1	14.2	-13.2	6.8	-4.1
324	1.2	21.5	34.2	-17.3	-16.3	-3.5	-1.7	28.2	-11.7
331	12.0	25.2	26.3	-8.5	9.3	4.5	5.9	3.8	5.6
332	9.4	20.5	23.0	-77.1	-3.0	19.7	2.1	11.2	3.4
341	-2.4	7.9	13.0	2.3	-2.9	10.7	7.9	5.2	-0.2
342	7.5	20.0	-7.4	4.4	12.3	1.9	6.9	9.2	-6.5

Table A5.3   (continued)

Industry	1988 –89	1989 –90	1990 –91	1991 –92	1992 –93	1993 –94	1994 –95	1995 –96	1996 –97
351	–1.8	25.4	–7.2	–5.5	–0.6	2.8	22.6	23.4	4.7
352	6.5	11.1	–3.5	–7.6	12.0	0.6	–7.1	9.8	7.3
354	1.5	–1.8	–3.0	14.1	2.9	–15.6	–9.7	–4.5	–5.9
355	–4.0	10.5	15.7	8.0	–0.6	7.5	7.3	18.1	–10.1
356	–6.1	11.3	26.9	10.4	–11.8	13.0	12.5	–46.6	2.6
361	6.9	8.0	1.3	1.8	12.3	–0.4	4.6	6.5	1.8
362	–0.7	35.0	11.4	0.0	–5.8	16.4	11.4	–3.5	–2.8
369	10.6	19.0	15.7	–9.8	–1.0	–1.1	11.6	6.9	2.2
371	8.2	19.9	6.4	0.9	–1.7	13.1	10.2	–2.7	0.2
372	–4.1	7.3	13.9	–8.1	–5.2	6.5	25.3	–10.1	9.3
381	5.9	13.1	–1.7	4.0	3.9	12.3	–2.5	13.7	–5.1
382	3.7	16.3	12.8	–6.7	0.4	3.5	10.6	10.1	3.7
383	0.1	13.9	–0.8	0.0	12.9	18.2	26.2	0.0	–13.6
384	3.5	28.7	6.5	2.8	–4.9	7.1	6.1	4.3	11.8
385	–1.9	7.5	–9.6	9.4	1.0	16.4	11.4	6.3	2.7
390	–2.4	7.1	1.8	3.5	5.7	6.4	10.6	–0.7	–1.3
300	**2.2**	**15.3**	**7.0**	**–0.2**	**2.6**	**8.0**	**11.0**	**3.9**	**0.1**

Note: The figures in bold denote annual TFP growth rates for manufacturing sector.

Source: Author's calculations.

Table A5.4   *Annual TFP growth rates by industry in Singapore*

Industry	1970 -71	1971 -72	1972 -73	1973 -74	1974 -75	1975 -76	1976 -77	1977 -78	1978 -79
311	2.1	-4.1	11.6	-14.8	-1.7	4.4	18.5	-3.4	-6.5
313	-10.3	-21.9	-0.3	-11.3	10.8	12.5	3.7	-0.7	-3.3
321	4.9	10.2	26.6	-50.0	-22.5	34.6	-2.3	10.9	15.0
322	1.0	10.7	-16.9	-19.6	-5.8	33.6	8.1	12.6	-5.9
323	-3.5	24.5	13.5	-9.4	-37.5	53.6	8.0	-16.2	-15.9
324	21.2	-7.0	-31.4	-6.7	24.7	5.5	-22.9	10.7	16.0
331	-24.1	-16.9	33.3	-53.9	-14.3	54.6	12.0	13.6	-4.4
332	-9.2	-9.4	1.7	-44.2	4.1	23.1	-1.3	-0.6	-16.0
341	5.2	9.0	18.2	-22.1	-22.9	17.3	9.8	4.9	14.5
342	-13.5	18.6	-1.0	0.7	-5.4	8.7	11.8	0.9	-11.0
351	-3.5	8.3	20.5	-29.6	-18.5	15.4	12.5	-2.5	11.6
355	-4.4	-35.4	40.2	-18.6	-35.6	33.1	-8.0	-3.0	55.6
356	7.5	3.3	-4.7	-21.2	-25.6	10.7	21.1	6.7	11.4
361+362	-11.0	-4.3	21.6	2.2	7.8	12.6	29.2	23.8	0.2
369	11.2	-2.8	38.0	-10.7	-0.4	-11.4	5.6	-8.0	16.6
371	-39.8	25.4	37.7	22.1	-87.8	1.8	27.7	33.6	11.2
372	-6.9	-59.2	34.5	-0.7	-4.0	-4.3	32.3	4.1	36.4
381	-22.1	-0.7	12.9	-10.9	-1.5	-1.1	6.1	3.4	4.6
382	1.2	17.9	4.4	-20.9	-3.7	-12.4	-4.4	-5.0	9.4
383	-27.4	4.5	-4.2	-16.4	-11.8	7.8	1.1	3.1	2.2
384	-14.6	-8.2	-13.2	10.3	-16.4	8.6	6.0	0.5	17.4
385	33.1	10.3	-30.6	-20.3	16.9	-4.6	-0.7	27.8	-7.6
390	5.6	0.5	3.2	8.4	-3.9	23.1	5.7	16.9	20.7
300	**-11.2**	**-0.7**	**5.1**	**-13.8**	**-11.5**	**8.6**	**5.0**	**3.6**	**6.2**

Industry	1979 -80	1980 -81	1981 -82	1982 -83	1983 -84	1984 -85	1985 -86	1986 -87	1987 -88
311	-14.2	18.4	-18.7	-3.7	-2.4	-6.3	2.6	11.4	8.4
313	-1.5	8.7	-3.5	-13.5	-5.7	-10.2	4.1	9.9	7.7
321	-1.3	-19.7	-10.8	5.2	-0.3	-5.4	32.7	26.5	-0.2
322	-3.9	0.5	-0.6	-3.7	5.7	-10.8	6.4	23.5	-1.5
323	-12.6	-12.1	2.3	-24.0	8.3	-4.3	6.8	19.6	26.4
324	-26.1	-12.2	-18.0	6.2	0.1	-24.9	5.1	17.8	1.2

Table A5.4   (continued)

Industry	1979 –80	1980 –81	1981 –82	1982 –83	1983 –84	1984 –85	1985 –86	1986 –87	1987 –88
331	−41.7	1.8	−17.1	6.3	−5.6	−6.5	1.0	12.5	25.3
332	5.1	5.7	−7.0	−6.1	9.7	−6.5	−6.7	−11.6	9.6
341	3.4	−28.1	−16.5	9.1	10.3	11.3	3.5	18.3	−2.2
342	−5.5	7.9	−9.6	1.1	−3.3	−8.9	−5.6	10.6	5.7
351	−3.5	−7.4	−10.4	−24.8	46.0	−5.4	24.6	50.7	38.4
355	−55.1	−14.0	−2.6	−1.8	−31.5	−27.9	15.3	28.9	−0.7
356	−9.6	−4.6	−8.6	−6.5	5.9	−3.9	2.8	20.2	1.4
361+362	−51.5	−16.3	−23.9	11.6	6.7	−62.5	−33.2	20.6	13.2
369	10.7	23.5	−1.9	−18.9	−45.9	−17.3	−24.5	−0.1	−0.7
371	4.8	−11.0	2.3	−31.6	−25.3	−25.9	25.3	26.3	9.0
372	−14.3	12.2	−37.7	11.1	14.4	−24.3	9.3	23.4	4.7
381	−10.6	−7.2	2.8	−12.0	−6.8	−17.1	9.5	10.7	5.5
382	0.9	23.7	−24.2	−27.7	−3.7	−5.4	−8.0	2.6	7.1
383	−9.1	−16.2	−9.8	4.7	23.0	−15.3	8.3	10.6	−10.6
384	10.1	−4.1	−22.8	−19.7	2.8	6.9	12.5	11.7	15.7
385	4.9	−24.1	4.5	−4.9	27.5	24.5	15.8	7.6	5.2
390	−9.8	−11.0	−26.8	2.9	−11.1	3.4	19.2	24.2	−16.1
300	**−5.4**	**−2.8**	**−12.5**	**−8.0**	**6.0**	**−9.1**	**6.3**	**13.5**	**1.1**

Industry	1988 –89	1989 –90	1990 –91	1991 –92	1992 –93	1993 –94	1994 –95	1995 –96	1996 –97
311	4.8	−1.6	−5.6	−6.6	−6.0	7.3	−5.4	14.3	−3.1
313	−34.8	−31.2	−11.4	12.8	9.7	15.6	4.3	1.2	10.5
321	−2.5	6.2	−9.5	−0.3	−0.6	10.1	−9.7	−6.9	15.4
322	−6.5	−3.8	−11.2	−4.3	−9.9	−3.5	−10.0	−0.6	2.8
323	9.0	−11.5	−9.4	1.9	−12.3	−0.6	3.7	−4.5	26.8
324	26.0	14.7	−23.2	9.4	12.9	3.8	4.4	19.4	−13.2
331	14.5	−6.4	−14.1	6.1	7.7	8.5	5.6	−6.0	2.3
332	7.1	−2.4	−0.8	13.0	3.1	−3.6	4.0	−1.5	−6.7
341	1.7	6.9	−10.6	−9.3	3.3	2.9	−5.6	−1.4	−4.7
342	3.1	2.3	−4.5	7.2	1.9	8.7	−2.1	−3.4	2.4
351	−22.9	−35.8	−17.2	−20.4	−0.8	−0.7	−38.4	−13.2	10.7
355	−5.7	−4.9	8.3	5.7	−2.3	5.5	12.5	−5.1	−0.6
356	9.1	−4.3	−6.0	−0.8	7.0	3.2	−7.1	−7.1	−5.5

Table A5.4   *(continued)*

Industry	1988 –89	1989 –90	1990 –91	1991 –92	1992 –93	1993 –94	1994 –95	1995 –96	1996 –97
361+362	69.1	–39.9	8.5	38.6	4.4	16.9	14.3	–34.0	–2.0
369	17.7	21.1	28.5	10.9	–1.2	3.9	7.0	–7.8	–17.0
371	6.5	–25.0	–13.1	11.6	–37.1	–9.5	2.2	–8.3	12.5
372	–4.6	10.5	–21.6	14.6	–6.9	–5.4	–49.5	–3.7	–8.7
381	4.1	–1.2	–0.5	7.0	–2.4	–2.6	–3.1	–9.7	–6.7
382	100.1	–17.7	–14.3	3.2	6.4	3.9	1.0	0.5	–7.3
383	–45.7	–4.2	–1.6	8.8	6.9	14.7	6.2	–16.4	–8.8
384	–4.8	–0.9	–15.1	9.2	–5.7	0.0	–17.3	–2.9	25.3
385	–2.5	–3.5	–14.0	15.3	12.1	5.4	4.9	6.1	4.0
390	–19.1	2.0	–7.7	–3.4	–6.3	1.9	9.0	–11.2	16.9
300	**–2.9**	**–8.6**	**–7.9**	**4.7**	**3.0**	**6.1**	**–1.1**	**–5.8**	**–3.1**

Note: The figures in bold denote annual TFP growth rates for manufacturing sector.

Source: Author's calculations.

Table A5.5   Annual TFP growth rates by industry in Taiwan

Industry	1981 -82	1982 -83	1983 -84	1984 -85	1985 -86	1986 -87	1987 -88	1988 -89	1989 -90
Food, beverages	1.0	11.0	1.4	2.0	0.6	7.9	-0.3	-2.2	-2.3
Textiles	-6.1	1.5	7.3	-0.7	17.1	2.2	-9.9	4.7	-2.0
Wearing apparel	13.4	-3.7	7.8	-13.9	7.4	5.6	-11.6	4.3	3.4
Leather, fur	3.7	-5.3	5.3	-1.6	8.5	-8.4	-8.5	-2.5	-2.2
Wood	-3.6	7.2	14.8	11.4	24.9	9.8	-12.8	-5.4	-13.3
Furniture	-14.7	4.6	6.6	-9.4	23.0	7.7	7.2	8.3	-8.5
Pulp, paper	-8.4	2.7	6.5	-2.4	14.1	0.7	-11.3	-6.7	-12.7
Printing	-19.1	-1.2	4.0	-12.2	8.9	-3.3	0.2	-6.9	-3.9
Chemical materials	6.6	18.9	17.1	5.9	15.1	-0.5	-1.0	-1.8	1.5
Chemical products	8.1	8.0	15.0	6.8	17.3	4.5	-4.3	-11.0	1.5
Rubber products	4.7	3.9	-4.7	0.5	4.4	4.4	-0.5	-5.6	6.7
Plastic products	4.6	8.9	8.7	6.1	23.4	7.3	2.3	-0.9	-2.0
Non-metallic	-7.0	9.0	2.4	2.7	3.1	9.7	9.1	7.4	5.5
Basic metal	0.2	14.7	12.2	-0.9	15.2	0.3	2.4	1.5	5.9
Fabricated metal	-12.7	6.7	6.0	-0.6	11.7	1.2	3.3	-0.5	-1.0
Machinery and equip.	-11.7	13.0	4.6	2.3	13.9	11.9	7.3	-3.7	-2.0
Electrical and electronic	1.1	10.2	9.8	-9.0	15.6	9.1	2.6	1.1	-1.4
Transport equipment	1.4	1.7	1.0	-12.8	10.1	16.2	-1.8	10.9	-2.0
Precision instruments	10.4	19.2	-6.0	-14.7	4.0	4.2	4.1	0.5	-10.0
Other industrial products	-5.1	8.5	4.9	-6.3	9.6	6.2	1.8	-6.1	-9.1
Manufacturing	**-0.6**	**7.3**	**6.7**	**-2.4**	**12.1**	**5.8**	**-0.7**	**0.4**	**-1.3**

Industry	1990 -91	1991 -92	1992 -93	1993 -94	1994 -95	1995 -96	1996 -97	1997 -98	1998 -99
Food, beverages	-2.2	2.1	-2.8	-0.6	-2.8	-1.0	-9.2	3.1	0.8
Textiles	7.7	-2.9	-8.4	0.3	-4.9	-3.8	-0.3	-6.7	-8.6
Wearing apparel	3.4	-6.4	-11.2	-23.3	-6.6	4.0	2.5	-6.2	-30.7
Leather, fur	3.5	-19.2	-5.3	-4.6	-12.1	3.8	-10.1	-8.6	-9.0
Wood	15.2	9.9	5.8	-13.3	-7.4	0.8	6.3	-6.5	-9.1
Furniture	10.9	9.7	1.9	2.3	2.9	12.4	3.9	-5.1	1.9
Pulp, paper	-10.4	-10.6	-11.6	-1.3	-1.4	-7.0	0.5	-4.9	1.0
Printing	-6.1	3.5	-4.6	-6.4	-4.6	-6.6	3.3	10.3	-6.7
Chemical materials	6.0	4.9	3.6	10.2	-1.3	-1.3	1.5	-3.2	-4.9

Table A5.5   (continued)

Industry	1990 -91	1991 -92	1992 -93	1993 -94	1994 -95	1995 -96	1996 -97	1997 -98	1998 -99
Chemical products	2.8	6.7	6.6	3.2	4.1	6.5	10.1	-0.1	-1.5
Rubber products	2.4	6.0	-4.8	-7.5	-4.6	-6.2	-9.8	-7.6	-4.1
Plastic products	4.9	-0.8	2.8	0.7	-5.6	6.2	-0.5	-15.7	-3.1
Non-metallic	4.3	4.6	0.8	1.7	3.2	-1.2	-0.8	-1.7	-6.9
Basic metal	6.0	-0.8	0.0	-7.3	-9.5	-4.4	10.1	-0.9	1.8
Fabricated metal	9.9	-0.6	-7.8	-2.7	-0.4	-7.1	-3.0	-7.4	0.1
Machinery and equip.	3.7	2.1	-1.6	-0.7	2.2	-1.5	-7.9	-10.3	1.2
Electrical and electronic	7.5	0.4	5.4	4.3	9.4	2.6	-2.7	-8.6	-2.3
Transport equipment	2.7	1.6	-9.8	-8.0	-4.2	-12.2	-5.1	-3.6	-12.3
Precision instruments	-6.4	-2.6	-3.1	-0.6	-1.7	-3.9	-6.9	-8.7	8.8
Other industrial products	-3.2	2.0	-1.2	-5.5	2.4	7.9	-0.6	-11.8	-6.8
Manufacturing	**4.1**	**0.7**	**-1.3**	**-0.7**	**0.2**	**-0.8**	**-1.4**	**-5.7**	**-3.1**

Source: Author's calculations.

NOTES

1. The book *Productivity and U.S. Economic Growth* by Jorgenson *et al.* (1987a) provides more details on the methodology.
2. Restrictions on parameter values for equation (A2.5) are similar to equation (A2.6).
3. For instance, the real GFCF of the tobacco industry in 1987 was 65 times higher than in 1977 and the real GFCF in 1984 was at least 17 times larger than in 1983.
4. Nevertheless, the analysis of output growth decomposition is still carried out for the footwear industry.
5. The negative GFCF in the beverages industry may be due to the sale of capital stock or being transferred out of Hong Kong.
6. The combined data mean that the figures are only available at the 2-digit level, which has been confirmed by the *UNIDO Industrial Statistics Yearbook*.
7. The attempt to incorporate the tobacco industry in the sample failed due to the sudden change in the estimated intercept and frontier coefficients; that is, the estimated frontier coefficient of labour swings drastically, say from 0.5 to 0.7.
8. For instance, the output–labour ratio of the petroleum and coal products industry in 1995 was 271.4 while other industries on average had 28.1.

9. On average, the output–labour ratio of the petroleum and coal products industry was more than 10 times higher than other industries. If the petroleum and coal products industry is included, the returns to scale, in the first three years dependent on estimated frontier coefficients, will be between 0.82 and 0.87, which seems very low and therefore unreliable empirically. If the returns to scale are calculated based on the mean coefficients, they become even lower, say, less than 0.8. According to the empirical model outlined in Chapter 3, the returns to scale based on estimated frontier coefficients should be close to or slightly greater than one, as estimated frontier coefficients are selected from the largest labour and capital coefficients among industries.

References

Abramovitz, Moses (1956), 'Resource and Output Trends in the United States Since 1870', *American Economic Review*, **46** (2), 5–23.

Aigner, D. J. and S. F. Chu (1968), 'On Estimating the Industry Production Function', *American Economic Review*, **58** (4), 826–39.

Aigner, Dennis, C. A. Knox Lovell and Peter Schmidt (1977), 'Formulation and Estimation of Stochastic Frontier Production Function Models', *Journal of Econometrics*, **6** (1), 21–37.

Aw, Bee Yan, Xiaomin Chen and Mark J. Roberts (2001), 'Firm-level Evidence on Productivity Differentials and Turnover in Taiwanese Manufacturing', *Journal of Development Economics*, **66** (1), 51–86.

Baltagi, Badi H. and James M. Griffin (1988), 'A General Index of Technical Change', *Journal of Political Economy*, **96** (1), 20–41.

Barro, Robert J. (1999), 'Notes on Growth Accounting', *Journal of Economic Growth*, **4** (2), 119–37.

Bauer, Paul (1990), 'Recent Developments in the Econometric Estimation of Frontiers', *Journal of Econometrics*, **46** (1–2), 39–56.

Bishop, Y. M. M., S. E. Fienberg and P. W. Holland (1975), *Discrete Multivariate Analysis: Theory and Practice*, Cambridge: MIT Press.

Bloch, Harry and Sam Hak Kan Tang (1999), 'Technical Change and Total Factor Productivity Growth: A Study of Singapore's Manufacturing Industries', *Applied Economics Letters*, **6** (10), 697–701.

Breusch, T. S. and A. R. Pagan (1979), 'A Simple Test for Heteroscedasticity and Random Coefficient Variation', *Econometrica*, **47** (5), 1287–94.

Caves, Douglas W., Laurits R. Christensen and W. Erwin Diewert (1982a), 'Multilateral Comparisons of Output, Input, and Productivity Using Superlative Index Numbers', *Economic Journal*, **92** (365), 73–86.

Caves, Douglas W., Laurits R. Christensen and W. Erwin Diewert (1982b), 'The Economic Theory of Index Numbers and the Measurement of Input, Output, and Productivity', *Econometrica*, **50** (6), 1393–414.

Chang, Ching-Cheng and Yir-Hueih Luh (1999), 'Efficiency Change and Growth in Productivity: The Asian Growth Experience', *Journal of Asian Economics*, **10** (4), 551–70.

Chavas, Jean Paul and Thomas L. Cox (1990), 'A Non-parametric Analysis of Productivity: The Case of U.S. and Japanese Manufacturing', *American Economic Review*, **80** (3), 450–64.

Chen, Edward K. Y. (1997), 'The Total Factor Productivity Debate: Determinants of Economic Growth in East Asia', *Asian Pacific Economic Literature*, **11** (1), 18–38.

Chen, Tain-Jy and De-piao Tang (1990), 'Export Performance and Productivity Growth: The Case of Taiwan', *Economic Development and Cultural Change*, **38** (3), 575–85.

Christensen, L. R., D. Cummings and D. W. Jorgenson (1980), 'Economic Growth, 1947–1973: An International Comparison', in J. W. Kendrick and B. Vaccara (eds), *New Developments in Productivity Measurement and Analysis*, Chicago: University of Chicago Press, pp. 595–698.

Christensen, L. R., D. Cummings and D. W. Jorgenson (1981), 'Relative Productivity Levels, 1947–1973: An International Comparison', *European Economic Review*, **16** (1), 61–94.

Chuang, Yih-Chyi (1996), 'Identifying the Sources of Growth in Taiwan's Manufacturing Industry', *Journal of Development Studies*, **32** (3), 445–63.

Coelli, T. J. (1995), 'Recent Developments in Frontier Modelling and Efficiency Measurement', *Australian Journal of Agricultural Economics*, **39** (3), 219–46.

Collins, Susan M. and Barry P. Bosworth (1996), 'Economic Growth in East Asia: Accumulation versus Assimilation', *Brookings Papers on Economic Activity*, **2**, 135–203.

Cornwell, Christopher, Peter Schmidt and Robin C. Sickles (1990), 'Production Frontiers with Cross-Sectional and Time-Series Variation in Efficiency Levels', *Journal of Econometrics*, **46** (1–2), 185 – 200.

Denison, Edward F. (1962), *The Sources of Economic Growth in the United States and the Alternatives Before Us*, New York: Committee on Economic Development.

Denny, Mike, Jeff Bernstein, Mel Fuss, S. Nakamura and L. Waverman (1992), 'Productivity in Manufacturing Industries: Canada, Japan and the United States, 1953–1986: Was the "Productivity Slowdown" Reversed?', *Canadian Journal of Economics*, **25** (3), 584–603.

Dollar, David and Edward N. Wolff (1994), 'Capital Intensity and TFP Convergence by Industry in Manufacturing, 1963–1985', in William J. Baumol, Richard R. Nelson and Edward N. Wolff (eds), *Convergence of Productivity: Cross National Studies and Historical Evidence*, Oxford and New York: Oxford University Press.

Dollar, David and Kenneth Sokoloff (1990), 'Patterns of Productivity Growth in South Korean Manufacturing Industries, 1963–1979', *Journal of Development Economics*, **33** (2), 309–27.

Dowrick, Steve and Duc Tho Nguyen (1989), 'OECD Comparative Economic Growth 1950–85: Catch-up and Convergence', *American Economic Review*, **79** (5), 1010–30.

Drysdale, Peter and Yiping Huang (1997), 'Technological Catch-up and Economic Growth in East Asia and the Pacific', *Economic Record*, **73** (222), 201–11.

Ermisch, John F. and W. G. Huff (1999), 'Hypergrowth in an East Asian NIC: Public Policy and Capital Accumulation in Singapore', *World Development*, **27** (1), 21–38.

Färe, Rolf, Shawna Grosskopf and C. A. Knox Lovell (1994a), *Production Frontiers*, Cambridge: Cambridge University Press.

Färe, Rolf, Shawna Grosskopf and Wen-Fu Lee (1995), 'Productivity in Taiwanese Manufacturing Industries', *Applied Economics*, **27** (3), 259–65.

Färe, Rolf, Shawna Grosskopf and Wen-Fu Lee (2001), 'Productivity and Technical Change: The Case of Taiwan', *Applied Economics*, **33** (15), 1911–25.

Färe, Rolf, Shawna Grosskopf, M. Norris and Z. Zhang (1994b), 'Productivity Growth, Technical Progress, and Efficiency Change in Industrialized Countries', *American Economic Review*, **84** (1), 66–83.

Farell, M. J. (1957), 'The Measurement of Productive Efficiency,' *Journal of the Royal Statistical Society, Series A*, **120** (3), 253–81.

Feige, Edgar L. and P. A. V. B. Swamy (1974), 'A Random Coefficient Model of the Demand for Liquid Assets', *Journal of Money, Credit, and Banking*, **6** (2), 241–52.

Felipe, Jesus (1999), 'Total Factor Productivity Growth in East Asia: A Critical Survey', *Journal of Development Studies*, **35** (4), 1–41.

Felipe, Jesus (2000), 'On the Myth and Mystery of Singapore's "Zero TFP"', *Asian Economic Journal*, **14** (2), 187–209.

Felipe, Jesus and J. S. L. McCombie (2001), 'Biased Technical Change, Growth Accounting, and the Conundrum of the East Asian Miracle', *Journal of Comparative Economics*, **29** (3), 542–65.

Førsund, Finn R., C. A. Knox Lovell and Peter Schmidt (1980), 'A Survey of Frontier Production Functions and of Their Relationship to Efficiency Measurement', *Journal of Econometrics*, **13** (1), 5–25.

Fuss, Melvyn and Leonard Waverman (1990), 'The Extent and Sources of Cost and Efficiency Differences between U.S. and Japanese Motor Vehicle Producers', *Journal of the Japanese and International Economy*, **4** (3), 219–56.

Gapinski, James (1997), 'Economic Growth in the Asia Pacific Region', *Asia Pacific Journal of Economics and Business*, **1** (1), 68–91.

Good D. H., M. I. Nadiri and R. Sickles (1997), 'Index Numbers and Factor Demand Approaches to the Estimation of Productivity', in H. Pesaran and

P. Schmidt (eds), *Handbook of Applied Econometrics*, Volume II: *Microeconometrics*, Blackwell, Oxford, pp. 14–80.

Griffiths, W. E. (1972), 'Estimation of Actual Response Coefficients in the Hildreth–Houck Random Coefficient Model', *Journal of the American Statistical Association*, **67** (339), 633–5.

Griliches, Zvi and Jacques Mairesse (1990), 'R&D and Productivity Growth: Comparing Japanese and U.S. Manufacturing Firms', in Charles R. Hulten, (ed.), *Productivity Growth in Japan and the United States*, Chicago and London: University of Chicago Press.

Hall, Robert E. (1988), 'The Relation between Price and Marginal Cost in U.S. Industry', *Journal of Political Economy*, **96** (5), 921–47.

Hall, Robert E. and Charles I. Jones (1996), *The Productivity of Nations*, NBER Working Paper No. 5812, Cambridge, MA: National Bureau of Economic Research.

Han, Gaofeng, Kali Kalirajan and Nirvikar Singh (2002), 'Productivity and Economic Growth in East Asia: Innovation, Efficiency and Accumulation', *Japan and the World Economy*, **14** (4), 401–24.

Harrison, Ann E. (1994), 'Productivity, Imperfect Competition and Trade Reform: Theory and Evidence', *Journal of International Economics*, **36** (1–2), 53–73.

Hayami, Yujiro and Junichi Ogasawara (1999), 'Changes in the Sources of Modern Economic Growth: Japan Compared with the United States', *Journal of the Japanese and International Economies*, **13** (1), 1–21.

Heshmati, Almas (2003), 'Productivity Growth, Efficiency and Outsourcing in Manufacturing and Service Industries', *Journal of Economic Surveys*, **17** (1), 79–112.

Hildreth, Clifford and James P. Houck (1968), 'Some Estimators for a Linear Model with Random Coefficients', *Journal of the American Statistical Association*, **63** (322), 584–95.

Hsiao, Cheng (1975), 'Some Estimation Methods for a Random Coefficient Model', *Econometrica*, **43** (2), 305–26.

Hsieh, Chang-Tai (1999), 'Productivity Growth and Factor Prices in East Asia', *American Economic Review*, **89** (2), 133–8.

Hsieh, Chang-Tai (2002), 'What Explains the Industrial Revolution in East Asia? Evidence from the Factor Markets', *American Economic Review*, **92** (3), 502–26.

Hu, Sheng-Cheng and Vei-lin Chan (1999), 'The Determinants of Total Factor Productivity in Taiwan', *Industry of Free China*, **89** (9), 1–50 (in Chinese).

Huang, Cliff J. and Jin-Tan Liu (1994), 'Estimation of a Non-Neutral Stochastic Frontier Production Function', *Journal of Productivity Analysis*, **5** (2), 171–80.

Huff, W. G. (1999), 'Singapore's Economic Development: Four Lessons and Some Doubts', *Oxford Development Studies*, **27** (1), 33–55.

Huggett, Mark and Sandra Ospina (2001), 'Does Productivity Growth Fall after the Adoption of New Technology?', *Journal of Monetary Economics*, **48** (1), 173–95.

Hulten, Charles R. (1992), 'Growth Accounting When Technical Change is Embodied in Capital,' *American Economic Review*, **82** (4), 964–80.

Hulten, Charles R. (2000), *Total Factor Productivity: A Short Biography*, NBER Working Paper No. 7471, Cambridge, MA: National Bureau of Economic Research.

Hulten, Charles R. and Frank C. Wykoff (1981), 'The Measurement of Economic Depreciation', in Charles R. Hulten (ed.), *Depreciation, Inflation, and the Taxation of Income from Capital*, Washington, D.C: Urban Institute Press, pp. 81–125.

Hwang, Insang (1998), 'Long-Run Determinant of Korean Economic Growth: Empirical Evidence from Manufacturing,' *Applied Economics*, **30** (3), 391–405.

Imai, Hiroyuki (2001), 'Structural Transformation and Economic Growth in Hong Kong: Another Look at Young's Hong Kong Thesis', *Journal of Comparative Economics*, **29** (2), 366–82.

Islam, Nazrul (1995), 'Growth Empirics: A Panel Data Approach', *Quarterly Journal of Economics*, **110** (4), 1127–70.

Islam, Nazrul (1999), 'International Comparison of Total Factor Productivity: A Review', *Review of Income and Wealth*, **45** (4), 493–518.

Jorgenson, Dale W. (1990), 'Productivity and Economic Growth', in E. Berndt and J. Triplett (eds), *Fifty Years of Economic Measurement*, Chicago: University of Chicago Press, pp. 19–118.

Jorgenson, Dale W. and Mieko Nishimizu (1978), 'U.S. and Japanese Economic Growth, 1952–1974: An International Comparison,' *Economic Journal*, **88** (352), 707–26.

Jorgenson, Dale W. and Zvi Griliches (1967), 'The Explanation of Productivity Change,' *Review of Economic Studies*, **34** (99), 249–83.

Jorgenson, Dale W., Frank M. Gollop and Barbara M. Fraumeni (1987a), *Productivity and U.S. Economic Growth*, Cambridge, MA: Harvard University Press.

Jorgenson, Dale W., Masahiro Kuroda and Mieko Nishimizu (1987b), 'Japan-U.S. Industry-Level Productivity Comparisons, 1960–1979', *Journal of the Japanese and International Economy*, **1** (1), 1–30.

Kalirajan, K. P. and M. B. Obwona (1994), 'Frontier Production Function: The Stochastic Coefficients Approach', *Oxford Bulletin of Economics and Statistics*, **56** (1), 87–96.

Kalirajan, K. P. and R. A. Salim (1997), 'Economic Reforms and Productive Capacity Realisation in Bangladesh: An Empirical Analysis', *Journal of Industrial Economics*, **45** (4), 387–403.

Kalirajan, K. P. and R. T. Shand (1999), 'Frontier Production Functions and Technical Efficiency Measures', *Journal of Economic Surveys*, **13** (2), 149–72.

Kalirajan, K. P., M. B. Obwona and S. Zhao (1996), 'A Decomposition of Total Factor Productivity Growth: The Case of Chinese Agricultural Growth Before and After Reforms', *American Journal of Agricultural Economics*, **78** (2), 331–8.

Kang, Jung M. and Jene K. Kwon (1993), 'The Role of Returns to Scale and Capital Utilization in Productivity Changes: The Case of Korean Manufacturing', *International Economic Journal*, **7** (1), 95–109.

Kim, Euysung (2000), 'Trade Liberalization and Productivity Growth in Korean Manufacturing Industries: Price Protection, Market Power, and Scale Efficiency', *Journal of Development Economics*, **62** (1), 55–83.

Kim, Jong-Il and Lawrence J. Lau (1994), 'The Sources of Economic Growth of the East Asian Newly Industrialized Countries', *Journal of the Japanese and International Economies*, **8** (3), 235–71.

Kim, Sangho and Gwangho Han (2001), 'A Decomposition of Total Factor Productivity Growth in Korean Manufacturing Industries: A Stochastic Frontier Approach', *Journal of Productivity Analysis*, **16** (3), 269–81.

Kim, Young Chin and Jene K. Kwon (1977), 'The Utilization of Capital and the Growth of Output in a Developing Economy: The Case of South Korean Manufacturing', *Journal of Development Economics*, **4** (3), 265–78.

Klenow, Peter J. and Andres Rodriguez-Clare (1997), 'The Neoclassical Revival in Growth Economics: Has It Gone Too Far?', in Ben S. Bernanke and Julio J. Rotemberg (eds), *NBER Macroeconomics Annual 1997*, Cambridge and London: MIT Press.

Koh, Soo-Wei, Shahidur Rahman and G. K. Randolph Tan (2002), 'Growth and Productivity in Singapore Manufacturing Industries: 1975–1998', *Asian Economic Journal*, **16** (3), 247–66.

Krugman, Paul (1994), 'The Myth of Asia's Miracle', *Foreign Affairs*, **73** (6), 62–78.

Kumbhakar, Subal C., Almas Heshmati and Lennart Hjalmarsson (1999), 'Parametric Approaches to Productivity Measurement: A Comparison among Alternative Models', *Scandinavian Journal of Economics*, **101** (3), 405–24.

Kumbhakar, Subal C., Shinichiro Nakamura and Almas Heshmati (2000), 'Estimation of Firm-Specific Technological Bias, Technical Change and

Total Factor Productivity Growth: A Dual Approach', *Econometric Reviews*, **19** (4), 493–515.

Kwack, Sung Yeung (2000) 'Total Factor Productivity Growth and the Sources of Growth in Korean Manufacturing Industries, 1971–1993', *Journal of the Korean Economy*, **1** (2), 229–65.

Kwon, J. K. and K. Yuhn (1990), 'Analysis of Factor Substitution and Productivity Growth in S. Korean Manufacturing,' in J. K. Kwon (ed.), *Korean Economic Development*, New York: Greenwood Press, pp. 144–66.

Kwon, Jene K. (1986), 'Capital Utilization, Economies of Scale and Technical Change in the Growth of Total Factor Productivity: An Explanation of South Korean Manufacturing Growth', *Journal of Development Economics*, **24** (1), 75–89.

Kwong, Kai-Sun, Lawrence J. Lau and Tzong-Biau Lin (2000), 'The Impact of Relocation on the Total Factor Productivity of Hong Kong Manufacturing', *Pacific Economic Review*, **5** (2), 171–99.

Lee, Jeong-Dong, Tai-Yoo Kim and Eunnyeong Heo (1998), 'Technological Progress Versus Efficiency Gain in Manufacturing Sectors', *Review of Development Economics*, **2** (3), 268–81.

Lee, Jong-Wha (1996), 'Government Interventions and Productivity Growth', *Journal of Economic Growth*, **1** (3), 391–414.

Lee, Young Hoon and Peter Schmidt (1993), 'A Production Frontier Model with Flexible Temporal Variation in Technical Efficiency', in Harold O. Fried, C.A. Knox Lovell and Shelton S. Schmidt (eds), *The Measurement of Productive Efficiency: Techniques and Applications*, Oxford and New York: Oxford University Press.

Leung, H. M. (1997), 'Total Factor Productivity Growth in Singapore's Manufacturing Industries,' *Applied Economics Letters*, **4** (8), 525–8.

Liang, Chi-yuan (1995), 'The Productivity Growth in Asian NIE: A Case Study of the Republic of China, 1961–93', *APO Productivity Journal*, Asian Productivity Organization, Tokyo, Japan, winter.

Liang, Chi-yuan and Dale W. Jorgenson (1999), 'Productivity Growth in Taiwan's Manufacturing Industry, 1961–1993', in Tsu-Tan Fu, Cliff J. Huang and C. A. Knox Lovell (eds), *Economic Efficiency and Productivity Growth in the Asia-Pacific Region*, Cheltenham, UK and Northampton, MA, USA: Edward Elgar, pp. 73–86.

Maddala, G. S. (1992), *Introduction to Econometrics*, 2nd edition, Upper Saddle River, NJ: Prentice-Hall.

Mahadevan, Renuka (1999), 'Total Factor Productivity Growth in Singapore: A Survey', *ASEAN Economic Bulletin*, **16** (1), 51–67.

Mahadevan, Renuka (2003), 'To Measure or Not To Measure Total Factor Productivity Growth?', *Oxford Development Studies*, **31** (3), 365–78.

Mahadevan, Renuka and K. P. Kalirajan (1999), 'On Measuring Total Factor Productivity Growth in Singapore's Manufacturing Industries', *Applied Economics Letters*, **6** (5), 295–8.

Mahadevan, Renuka and Kali Kalirajan (2000), 'Singapore's Manufacturing Sector's TFP Growth: A Decomposition Analysis', *Journal of Comparative Economics*, **28** (4), 828–39.

Mahadevan, Renuka and Sangho Kim (2003), 'Is Output Growth of Korean Manufacturing Firms Productivity-Driven?', *Journal of Asian Economics*, **14** (4), 669–78.

Meeusen, W. and J. van den Broeck (1977), 'Efficiency Estimation from Cobb–Douglas Production Functions with Composed Error', *International Economic Review*, **18** (2), 435–44.

Morrison, Catherine J. (1990a), 'Decisions of Firms and Productivity Growth with Fixed Input Constraints: An Empirical Comparison of U.S. and Japanese Manufacturing', in Charles R. Hulten (ed.), *Productivity Growth in Japan and the United States*, Chicago and London: University of Chicago Press.

Morrison, Catherine J. (1990b), *Market Power, Economic Profitability and Productivity Growth Measurement: An Integrated Structural Approach*, NBER Working Paper No. 3355, Cambridge, MA: National Bureau of Economic Research.

Nadiri, M. Ishaq and Ingmar R. Prucha (1999), *Dynamic Factor Demand Models and Productivity Analysis*, NBER Working Paper No. 7079, Cambridge, MA: National Bureau of Economic Research.

Nadiri, M. Ishaq and Seongjun Kim (1996), *R&D, Production Structure and Productivity Growth: A Comparison of the US, Japanese, and Korean Manufacturing Sectors*, NBER Working Paper No. 5506, Cambridge, MA: National Bureau of Economic Research.

Nakajima, Takanobu, Masao Nakamura and Kanji Yoshioka (1998), 'An Index Number Method for Estimating Scale Economies and Technical Progress Using Time-Series of Cross-Section Data: Sources for Total Factor Productivity Growth for Japanese Manufacturing, 1964–1988', *Japanese Economic Review*, **49** (3), 310–34.

Nelson, Richard R. and Howard Pack (1999), 'The Asian Miracle and Modern Growth Theory', *Economic Journal*, **109** (457), 416–36.

Nishimizu, Mieko and John M. Page (1982), 'Total Factor Productivity Growth, Technological Progress and Technical Efficiency Change: Dimensions of Productivity Change in Yugoslavia, 1965–78', *Economic Journal*, **92** (368), 920–36.

Nishimizu, Mieko and Sherman Robinson (1984), 'Trade Policies and Productivity Change in Semi-industrialized Countries', *Journal of Development Economics*, **16** (1–2), 177–206.

Norsworthy, J. R. and David H. Malmquist (1983), 'Input Measurement and Productivity Growth in Japanese and U.S. Manufacturing', *American Economic Review*, **73** (5), 947–67.

Okuda, Satoru (1994), 'Taiwan's Trade and FDI Policies and Their Effect on Productivity Growth', *Developing Economies*, **32** (4), 423–43.

Okuda, Satoru (1997), 'Industrialization Policies of Korea and Taiwan and Their Effects on Manufacturing Productivity', *Developing Economies*, **35** (4), 358–81.

Park, Seung Rok and Jene K. Kwon (1995), 'Rapid Economic Growth with Increasing Returns to Scale and Little or No Productivity Growth', *Review of Economics and Statistics*, **77** (2), 332–51.

Pilat, Dirk (1995), 'Comparative Productivity of Korean Manufacturing, 1967–1987', *Journal of Development Economics*, **46** (1), 123–44.

Prasad, Eswar (1997), 'Sectoral Shifts and Structural Change in the Japanese Economy: Evidence and Interpretation', *Japan and the World Economy*, **9** (3), 293–313.

Rao, Bhanoji and Christopher Lee (1995), 'Sources of Growth in the Singapore Economy and Its Manufacturing and Service Sectors', *Singapore Economic Review*, **40** (1), 83–115.

Republic of China, Directorate-General Budget, Accounting, and Statistics (2000), *The Trends in Multifactor Productivity, Taiwan Area, Republic of China*, Executive Yuan, R.O.C.

Rodrigo, G. Chris (2000), 'East Asia's Growth: Technology or Accumulation?', *Contemporary Economic Policy*, **18** (2), 215–27.

Rodrik, Dani (1998), 'TFPG Controversies, Institutions and Economic Performance in East Asia,' in Yujiro Hayami and Masahiko Aoki (eds), *The Institutional Foundations of East Asian Economic Development*, New York: St. Martin's Press.

Salim, Ruhul A. (1997), *Market-Oriented Economic Reforms, Capacity Realization, and Technical Progress in Bangladesh Manufacturing*, unpublished PhD thesis, Australian National University, Canberra, Australia.

Sarel, Michael (1995), *Growth in East Asia: What We Can and What We Cannot Infer from It*, IMF Working Paper 95/98, International Monetary Fund.

Sarel, Michael (1997), *Growth and Productivity in ASEAN Countries*, IMF Working Paper 97/97, International Monetary Fund.

Sato, Kazuo (2002), 'From Fast to Last: The Japanese Economy in the 1990s', *Journal of Asian Economics*, **13** (2), 213–35.

Singh, Nirvikar and Hung Trieu (1999), 'Total Factor Productivity Growth in Japan, South Korea, and Taiwan', *Indian Economic Review*, **34** (2), 93–112.

Solow, Robert (1956), 'A Contribution to the Theory of Economic Growth', *Quarterly Journal of Economics*, **70** (1), 65–94.

Solow, Robert (1957), 'Technical Change and the Aggregate Production Function', *Review of Economics and Statistics*, **39** (3), 312–20.

Stevenson, Rodney E. (1980), 'Likelihood Functions for Generalized Stochastic Frontier Estimation', *Journal of Econometrics*, **13** (1), 57–66.

Swamy, P. A. V. B. (1970), 'Efficient Inference in a Random Coefficient Regression Model', *Econometrica*, **38** (2), 311–23.

Swamy, P. A. V. B. and George S. Tavlas (1995), 'Random Coefficient Models: Theory and Applications', *Journal of Economic Surveys*, **9** (2), 165–96.

Swan, Trevor W. (1956), 'Economic Growth and Capital Accumulation', *Economic Record*, **32**, 334–61.

Swee, Goh Keng and Linda Low (1996), 'Beyond "Miracles" and Total Factor Productivity: The Singapore Experience', *ASEAN Economic Bulletin*, **13** (1), 1–13.

ten Raa, Thijs and Pierre Mohnen (2002), 'Neoclassical Growth Accounting and Frontier Analysis: A Synthesis', *Journal of Productivity Analysis*, **18** (2), 111–28.

Thomas, Vinod and Yan Wang (1996), 'Distortions, Interventions, and Productivity Growth: Is East Asia Different?', *Economic Development and Cultural Change*, **44** (2), 265–88.

Timmer, Marcel P. (2002), 'Climbing the Technology Ladder Too Fast? New Evidence on Comparative Productivity Performance in Asian Manufacturing', *Journal of the Japanese and International Economies*, **16** (1), 50–72.

Timmer, Marcel P. and Adam Szirmai (2000), 'Productivity Growth in Asian Manufacturing: The Structural Bonus Hypothesis Examined', *Structural Change and Economic Dynamics*, **11** (4), 371–92.

Tinbergen, Jan (1942), 'Zur Theorie der langfristigen Wirtschaftsentwicklung', *Weltwirtschaftliches Archiv*, **55** (1), 511–49.

Toh, Mun Heng and Linda Low (1996), 'Differential Total Factor Productivity in the Four Dragons: The Singapore Case', *Journal of International Trade and Economic Development*, **5** (2), 161–81.

Toh, Mun Heng and Wai Choong Ng (2002), 'Efficiency of Investments in Asian Economies: Has Singapore Over-invested?', *Journal of Asian Economics*, **13** (1), 52–71.

Tsao, Yuan (1985), 'Growth without Productivity: Singapore Manufacturing in the 1970s', *Journal of Development Economics*, **19** (1–2), 25–38.

Tuan, Chyau and Linda F. Y. Ng (1995), 'Hong Kong's Outward Investment and Regional Economic Integration with Guandong: Process and Implications', *Journal of Asian Economics*, **6** (3), 385–405.

United Nations Industrial Development Organisation (1999), *International Yearbook of Industrial Statistics*, United Nations.

Wolff, Edward N. (1991), 'Capital Formation and Productivity Convergence over the Long Term', *American Economic Review*, **81** (3), 565–79.

Wong, Fot Chyi (1993), 'Patterns of Labour Productivity Growth and Employment Shift in the Singapore Manufacturing Industries', *Singapore Economic Review*, **38** (2), 231–51.

Wong, Fot Chyi and Wee Beng Gan (1994), 'Total Factor Productivity Growth in the Singapore Manufacturing Industries During the 1980s', *Journal of Asian Economics*, **5** (2), 177–96.

World Bank (1993), *The East Asian Miracle: Economic Growth and Public Policy*, Oxford and New York: Oxford University Press.

Young, Alwyn (1992), 'A Tale of Two Cities: Factor Accumulation and Technical Change in Hong Kong and Singapore', in Olivier J. Blanchard and Stanley Fischer (eds), *NBER Macroeconomics Annual 1992*, Cambridge and London: MIT Press.

Young, Alwyn (1994), 'Lessons from the East Asian NICs: A Contrarian View', *European Economic Review*, **38** (3–4), 964–73.

Young, Alwyn (1995), 'The Tyranny of Numbers: Confronting the Statistical Realities of the East Asian Growth Experience', *Quarterly Journal of Economics*, **110** (3), 641–80.

Yuhn, Ky Hyang and Jene K. Kwon (2000), 'Economic Growth and Productivity: A Case Study of South Korea', *Applied Economics*, **32** (1), 13–23.

Index